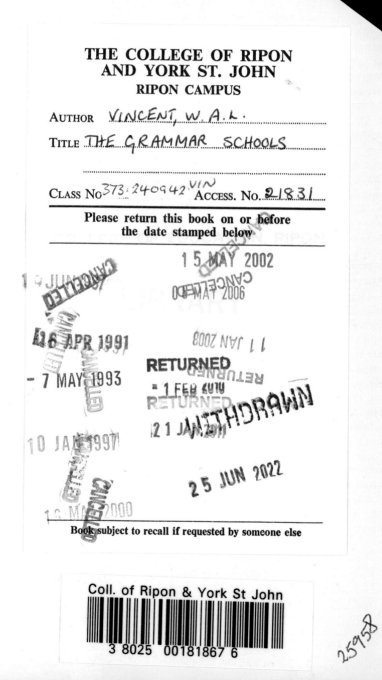

THE GRAMMAR SCHOOLS

By the same Author

The State and School Education 1640–1660 in England and Wales (s.p.c.k.)

W. A. L. VINCENT

THE GRAMMAR SCHOOLS

Their Continuing Tradition
1660–1714

JOHN MURRAY
50 ALBEMARLE STREET LONDON

© W. A. L. VINCENT 1969

PRINTED IN GREAT BRITAIN
FOR JOHN MURRAY
BY COX AND WYMAN LTD, LONDON,
FAKENHAM AND READING

7195 1845 8

CONTENTS

ILLUSTRATIONS

PREFACE

There have been many histories of individual schools since the publication in 1908 of Professor Foster Watson's comprehensive study in *The English Grammar Schools to 1660: their Curriculum and Practice*. So far as I know, there has been no attempt in one volume to continue the story of the grammar schools from 1660 onwards and to examine the causes of the decay and disappearance of many of these schools in the eighteenth century. My own previous foray into this field of study was concerned with the proliferation of endowed grammar schools before the Restoration and the educational ferment during the decades from 1640 to 1660. There was no difficulty, therefore, in deciding the *terminus a quo* for a further investigation of the old-established schools.

Less easy to determine was a *terminus ad quem* for this study. The first, and indeed only, landmark in the history of the grammar schools after 1660 is the publication in 1818 of Nicholas Carlisle's *A Concise Description of the Endowed Grammar Schools in England and Wales*. This might have served the purpose of providing a terminal date. Another possibility was to end the survey with the report of the Schools Inquiry Commission which was published in 1868. The factors which finally determined me in the demarcation of the territory were the desire to make generous use of the manuscripts of Christopher Wase and the desirability of maintaining a harmony of design and proportion and of keeping the research within bounds.

More than twenty-five years ago my attention was directed to the Wase school collection by Mr. H. E. M. Icely who was then Reader in Education in the University of Oxford. Subsequently Mr. P. J. Wallis has performed a signal service by contributing to the *Bodleian Library Record*, Volume IV, No. 2 (August 1952), an introduction to these papers and an index to the seven hundred and four schools which are mentioned in them. An account of the purpose and method of the Wase inquiry is given in the second chapter of this book. The results of Wase's inquiry are contained in four volumes of manuscripts, deposited in the Bodleian Library, which provide a rich source for educational history in the seventeenth century and particularly for the 1670s.

In quoting from manuscripts, abbreviations have been extended, and indicated by letters in italics, where such extensions make for ease in reading. Otherwise the spelling and punctuation of the original texts have always been preserved.

In common with all who were privileged to be his pupils I owe much to the late Dr. Claude Jenkins, Canon of Christ Church and Professor of Ecclesiastical History in the University of Oxford, who directed my first steps in research and prepared the way for this second venture. To one of his pupils, Dr. Anne Whiteman of Lady Margaret Hall, Oxford, I gladly acknowledge my indebtedness because she read and criticized the book in manuscript and acted as my mentor throughout the whole project.

W.A.L.V.

I

INTRODUCTORY

1. Aims and Scope of the Inquiry

Two impressive aspects of educational history in the first sixty years of the seventeenth century are the truly astonishing number of grammar schools which existed and flourished, and the genuine anxiety shown by the Long Parliament and the Protectorate Government to preserve them in the midst of political and social upheaval. It is usually agreed that in the eighteenth century the keynote of the history of these schools is decline. The traditional picture is that the old endowed schools were stuffy, inflexible, hidebound institutions, pursuing narrow and rigid curricula unsuited to the needs of the times, and not surprisingly outstripped by the more efficient and modern dissenting academies and private schools. In this context the years from 1660 to 1714 seem to be a period of repose. The aim of this study is to focus attention upon the grammar school system in England and Wales during these fifty-four years following the Restoration.

A very necessary question in such an inquiry is how much got off the statute books into practice in the schools. Doubtless there was a gulf between injunction and performance, a considerable difference between what was said ought to be done and what actually was done. Certainly we need to ask for whom the schools were intended; but it is more important to our purpose to know who were actually educated in them. The qualifications required of aspiring schoolmasters are interesting; but were the conditions of employment such as to attract men of quality and did teachers operate for the good of their schools? We must ask questions not only about the constitution but also about the conduct of governing bodies. And what of the educational practice in the schools? Did it match the prescriptions laid down in school statutes and how far did it satisfy the intellectual and moral requirements of society?

In this investigation of grammar school life in the later Stuart period there is another important purpose. At the outset attention is directed to the contrast between the achievement and expansion of grammar schools in Tudor and early Stuart times and the decadence of many of these schools which became clear in the eighteenth century. From the study of the constitution and practice of the grammar schools in later Stuart times it is hoped to shed light upon the causes of their subsequent decline.

In the second chapter there is an account of the purpose, method and result of the inquiry, on a national scale, into the free grammar schools instigated by Christopher Wase in 1673. This raises the questions why he abandoned his design and how his inquiry ties up with the book which he published in 1678. There follows an examination of the meaning of the term 'free school'. One problem here is the almost total exclusion of girls from the schools. Next comes a survey of the educational practice of grammar schools, the twofold aims of giving instruction in the classics and producing Christian citizens, the material, method and hours of study, library facilities, and the stern discipline which attended the pursuit of learning. For the historian, the significance of this educational practice lies, no doubt, in its relation to the changing needs and demands of society. In this connexion the views of contemporary writers on education are interesting as showing that there was a body of opinion which looked and hoped for reform in the school curriculum. More important for the future of the grammar schools were the unwillingness and inability of school trustees and teachers to introduce new methods and material of study. In successive chapters there is information about men who were engaged in the exacting task of teaching, about the conditions and rewards of their labours, and about the theory and practice of school governance. In the later Stuart period schoolmasters were required to satisfy not only governing bodies, about their academic qualification and manner of life, but also the ecclesiastical and civil authorities, about their conformity to the establishment in Church and State. It seems unlikely, however, that there was any drastic uprooting of schoolmasters at the Restoration or as a result of the Romanizing campaign of James II or the events of 1688. An attempt has been made to quantify findings about the number of graduates, clergymen and pluralists in the ranks of the schoolmasters

and about their length of service. An examination of rates of pay
in the teaching profession reveals a marked disparity in the incomes of schoolmasters and makes understandable the not uncommon practice of combining scholastic with preaching and
parochial duties.

As already mentioned, an important part of the purpose of
this study is to test, in the light of evidence from the history of
grammar schools in the later Stuart period, the validity of general
assumptions about the decline of many schools in the eighteenth
century. In the years following the Restoration the grammar
schools were apparently regarded with disfavour in some influential quarters since, it was held, they had produced rebels
and regicides and since the reading of classical authors incited
to revolution. Furthermore, there were some who maintained
that the old-established schools were doing a disservice by producing a superfluity of learned youths for the professions. Whether
for these or other reasons the era of lavish outpouring of wealth
for the endowment of grammar schools was over. There is
evidence that in some schools at the end of the seventeenth
century endowments, generous at the time of foundation, were
proving inadequate and that, as a result, school authorities were
driven to repudiate the objectives of founders by introducing or
raising fees and restricting the number of free places. In the
absence of further benefactions, poorly endowed schools depended for survival upon attracting fee-paying pupils from
within and especially from beyond their immediate localities.
At the same time a falling demand for a classical education was
apparent in some areas. Where an English department already
existed or where it was introduced to meet popular demand it
almost inevitably led to the reduction or disappearance of grammar teaching. In a worsening situation school governors appear
to have done little or nothing to stay the decline of schools and,
all too often, their governance was characterized by indifference,
inefficiency and downright dishonesty.

On these points the further study of the grammar schools,
undertaken in this book, indicates that generalized assertions,
regularly made by writers on educational history about the
decline of the grammar schools, do not need to be radically
changed. It is, of course, obvious that at all periods of their

history grammar schools were largely dependent for their success or failure on the quality of schoolmasters. It is likely that, in general, the practice of combining schoolmasterships with parochial duties was detrimental to schools. But statistical evidence gives no ground for supposing that inefficiency and dual employment among schoolmasters were on the increase in the seventeenth and eighteenth centuries or that schools deteriorated because the quality of the schoolmasters deteriorated. And to assert, as Mr. A. F. Leach did, that the conjunction of the offices of schoolmaster and parish priest was fatal to the grammar schools, is to do less than justice to the evidence.

An important motif in the conventional picture is one which shows the dissenting academies as triumphing over the endowed grammar schools. In Chapter IX we review the whole field of private teaching in the later Stuart period and attempt to assess the effect upon the old-established schools of competition from private teachers and private institutions. Home and private tutors and private schools were familiar parts of the educational system in the seventeenth and eighteenth centuries. In the first half of the seventeenth century they played an indispensable part in the general expansion of secondary learning. After the Restoration the grammar schools were losing their hold and educating a decreasing percentage of boys. Were, then, private teachers and private institutions on the increase and attracting pupils from the public grammar schools? May we confidently assert that the proportion of boys receiving secondary education in the eighteenth century did not fall below the level for the seventeenth century? The answers to these questions, provided by an examination of available evidence, give no encouragement to assume that the flight from the grammar schools was compensated by a movement towards one or other of the forms of post-primary learning provided by private ventures in education in the seventeenth and eighteenth centuries.

The inquiry into the grammar school system undertaken in this book is rewarding because the conditions of schools and schoolmasters deserve to be studied for their own sake and because the educational practice in the grammar schools continued with little change throughout the eighteenth century and into the nineteenth century. But to study the constitution and practice of the grammar schools in the later Stuart period is to arrive at a clearer understanding of the causes of their decadence in the eighteenth century and to conclude that the decline of the grammar schools was the significant and decisive factor in the history of secondary education for two hundred years after the Restoration.

So much for the aims and extent of the inquiry. As a prelude to our review of the grammar school system between the years 1660 and 1714 it is necessary now to give some account of the expansion of the grammar schools in the preceding years and of educational developments in the two decades from 1640 to 1660. Finally in this introductory chapter we shall consider the remarkable transformation in the fortunes of many grammar schools after the Restoration and establish the theme of decline which is central to our study. It is in the eighteenth century that the retreat from the endowed schools becomes unmistakably clear. But, as we shall hope to show, it is in the later Stuart period that we may see the signs of subsequent decay.

2. The Expansion of the Grammar Schools

Writing of the English grammar school Mr. G. Davies says that 'it was richly supported by the middle classes which poured their wealth into the endowment of education between 1560 and 1650 probably to a greater extent relatively than during any other hundred years in English history'.[1] To this statement may be added the impressive testimony of Professor W. K. Jordan's research which reveals that in the years from 1480 to 1660 donors in ten counties of England[2] bequeathed the huge sum of £833,493 12s. for education and that 'the great, the prodigal, outpouring came in the early Stuart period, when in four decades the enormous total of £383,594 1s. was provided for the several, and interrelated, educational uses'. Of this latter sum £220,599 15s. was bestowed for the founding of grammar schools.*

'All classes shared importantly in this epical undertaking,' wrote Professor Jordan, 'but it was the merchant wealth of

---

* 'The great achievement is all the more impressive,' wrote Professor Jordan, 'when we reflect on it in terms of the number of schools actually founded during the age. In this era, we must recall, £500 would build and endow a school of fair strength; £1,000 was quite sufficient for a school of notable resources'. During the period 1480–1660 benefactors in the ten counties founded and endowed 437 schools. (W. K. Jordan, *Philanthropy in England 1480–1660*, London, 1959, pp. 289–90.)

London, of Bristol, of Norwich, and even of the raw new towns
of the West Riding that first conceived and then completed this
grand design.' Using as his main source 'the many thousands
of wills proved in England during the period 1480–1660'[1]
Professor Jordan attributes the lavish prodigality of the London
merchants to their belief that learning was the most effective
means to destroy and to prevent the evils of poverty and ignorance which they themselves had experienced and that a rising
standard of education was necessary to meet the intricacies of
commerce and financial operations and also to create a nation
of God-fearing men capable of perceiving religious truth and
protecting it against its enemies.[2] But, as Mr. K. Charlton has
reminded us, an explanation of the motives for educational
philanthropy in pre-Restoration times must allow for the fact
that men who had achieved wealth and who desired also to raise
their social standing found in educational endowment an acceptable form of charitable giving which had formerly found an
outlet in bequests for religious purposes.[3] And indeed the tendency to bestow money for secondary education rather than for
seemingly humbler institutions for elementary education may
be indicative of self-interest and ambition in some of the donors.
It is certain that this provision for more advanced education
without adequate care for the earlier stages of learning seriously
inconvenienced the grammar schools when eventually the demand for elementary instruction outgrew the demand for classical studies. We shall return to this point in a later chapter.

Whatever the motives for philanthropic effort in the cause of
education the result was that the first sixty years of the seventeenth century was a period when the grammar schools of
England and Wales flourished, and when education preparatory
to the university was available to all who wished to avail themselves of it. In the 1670s Christopher Wase collected information
about free grammar schools and a list of seven hundred and four
schools which are mentioned in his manuscripts has been compiled and arranged according to counties by Mr. P. J. Wallis.
Not all these schools were in fact free grammar schools and the
number of seven hundred and four schools may be compared
with my list of one thousand three hundred and twenty grammar
schools in England and Wales which were in existence between

The Grammar Schools at Adderbury and
Chipping Norton, Oxfordshire

An eighteenth century Parson's School by Samuel Wale

1600 and 1660.[1] This latter list is doubtless incomplete though an effort was made to include in it no school for which the evidence is not really accurate. It does not contain the names of schools which are expressly stated to be private schools and which were offering the same education as the endowed schools.[2] Two years after its publication Mr. Wallis suggested that the number of grammar schools might not unreasonably be estimated as not less than two thousand.[3] Subsequently he has told us that recent research indicates that, including the private fee-paying establishments, there were more than four thousand grammar schools in the seventeenth century.[4]

Some few of these schools, notably Eton, Winchester and Westminster, had already acquired a fame which extended beyond their immediate locality, and it was the practice among certain of the country gentlemen to send their sons to these schools as boarders rather than to the neighbouring grammar school. There was nothing new in this practice which, although not widespread, had continued throughout the seventeenth century. John Wallis who was at Felsted School in Essex from 1630 to 1632 wrote that at this school, although it was situated in a country village, there were 'at that time above an hundred or six score Scholars; most of them Strangers, sent thither from other places, upon reputation of the School; from whence many good Scholars were sent yearly to the University'.[5] In 1632 William Ullock, who ten years later became master of his old school, was sent to Repton from Tallentire in Cumberland.[6] The Civil War affected the schools adversely in some cases, but no doubt in other cases the number of boarders was increased by the sons of royalists who had been compelled to abandon their homes. The fame and reputation of a schoolmaster was able to attract pupils to him and away from their own neighbourhood. Thomas Chaloner was expelled from the mastership of Shrewsbury School when the town fell to the parliamentary forces on 22 February 1644–45.* During the next eighteen years Chaloner moved to nine different places in Shropshire, Staffordshire and North Wales, as he received invitations to assume a new mastership or as a parliamentary committee drove him out. To the

* Here and elsewhere dates are stated in this way because until 1752 the Julian calendar was in use in this country and the legal year began not on 1 January but on 25 March.

B

school which he started at Birch Hall, near Ellesmere, came ninety-eight pupils in five months, and to Hawarden, a hundred and fifty boys in three months. Twenty-two boys, most of whom had already been at Birch Hall and Hawarden, followed him when he moved to Overton in Flintshire.[1] Samuel Butler was another whose reputation was such that when during the Commonwealth he went to Tiverton to become master of Blundell's School 'he brought several Gentlemens Sons with him; so that he had Scholars from many parts of the Kingdom'.[2] In 1675 a boy named Vaux came from Cumberland to Rugby School to be taught by Robert Ashbridge whose pupils included James Pettiver, who was to distinguish himself as a naturalist, Ambrose the son of Sir Thomas Cave of Stomford Hall in Leicestershire, and the sons of well-known local families like the Dixwells, Boughtons, Shuckburghs and Caldecotts.[3] When in 1690 Edward Leeds, high master of Bury St. Edmunds School, published his *Methodus Graecam Linguam Docendi* he included in it a list of county families whose sons were his pupils at that time, some of whom like the Beckwiths, Legards, Widdringtons and Greys came from as far away as Yorkshire, Durham and Northumberland. Two grandsons of the earl of Salisbury were at Oundle School in 1665,[4] the son of Sir Thomas Slingsby, baronet, entered St. Albans School in 1673–74[5] and Oakham School in Rutland boasted the two sons of Sir Richard Wingfield of Tickencote in the 1660s.[6] Richard, the son of Sir Thomas Burton of Brampton in Westmorland, the three sons, William, John and Ferdinand, of Sir William Forster or Forrester of Bamburgh in Northumberland and John the son of Henry Hilton, esquire 'by custom of the place called Baron Hilton' were among those who were sent to St. John's College, Cambridge from Durham School by Thomas Battersby who was master from 1667 to 1691. To the same college in 1718 came Brownlow Cecil, the future marquis of Exeter, from Northampton Grammar School, and the sons of a baronet and a knight from Thetford School in Norfolk in 1673 and 1674.[7]

The statesmen of the Interregnum were careful to conserve the old endowed grammar schools and showed their confidence in the education given by these schools by sending their sons to them. The register of Pocklington Grammar School in Yorkshire, beginning on 23 September 1650, shows that within one year there were admitted seventy-six sons of the most important families in that county, including Fairfaxes, Savilles, Beaumonts, Darleys and Wilberforces.[1] The list of scholars admitted to Westminster School included the two younger sons of William Russell, earl of Bedford, and four sons of Edward Montagu, earl of Manchester.[2] To Felsted School went four sons of Oliver Cromwell[3] and to Eton the Protector sent his ward, a boy named William Dutton, in the care of the Puritan poet, Andrew Marvell.[4]

Recourse to Professor Jordan's work furnishes the interesting information that though there was during the period of the Puritan Revolution an inevitable falling-off in charitable bequests yet the sum of money bequeathed for education was not much less than that given for the same purpose during the last forty years of the sixteenth century. From 1640 to 1660 donations to educational uses amounted to £130,461 9s., of which almost £90,000 was for grammar school foundations, and represented an annual rate of giving only slightly below that for the early Stuart period.[5]

3. The State and the Schools, 1640-60

In a sermon preached before the House of Commons on Sunday, 29 November 1640, Mr. John Gauden referred to 'the noble endeavours of two great and publique spirits, who have laboured much for truth and peace, I meane Commenius and Duraeus' and suggested that it would be 'worthy the name and honour of this State and Church to invite these men to you'.[6] John Amos Comenius was a Bohemian, a minister of the Unitas Fratrum, a Bohemian sect, and a refugee who had settled at Leszno in Poland. He was the leading educationist of his day and the author of books of theory and method and of textbooks for the use of the class.[7] John Dury, a Protestant divine, was chiefly concerned to promote ecclesiastical peace by bringing about a reconciliation between Lutherans and Calvinists. He was also an enthusiast for educational reform and believed that 'to frame a right course for the education of children, and for the perfection of humane learning, is a most laudable publique good worke as well for this age, as for posterity.'[8]

The invitations, to Comenius in Poland and Dury in Denmark,

were eventually sent by their friend Samuel Hartlib who acted apparently on his own behalf and on behalf of a small group of influential patrons including John Pym, the member for Tavistock, and John Selden, the member for Oxford University, in the Long Parliament.[1] In September 1641 Comenius, Hartlib and Dury were together in England and it might well seem that, given the support of parliament, a programme of educational reconstruction was on the point of execution.[2]

Already the parliament had given intimations of its interest in public education. On 16 April 1641 the House of Commons instigated an inquiry into the state of the hospitals and free schools in England and Wales and on 15 June it resolved that all the lands, which it proposed to take from deans and chapters, should be 'employed to the Advancement of Learning and Piety'.[3] In October Comenius wrote to his friends at Leszno: 'They are eagerly debating on the reform of schools in the whole kingdom in a manner similar to that to which, as you know, my wishes tend, namely that all young people should be instructed, none neglected.'[4] But civil war was then only ten months off and parliament had little time to give to the question of national schooling.

It was, of course, to be expected that in the turmoil of civil war there would be some dislocation in the educational system. But the extent to which the educational life of the country was disturbed must not be exaggerated. The fortunes of schools and schoolmasters varied considerably during the distracted times. Shrewsbury School was closed for a short time after the town fell to the Parliamentarians on 22 February 1644–45[5] and St. Peter's School was moved to new premises when, at the end of the siege of York in 1644, the building in the Horsefair lay in ruins.[6] In the west country Blundell's School was in the thick of the fighting and the war left its mark on the school buildings as witness the entries in the school account book for sums of money, amounting to a hundred and eighty-two pounds, which were spent for repairs after the Parliament men had been quartered there.[7] But some schools at any rate were flourishing in these days of civil war. In January 1646–47 the usher of Repton School, Thomas Whitehead, received an increase in salary as a reward for his loyal service during the past three and a half years, 'the

multitude of schollers having been extraordinary'.[1] At Harrow
the school building proved inadequate to accommodate the large
number of pupils.[2]

For many schools and schoolmasters war meant financial
hardship since inevitably there was a falling-off in the payment
of rents which supplied endowments and salaries. The trustees
of schools sometimes found it impossible to collect their rents
either because travel was difficult in the disturbed state of the
country or because tenants were hard pressed by taxation. Thus
the fact that, at St. Paul's School, Campden Exhibitions to
enable boys to go to the universities were not awarded from 1640
to 1654 is probably to be explained by the difficulty of collecting
rents from a county as far away as Northumberland.[3] Failure
to collect the rent-charge from an estate in Essex meant that the
master and usher of the Perse School, Cambridge, were paid half
their salaries from 1644 to 1648 when arrears were made up in
full.[4] At Rugby Raphael Pearce, who was in charge of the school
from 1641 until shortly before his death in 1651, received two
shillings and sevenpence of the twelve pounds which was his
annual salary and was reduced to selling timbers, which had
probably fallen from parts of the school buildings, and breaking
up school beams and benches to provide fuel for himself and his
family. Pearce was the victim of unscrupulous tenants who held
back the payment of rents in one or more years because their
land had been damaged by breastworks thrown up across it. In
fact less than one acre out of ten had suffered.[5]

As we have seen, the opportunity for a reform of public education, which the visits of Comenius and Dury had seemed to
promise, was lost by the outbreak of civil war. On 21 June 1641
Comenius left England. But the desire for educational reform
was not diminished and, throughout the period of the Long
Parliament and Protectorate, Hartlib and Dury and a host of
authors gave expression to the need. The writings of the time
show that men's minds were exercised by the subject of education
and its place in a well-ordered community. They recognize that
if learning deteriorates the health of the State must suffer. They
call for an extension of education to embrace all children, rich
and poor. Moreover, they express the conviction that it is the
duty of the government to establish a national system of schooling.

Comenius had already drawn attention to the subject of national systems of schooling in his book *The Great Didactic* which was published in Czech in 1632. The scheme which he envisaged included a so-called Vernacular School in every hamlet and village, where children of both sexes between the ages of six and twelve years should be taught, and a Latin School in every city for pupils between the ages of twelve and eighteen whose abilities fitted them for higher learning. The subject was treated by Samuel Harmar in 1642 in a pamphlet, *Vox Populi, Or Glostersheres Desire,* which took the form of a petition to parliament. Harmar pointed to the evils of vagrancy and crime which resulted from allowing children to run the streets when they should have been in school. He begged, therefore, 'that the Lords and Commons of both the Houses of Parliament will be pleased to take it into their wise and grave consideration carefully to Plant Orchards of young stockes, meaning young Nurseries of generall Schooling in every Parish throughout the Land, with a carefull Gardner or Grafter over them'.

He proposed that the cost of education should be met by a tax on men's estates and answered the objection that poor parents could not afford to keep their children at school with the suggestion that children might earn twopence a day by spinning, or knitting, and by working on hemp and flax before and after school. In 1648 William Petty, afterwards Sir William Petty, pleaded for schools for poor children as well as rich on the ground that 'many are now holding the plough, which might have been made fit to steer the state'. His plan, which was propounded in *The Advice of W.P. to Mr. Samuel Hartlib, for the Advancement of some particular Parts of Learning,* was for literary work-houses where all children above the age of seven years should be taught to read and write and to do something towards their living. In his *Londons Charity inlarged,* 1650, Samuel Hartlib appealed for a grant of a thousand pounds to provide work for the poor of London and education for the children of the poor. Free, compulsory and State-inspected schools were advocated by James Harrington in *The Commonwealth of Oceana,* a work which was dedicated to Lord Protector Cromwell and published in 1656. Children between the ages of nine and fifteen were to be taught in these schools, free of charge if their parents could not afford to pay fees. Parents who neglected to send their children to school were to be punished by the magistrates who were also to be responsible for inspecting the schools.

Such, then, were some of the visions of Commonwealth reformers. We turn now to the educational policies of the Commonwealth government. The Long Parliament met on 3 November 1640. In the following year, as we have seen, it ordered an inquiry into the state of the free schools and resolved that the revenues of lands taken from deans and chapters should be devoted to the advancement of learning and piety. The eventual effects of this resolution may be illustrated from the histories of the grammar schools at Gloucester and Chester. The sequestration of the estates of the dean and chapter of Gloucester in 1645 was followed in 1646 by an augmentation of thirty pounds a year to the schoolmaster, William Russell, whose stipend had formerly been £19 6s. 8d.[1] At Chester in 1646 augmentations payable out of the revenues of the dean and chapter raised the salary of the master, Mr. Greenhalgh, from twenty-two pounds a year to fifty-eight pounds and that of the usher, John Pack, from ten pounds to nineteen pounds a year.[2]

Further indications of the attitude of the parliament towards public education were forthcoming in 1642 when the House of Commons proposed to confiscate the revenues of archbishops, bishops, deans, deans and chapters, and of malignants who had taken up arms,[3] and in 1643 when ordinances were passed for the sequestering of the estates of notorious delinquents and of the Crown.[4] In each case the parliament provided that such part of the revenues as was used to support schools should be exempted from seizure. In 1645 and 1646 the Long Parliament took steps to ensure that the elections of scholars to Westminster, Winchester and Eton and thence to the universities should be resumed and maintained.[5] The measures of 9 October 1646, for abolishing the government of the Church by archbishops and bishops, and of 30 April 1649, for abolishing deans and chapters, contained provisions that all money which had hitherto been used for the maintenance of schools should continue to be employed as before.[6] The same desire to preserve existing educational institutions was apparent when the parliament relieved universities, colleges and schools of the obligation to contribute to the monthly assessments which were levied between 1647 and 1652 for the upkeep of the army.[1] On 8 June 1649 the Long Parliament voted an annual grant of money in aid of education. By the 'Act for Maintenance for Preaching Ministers, and other Pious Uses' the first-fruits and tenths, which had formerly been payable to the Crown, were transferred to trustees who were to use them to pay yearly all such salaries as had been settled by the parliament 'for preaching the Gospel, Preaching Ministers, or Schoolmasters or others in England and Wales'. A noteworthy provision was that if the income from these sources fell short of twenty thousand pounds, the balance should be made up by the Exchequer from some other part of the annual revenue.[2]

To the Long Parliament belongs the distinction of having instituted the first organized movement for a system of national schooling in Wales. Under the authority bestowed on them by 'An Act for the better Propagation and Preaching of the Gospel in Wales', which passed into law on 22 February 1649–50, commissioners used the profits of ecclesiastical livings to establish more than sixty new schools in the Principality.[3] Eleven of these schools had a master and an usher and two others had two masters. It may be assumed, therefore, that these at any rate were grammar schools.[4] On 1 March an Act, which has not been preserved but which no doubt was similar in substance to that for Wales, constituted Commissioners for the Propagation of the Gospel in the Four Northern Counties of Northumberland, Cumberland, Westmorland and Durham.[5] Evidence of the work of the commissioners in the county of Durham between 1650 and 1653 is afforded by grants to establish teachers at Sunderland, Ferry Hill, Whickham, Stanhope, Staindrop, Brancepeth, Easington, Shincliffe and Lanchester.[6]

Probably not more than twenty-one of the schools set up in Wales were still in existence at the Restoration. It seems likely that some of them failed because they were situated in places remote from towns. Only two of the nine schools founded in the county of Brecon can be traced after 1653. Nine schoolmasters, only two of whom were replaced, gave up their schools in order to enter the ministry. Seven others who had been appointed to the new schools did not teach during the Protectorate period and their schools were closed. One new school was founded by authority of the State, at St. David's in Pembrokeshire by an order of 17 May 1654.[1]

The story of the schools in Wales after 1653 is a disappointing one. Nevertheless, interest in public education did not die with the Long Parliament. The provisions which had been made by the parliament to safeguard existing schools were continued by the Protector and his Council. Educational endowments were still exempted from seizure and from assessments which were levied in June 1657 and January 1659–60 for the maintenance of the army.[2] Trustees, who exercised their power under the direct control of the Protector and his Council, kept under review all existing grants in aid of schoolmasters and paid allowances and augmentations.[3] Thus in June 1656 the Council recommended to the Trustees for Maintenance of Ministers that they should settle forty pounds a year on Mr. Taylor, the schoolmaster of Huntingdon, and thirty pounds a year on Edward Smith, the schoolmaster of Grimston in Norfolk.[4]

Throughout the period 1640–60 various Commissions of Charitable Uses improved the efficiency of schools by rousing school governors to a keener sense of responsibility, putting school finances in order, raising schoolmasters' salaries and ensuring that they were regularly paid. Among those who benefited from the ministrations of the commissioners were the master and usher of King Edward VI Grammar School, Chelmsford who in 1646 received arrears of pay[5] and the master and usher of Hartlebury Grammar School who in 1654 had their annual salaries raised from fourteen to thirty-two pounds, and from six to ten pounds respectively.[6] In 1653 a Commission of Charitable Uses took steps to remedy the deplorable conditions at Rugby School, to which attention has already been drawn. The commissioners ordered the payment of arrears, amounting to more than seven hundred pounds, which was to be used to repair the school buildings and almshouses, to pay the schoolmaster's salary regularly, and to make compensation to the present schoolmaster and to the widow of the former schoolmaster, Raphael Pearce.[7]

The record of achievement is, then, that existing schools were protected in the midst of violent changes in Church and State, that new schools were brought into existence, especially by the Acts for the Propagation of the Gospel, and that money grants for the upkeep of schools and maintenance of schoolmasters were readily forthcoming. All this, remarkable as it is, obviously falls short of the programme of general educational reform which seemed possible in the early days of the Long Parliament and which was restated by reformers throughout the Commonwealth period. Nevertheless, the instances of State intervention in the field of learning, which have been considered, indicate that the question of national schooling remained prominent in the minds of statesmen, and witness to the Puritan belief that it was the duty of the government to bring free and popular education within reach of all children of all social groups. These experiments in the educational sphere were brought to an end by the Restoration. The evidence supports the view that, if the Puritan government had survived, the ideas of Comenius, Hartlib and Dury would have been put into practice and a national system of education realized.

4. The Decline of the Grammar Schools

The first impressive fact about the educational system in the later Stuart period is its continuing expansion. New schools were founded and established schools were strengthened by the provision of additional endowments. Of the seven hundred and ninety-nine schools listed in the *Report of the Schools Inquiry Commission*, which was published in 1868, five hundred were founded more than two hundred years before,[1] and one hundred and forty-seven were founded between 1660 and 1714.[2] And yet when at the beginning of the nineteenth century Nicholas Carlisle made his inquiries, fifty-seven of the four hundred and seventy-five grammar schools which he described had become elementary schools, twenty-four or twenty-five were no longer in existence, while his failure to obtain any information from seventy-two schools suggests that the fortunes of some of them were at a low ebb.

These facts are of particular interest to the educational historian whose field of study is the later Stuart period since in his survey of the grammar school system he may hope to unearth factors contributory to the decline of this sort of education after its expansion and achievement in Tudor and early Stuart times. Before we embark on this investigation, however, it will be well to consider the accepted view that in general the grammar schools entered upon an unhappy period of decadence in the eighteenth century. We may begin by examining the condition of these schools in one county, that of Oxfordshire, when at the beginning of the nineteenth century Nicholas Carlisle published his findings.

In 1818, after two and a half centuries of its history, the grammar school at Chipping Norton was still providing a classical education for between forty and seventy boys. At Woodstock Samuel Jackson had twenty or thirty boys in the school and was giving a sound education in the classics at a charge of one guinea a quarter, and elementary instruction at a charge of half a guinea, to the sons of freemen while boarders paid from twenty-five guineas to forty pounds a year. The master of Charlbury Grammar School, Thomas Oakley, taught classics in return for the stipend of forty pounds which had been fixed in 1675 and which he augmented by taking 'one or at most two young Gentlemen of respectability' as boarders and preparing them for entry to the university. No one with qualifications to teach classics would accept the stipend of £17 10s. which was offered at Steeple Aston and under John Jepson, who was the first layman to hold this post which customarily went to the rector of the parish, the ancient grammar school was an elementary school for about sixty children. The mastership of Ewelme Grammar School was a sinecure, there were about six boys at Lord Williams' School, Thame and at Magdalen College School, Oxford there were few if any pay boys, as those who were not on the foundation were known.[1] The school at Dorchester had probably ceased to be a grammar school in all but name as early as 1746 when Jacob Applegarth who was not qualified to teach classics was appointed to the mastership at a salary of ten pounds a year, and only elementary instruction was given at the schools which had formerly offered grammar, at Bampton, Burford, Watlington, and at Nixon's School in Oxford. The grammar school at Henley had lost its existence in 1778 when it was combined with a charity school,[2] and the grammar school at Banbury was no longer remembered and all record of its endowment had disappeared.[3]

As this evidence from Oxfordshire suggests the grammar schools have had varied histories and in the eighteenth century it seems that it was almost a matter of chance whether a school would flourish or fail. Some schools continued throughout the century with no drastic change in their fortunes, neither in great repute nor in sad decline, supplying a classical education and from time to time sending boys to the universities while others rose to a position of eminence by the end of the century. But it is also true that in many grammar schools there was a fall in the number of pupils throughout the eighteenth century so that some schoolmasters came to regard their posts as sinecures, while others continued to teach classics to a few free boys and coached privately in their own homes or ceased to take boys on the foundation and used the school building for their private pupils. Unfortunately the evidence is too scattered and limited to permit any quantitative analysis of how these and other considerations affected the grammar schools, but some examples will show how individual institutions fared in the eighteenth century. We shall consider in turn schools which maintained or improved their position and schools which declined.

Northampton Grammar School had an uneventful and not unsuccessful history throughout the eighteenth century with little more to remark than the long tenures of its masters, one of whom, John Stoddart, was blind for twenty-five of the thirty years during which he ruled the school from 1797 and who in 1818 had about eighty-five boys including thirty boarders.[1] Southwell Minster Grammar School seems to have continued to serve its purpose and at the end of the century the number of scholars had grown too large for the premises so that in 1790 the master, Magnus Jackson, received fourteen pounds for repairing and enlarging the schoolroom and in the following year obtained the lease for forty years of a piece of land upon which to build a new schoolroom.[2] In Hampshire the grammar school at Alresford had considerable attraction for persons of high social standing when Richard Steele was master from 1796 to 1818[3] and Southampton School which had enhanced its reputation during Richard Mant's mastership from 1770 to 1795 had become entirely a boarding school in 1819.[4] According to Richard Surtees, Houghton le Spring Grammar School had been restored 'from a low ebb' by Thomas Griffiths, 'a sound, thoroughbred scholar', who became master in 1738 and who bequeathed his books to his successors,[5] and in 1818 was flourishing under

William Rawes who had thirty boarders who paid the high fee of fifty guineas.[1] At Beverley Grammar School John Clarke began his mastership in 1736 by rebuilding the schoolroom, in 1743 had a hundred boys in his school and when he retired in 1751 left the library full of books.[2] In Sussex its modest endowment which provided only twenty pounds a year for the master did not prevent Midhurst Grammar School from maintaining a good reputation into the nineteenth century so that Carlisle could write: 'This Institution has, for some years past, been a Classical School of very great Eminence, – annually sending Students to The Universities, and ranking among its Pupils, besides many independent Members, several lately admitted upon the Foundation of the most respectable Colleges in each'.[3] Already in the eighteenth century the nine schools, Winchester, Eton, St. Paul's, Westminster, Merchant Taylors', Rugby, Harrow, Shrewsbury and Charterhouse, which in 1861 were placed in a special category and designated 'public schools',[4] were winning a position of eminence and becoming the exclusive preserve of the sons of gentlefolk and of the wealthy.

The public schools did not differ originally from grammar schools which had been founded to receive boys from all parts of the country and not from the particular locality. All schools which were non-local in character were in this sense public schools. All alike in their earlier days attracted boys from the country and from the town, the sons of the nobility and gentry, clergy and tradespeople. The lack of differentiation is further attested, as Mr. A. F. Leach showed, by the facts that orders for the school at Saffron Walden in Essex in 1525 directed that 'the order and use of Winchester and Eton' should be followed[5] while the master of Cuckfield Grammar School in Sussex was to take Eton as his model for curriculum and school hours and to make any modifications that were necessary from time to time so that the school practices were kept in line with changes that were made at Eton.[6] 'At the close of the eighteenth century, the distinction between the "public schools" and the rest of the grammar schools is well established', wrote Professor R. L. Archer. 'The public schools were merely those of the grammar schools which had increased in numbers and prestige while the rest declined'. Not all grammar schools declined and not all those

which increased in number were included in the special group
of nine public schools, nor is it sufficient to say that 'two changes
had occurred which served to differentiate them; they had increased the numbers of their staff, and they had become board-
ing-schools'.[1] Indeed, as Mr. W. O. Lester Smith wrote, 'It is
doubtful . . . whether any description will serve which does not
draw attention to the social and economic aspect.'[2] The antecedents of boys who were attending these nine schools in the
eighteenth century have been investigated by Dr. N. Hans who
concludes that 'the aristocratic character of these schools is quite
evident' and that this fact is 'still more pronounced if we separate
the two leading schools – Eton and Winchester'.[3] It is indeed
difficult to explain why these schools flourished by attracting the
sons of the nobility and the well-to-do though it is their resulting
social status and exclusiveness which mainly distinguished them
from other grammar schools.

But these schools were among the fortunate exceptions and
other evidence gives justification to Lord Kenyon's description
in 1795 of the grammar schools as 'empty walls without scholars'
and adds weight to his comment that whoever examined the
grammar schools in various parts of the country would realize
the 'lamentable condition' to which most of them had been reduced, and to his own knowledge of some schools in which 'there
was not a single scholar . . . though there were very large endowments to them'.[4] Berkhamsted School in 1743 had only five boys
and in the following year it was commented that the master,
Evan Price, 'might as well lock up the doors of the school and at
the furthest part of Wales receive the wages of a sinecure'; in
1813 the master had only one scholar to teach and the usher was
living in Hampshire.[5] When John Evanson became master of
Oundle School in 1779 there were four boys in the school and
six years later there were none; in 1788 the number of boys had
risen to ten, of whom seven were boarders.[6] The ill-health of the
master, Joseph Shipston, may account for the fact that the
number of scholars at Chesterfield Grammar School in Derbyshire dwindled after 1773; but the decline continued under his
successor, Thomas Field, who was promoted from the ushership
in 1794, so that the school became 'of little public benefit'.[7]
Benjamin Preedy, master of St. Albans School, reported to the

corporation on 3 February 1762 'that he had no scholars to teach'[1] and Carlisle's information was that from 1754 to 1803 the number of boys in the school 'seldom exceeded 7 or 8' and that most of these were the masters' private pupils.[2] In 1767 there was only half the full number of forty King's Scholars at the King's School, Worcester and from 1768 to 1771 the duties of master and usher were performed by one man, Thomas Goodinge.[3] In a letter to the bishop of Lichfield and Coventry in 1794 the governors of Ashbourne Grammar School in Derbyshire complained about 'the present deserted and neglected state of the said School', about the master, William Langley, who then had one scholar and who had for many years taught only two or three, and about the under master, Fairfax Nortcliffe, who neglected the free scholars for the sake of private pupils whom he taught in his own house.[4] Steyning Grammar School in Sussex during John Morgan's mastership from 1778 to 1817 was of little benefit to the town[5] and a correspondent in *The Gentleman's Magazine* of September 1804 witnessed that at the beginning of the nineteenth century the school had ceased to function.[6] When the usher of Derby Grammar School died in 1813 it was found unnecessary to replace him since there were so few boys in the school and the master, James Bligh, received the two salaries which amounted to sixty pounds.[7] For many years up to 1806 Colchester Grammar School in Essex was ruled over 'by a Gentleman who paid no attention to the duties of a Schoolmaster' and who had not taught anyone 'for several years' while at North Leach Grammar School in Gloucestershire in 1818 the curriculum was confined to the classics and three free scholars were taught by the master, John Nelson, and the usher, Thomas Tordiffe, who for their labours received respectively two-thirds and one-third of the income which was estimated to be six hundred pounds.[8] In the same year Carlisle reported that at Clare Grammar School in Suffolk classics had not been taught 'for some time past' and that the grammar school at Kingston-on-Thames with 'not more than four or five boys' was reckoned to be 'of very little use to the Town'.[9]

If we bear in mind the incredible amount of money and effort which was invested in grammar school education in the sixteenth and early seventeenth centuries and how disappointingly meagre were the results in the eighteenth century the question that poses itself from the very beginning is why so little came out of so much. In our survey of the grammar school system in the later Stuart period we must, then, consider the possibility that even when new schools were being founded, and established schools were receiving benefactions, these schools carried within themselves the seeds of their own decay.

The historian of the later Stuart period is fortunate in having at his disposal the material concerning the grammar schools in England and Wales which was collected by Christopher Wase between the years 1673 and 1677 and to which reference will be made throughout this work. This material remains in manuscript form in the Bodleian Library, where it was deposited in 1934 by Corpus Christi College, Oxford,[1] and has been largely neglected as a source for the history of education. Since it furnishes an educational survey on a national scale of the sort which was not again attempted until at the beginning of the nineteenth century Nicholas Carlisle made his investigation, it will be necessary to give some account of the purpose, method and result of Wase's inquiry.

The Writing School at Christ's Hospital, 1816

Loving Brother.

By my long Silence you may well conclude I have wholly forgot you, and your concerns, which I promised to endeavor to serve you in those parts. But I assure you I have not been unmindfull of you; upon my returne from London I did by the first opportunity disperse among friends your papers of Inquiries, but to this day have not had one answer returning but to them. What ever the Reason is, I find a very great backwardness and unwillingness in persons hereabouts to answer the Queries. I have severall times called for the Answers, and have had promises thereof, but all have hitherto failed, so that I now even despaire of obtaining them. I have sent you a breife account of the neighbour free-Schoole of Boxford which I could have sent you much sooner but was unwilling it should come alone (as now upon force it doth) I have given you withall a sight of such orders, and directions as the Governors have thought fit among themselves to make and establish for the better governing of the said Schoole, whither they will doe you any Service or no in yor designe I know not, but upon perusall you will find them such, as the right observing of which would not a little conduce to the well ordering, and flourishing of the said Schoole. If you are yet carrying on this worke I wish you all success therein, and that other friends may doe you better Service then I see I am able, though not unwilling, to do you. If yet any account should come to my hands from any to whom I have given your Inquiries I shall by the first dispatch it to you. your daughter Hannah is (God be thanked) in good health, as you will understand by this inclosed from her, and so for through with all yor friends & relations in these parts. One of my Sist. viz Eliza is lately married to Norwich, where I hope God hath provided her a good Husband, and another viz Martha is near upon marrying to a young clergy-man, neare Ipswich. Aunt Scott is at present here, and in health. With Love, and Respects from her Bro: Whiting and sister, Service from my Selfe I rest

Groton. Aprill. 23.
1677.

Our love to Cos. Christopher.

yors to command
Ste: Newcomen.

A letter from Stephen Newcomen in the
Wase Collection

II

THE WASE INQUIRY

In the years following the Restoration the educational system of the grammar schools in England and Wales fell into some disfavour. The value of the ancient languages in education was questioned in some influential circles, and critics went so far as to suggest that the evils of civil war which had lately disrupted the country might be attributed to the training given in the classics. This opinion had been expressed in 1651 by Thomas Hobbes in his *Leviathan* when he wrote that 'by reading of these Greek, and Latine Authors, men from their childhood have gotten a habit (under a false shew of Liberty,) of favouring tumults, and of licentious controlling the actions of their Soveraigns; and again of controlling those controllers, with the effusion of so much blood'.[1]

A supporter of the grammar schools was Christopher Wase who in his book *Considerations concerning Free Schools, as settled in England*, published in 1678, made a strong plea for their continuation and increase in numbers.

> There is an opinion commonly receiv'd that the Scholars of England are overproportion'd to the preferments for letter'd Persons. Hereupon the Constitution of Free Schools cometh to be question'd, as diverting those, whom Nature or Fortune had determin'd to the Plough, the Oar, or other Handicrafts, from their proper design, to the study of Liberal Arts, and even Divinity it self.[2]

To this complaint that already there were too many scholars to fill the needs and opportunities in the learned professions Wase answered:

> All Trades think themselves overstock'd; some have fancied the World to be so, that if men did not in Wars kill one another, they must eat one another. This supposition may yet be perhaps ill-grounded. All men are not thriving in any

profession. Some in all would live upon the Earth. Magistrates here moderate and by the Prudence of their Orders remove obstructions to Trade, that Work be not wanting to the Industrious; as also provide encouragements for Industry, that Laborers be not wanting to the Work.

The charge brought against the schools that 'the multiplying these Foundations' was 'dangerous to the Government' called for an answer since 'these jealousies have gain'd upon the Prudent, the Powerful, and not the least, upon the Scholar'. Wase sought to combat the allegation that the 'late civil Commotions' could be attributed to the education given in the endowed schools and pointed out that 'Grand Authors of the Troubles were Politicians of a higher form; and noted Officers that executed their designs were many men illiterate, pure Instruments, beneath such ingenuous breeding'.[1]

Wase's book, interesting as it is as a defence of free schools, is disappointing because, as Falconer Madan remarked, 'there are few details, and very little attempt at a list of Schools, or notes of actual curricula or statistical information of any kind'.[2] And yet since 1673 Wase had been corresponding with schoolmasters and had been collecting information with a view to publishing his findings and furnishing a comprehensive account of free grammar schools in England and Wales.

During the time when he was pursuing his inquiries about the grammar schools Christopher Wase was Architypographus and Superior Bedell of Civil Law in the University of Oxford.[3] In a letter of 1 October 1674, William Duncumbe, the schoolmaster of Kingsbridge Grammar School in Devon congratulated him on his 'Election in ye University to so suitable an imployment' and on 13 September 1675 he wrote: 'I hope you may be an Instrument of much good in ye University where ye Providence of God hath so unexpectedly brought you.'[4] Wase's election to these offices in the university had indeed been unexpected and unusual after a varied and eventful career.

Christopher Wase was admitted to King's College, Cambridge in 1645 as a scholar from Eton. He became a fellow of his college and graduated B.A. in 1648. His loyalty to the royalist cause was clearly revealed when his translation of the *Electra of Sophocles* was published at the Hague in 1649. The book was dedicated to Princess Elizabeth, the daughter of Charles I, and in an appendix Wase expressed his earnest hope and expectation that Charles II would soon be restored to the throne.[1] This display of partisanship cost him his fellowship and he fled from the country only to be captured at sea. He escaped from his prison at Gravesend, saw service in the Spanish army fighting against the French and for a short time was a prisoner of war.[2] After his release he was enabled to return to England by John Evelyn who recorded the circumstances in his diary for February 1652:

> I brought with me from Paris, Mr. Chr: Wase, sometime before made to resigne his Fellowship in Kings Coll: Camb: because he would not take the Covenant; he had ben a Souldier in Flanders, came miserable to Paris, where both [h]is excellent learning & some relation he had to Sir R: Browne, made me beare his Charges into England: I also clad, & provided for him, 'til he should find some better Condition, for he was worthy of it, both for his exceeding greate Erudition & no lesse modesty.[3]

Wase now found employment as tutor to the eldest son of Philip Herbert, first earl of Montgomery, until on 25 March 1656 he was appointed to the mastership of Dedham Grammar School in Essex.[4] From Dedham he moved in 1662 to Tonbridge School in Kent where he continued as master until 1668. During Wase's mastership at Tonbridge the school, together with some other schools, was adversely affected by the Fire of London in 1666. In a letter of 15 July 1674 John Stileman promised to send to Wase an account of exhibitions from the school to the universities, 'how much they are now diminished by the fire, and when they are like to returne to their first Valew'.[5] Wase gave up schoolmastering and with the influential support of John Evelyn obtained a post as an under-secretary of state. On 16 March 1668–69 Evelyn wrote: 'To Lond: to place Mr. Wase about my L: Arlington', and on 2 April he recorded that he had 'now placed Mr. Wase, with Mr. Williamson Secretary to the secretary of state, & Cleark of the Papers'.[6]

On 10 October 1671 in his absence and without his knowledge Wase was elected Architypographus and Superior Bedell of

Civil Law in the University of Oxford.[1] The curious circumstances of his election are related by Anthony Wood. Dr. John
Fell, dean of Christ Church, supported the candidature of a
member of his own college, Thomas Bennet, whose election
seemed certain when the two other candidates, Noah Parkinson
of Hart Hall and Gowin Knight of Merton College, withdrew.
The masters, however, resented the attitude of Dr. Fell who 'was
resolved to get his man in meerly by his authority, without any
application to them' and that of Bennet who did not apply
'himself, according to the manner, with cap in hand to gain
votes'. And so

> when the election was to be on the 10th of the same month,
> a majority of the masters joyned together, (headed and en-
> couraged chiefly by a clownish factious person) did in
> despight of Dr. Fell, his mandamus and authority, of the
> heads of houses, seniors, and the sober party, set up and
> chuse a meer stranger, who lived remotely from Oxon,
> named Christop. Wase, (sometime fellow and bach. of arts
> of King's coll. in Cambridge, and afterwards a schoolmaster
> at several places) to the very great discomposure of Dr. Fell,
> and something to the discredit of the university, as if not
> able to afford a man to execute the said office. Afterwards
> Wase came to Oxon, was sworn and took possession of his
> place: But Dr. Fell, who had received a character of him,
> would never let him execute the archityp. place, because, as
> he usually said, he was not fit for it, as being not a person of
> sobriety, &c. So that from the death of Mr. Clarke to this
> time, the superior beadleship of the civ. law and the archi-
> typographer's place hath been disjoyned.[2]

Dr. Fell's opposition explains the sympathetic comment of
Nicholas Roberts, the master of Carmarthen Grammar School,
in his letter of 23 October 1673. 'I am sorry to understand,' he
wrote, 'that there is yet a distance between the Architypographus
and the grand Promoters of printing.'[3] On 19 July 1676 Thomas
Leigh asked Wase if he was 'now allow'd al ye privileges of ye
Architypography'.[4]

Nearly two years after his election Wase began his inquiries
into free schools in England and Wales. The purpose and

method of the project are expressed in 'A Certificat in order to the Collecting and Reporting the State of the present English Free-Schools'. This document, dated 'Oxon. Aug. 16. 1673', is signed by the bishop of Bath and Wells, vice-chancellor, and Dr. Thomas Bouchier, regius professor of Civil Law, in the University of Oxford, who testify their 'sense of the undertaking whereby the Compiler of the Work may stand recommended to the Registers, Officers in the respective Dioceses, or any who may assist him in those Enquiries', and 'own the industry of Christopher Wase Superior Bedle of the Civill-Law in the said University in making this Collection'. The certificate concludes with the

> Enquiries. 1. From Registers. What Free-Schools in each Diocese? 2. From School-masters for their particular Schools. 1. Who Founder? 2. When Founded? 3. How Endowed? 4. What School-Master and succession of Masters? if at hand; otherwise such as are in memory to have been eminent, or Authors of any extant Work. 5. What Exhibitions and in whether University? 6. Who Governors, Patrons & Visitors? 7. What Libraries in them or in Towns adjoining, with what Manuscripts?[1]

Wase obtained a list of schools in each diocese from the registrar and for the most part corresponded directly with the schoolmasters. Sometimes the papers were sent to the registrars who collected the material from the schoolmasters in their dioceses and returned the answers to Wase. Joseph Harvey wrote from Hereford on 4 February 1673–74: 'Mr Register sent mee word, that you had sent to most of them of yourselfe, & receivd their Answers to *your* enquiries; Hee has sent you here inclosd a more exact account then before of all the Schooles in the Diocesse'. Harvey noted that the schoolmasters had been 'especially carefull' to give Wase a list of the succession of masters.[2] On 9 July 1676 Robert Herne was 'With Dr Robert Twelves, the present Register of ye Diocesse of Ely, and desired an account of the number of free-schools in his Diocesse'. On the following day Herne sent to Wase the account which he had received from the registrar who intended to make further inquiry 'this weeke at ye Visitation'.[3] The registrar of the diocese of Chester wrote to Mr. Moreton, the master of the free school at Mottram:

> You are desired on the behalfe of Christopher Wase Superior Bedell of the Civill Law in the Universitie of Oxon (Who purposes to report the state of the present English Free schooles) to send with convenient Speed the best information you can give or answer to the Queries under written unto the Registres Office in Chester.

To the seven questions contained in the certificate the registrar added an eighth: 'Whatt other particulars equally remarkable'.[1] A similar letter to the schoolmaster at Ormskirk in Lancashire is preserved in the manuscripts.[2] The plan and patronage of Wase's inquiry is further attested in 'An Accompt of the Free Grammar Schoole of Presteigne in the County of Radnor in the Diocesse of Hereford' which was written by Samuel Rickards, the master of the school,

> in answer to a Certificate in order to the Collecting and reporting the State of the present English Free-Schooles and to each particular enquiry therein Contained & Directed to the Registers of Dioceses and Schoole Masters of particular Free-Schooles from the Right Reverend Father in God Peter L: Bishop of Bath & Wells and Later Vice Chancelor of Oxon and Thomas Bouchier Dr. of Laws Regius Professor of the Civill Law in Oxon.[3]

The difficulty of making 'a perfect collection of these schooles' was remarked by Oliver Doyley, fellow of King's College, Cambridge who pointed out that it would not be easy 'to travell about the nation to gett due information' and that Wase could hardly expect 'all the materials for this worke' to be brought to his 'owne doore'.[4] Another friend, Thomas Leigh, thought that so far as the 'great schools' like Winchester College were concerned Wase could not 'faile of an exact account of ye respective Masters; but of ye smaller schools, that are dispers'd up & down ye countrey,' Leigh wrote on 20 September 1673, 'I doubt you wil find ye returns come in very defective as to Masters'.[5] A letter of 7 November 1673 from John Martin, the schoolmaster of Burford in Oxfordshire, shows that there was some justification for Leigh's feeling of uncertainty. With two or three friends Martin had 'made a long & tedious search over all ye writings belonging to ye Towne in publick, but could not find one of ye Wardens bookes'. And therefore, he wrote to Wase: 'You must take ye succession of ye Masters, as I had them, from ye ancientist & knowingst men in Towne.'[1]

Wase's purpose was the continuance and increase of free schools; but the opinion was expressed that his investigation might ultimately do more harm than good to the cause of education which he was so deeply concerned to help. 'Ye designe is not alike approved by all,' wrote Oliver Doyley. 'I heare some think the consequence of it may not be so good as you intend it they fearing that when the great number of free schools throughout the nation shall be collected together, & exposed to publicke view, it may be a meanes to supersede any further charity of that kind as a thing superfluous.'

Doyley's aim was not to discourage Wase, but, as a friend, he begged him to consider carefully before involving himself in 'uncertaine charges' about the inquiry which would cost him so much 'time & paines'.[2] John Rowland, the rector of Foots Cray in Kent, was a friendly correspondent who had doubt about the project. 'I might have saluted you with the Title of great Benefactor for free Grammer Scholes,' he wrote on 1 March 1673–74. 'Yet I think it very disputable, whether the great charity of Benefactors erecting so many free scholes in times of Ignorance, have not, through Mens Ingratitude, cast a greater scorne upon Learning, and learned Men, than if there were now noe free scholes at all.' Rowland concluded therefore that one of Wase's 'chief ends, of stirring up more Benefactors, unless it bee for other good ends, and purposes than the building of more free Scholes, will doe learning noe service at all'.[3]

In spite of their misgivings about the prudence and outcome of the undertaking Doyley and Rowland were among Wase's friends and supporters who in various parts of the country did their utmost to obtain information for him. Rowland contributed material and on 8 December 1674 wished Wase 'good speed' in the 'laborious and usefull work' he had undertaken. 'It may prove a bridle to future usurpation. Had the overseers in their respective Liberties not been so remiss or corrupt; much of your pains might have been spared. It were well, if some person of your Abilities, would doe the like in the Preferments of the Church.'[1]

William Walker, the master of Grantham School, was very much concerned with Wase's design in the county of Lincolnshire. In a letter dated 17 June 1674 he expressed his wishes for its good success and his assurance of help. 'As my good will is not wanting,' he wrote, 'so neither shall my power be wanting to serve it, and you therein, when I shall have opportunity.'[2] William Rochford, whose letter from Addington in Buckinghamshire is dated 27 August 1675, was evidently in sympathy with the design. He wrote to give an account of his efforts and informed Wase that since he was 'of late yeares a great stranger' in Northamptonshire he had written to a minister of his acquaintance to ask for 'the best satisfaction he could gaine, as to the Origines of the Scholes in those parts, their founders, and endowments, &c'.[3] Information about the free schools in North Wales was sent by Hugh Pugh, rector of Llanbedr, warden of Ruthin School and Hospital. 'I wish you good successe in this your worthy designe,' he wrote on 7 April 1676,

> and doubt not but god will prosper your endeavours herein, since intended for soe good and noble an end. for hereby you doe right unto, and perpetuate the memory of the generous founders and bountifull benefactors, of their respective schooles, and encourage others to imitate their good examples. And cheifly, you leave a Record for future ages, whereby each schoole may produce an evidence, if questioned for its right an [sic] revenue, which otherwise time or covetousnesse may devour and destroy.[4]

His friend and helper, Thomas Leigh, in an undated letter from Bishop's Stortford in Essex sent an account of the free school at Moulton in Lincolnshire which he had obtained from his former pupil the Reverend Edward Whiston, vicar of the parish. Whiston also informed him that there were 'free schooles not farre off thence at Spalding & Holbeech' but was unable to give any details about them. Leigh, however, was 'lesse solicitous' about this since he understood that the bishop of Lincoln had 'ingaged to promote' the design throughout his diocese.[5]

There is evidence that the archbishop of Canterbury and some bishops gave influential support to Wase. On 30 August 1673 the secretary, Dr. Robert Thompson, wrote from Lambeth that he had 'comunicated the paper' which Wase had sent, to the archbishop who was very willing to give all the help he could in order to further the design. Thompson added: 'The Enquiries differ very little from what I formerly made to ye Registers of Canterbury and Essex, But that there may be no mistake I have since repeated *your* desire to yem in *your* own words.'[1] In September Thomas Leigh expressed his pleasure that Wase's design was 'owned by such great persons' and declared that his own labours in Essex had been 'superseded' by the 'particular enquiries' of the archbishop's secretary in some parts of the county.[2] The bishop of Lincoln, in a letter of 21 May 1674, promised to do his utmost to serve Wase in his 'good Designe' and asked for '2 or 3 dozen of those papers you printed concerning schooles' so that he might distribute them during his forthcoming visitation to the diocese.[3] The bishop of Worcester 'by reason of his weakenesse was not able to goe the Visitation himself', but Nathaniel Salter informed Wase on 13 October 1674 that he had 'desird his Lordship's Secretary to recommend it to the Clergy'.[4] Richard Healy received assurance from Mr. Thurlby, the bishop's secretary, that papers had been sent by him in the bishop's name to all the free schools in the diocese of Bath and Wells[5] and Hugh Pugh in North Wales was helped by Mr. Humphreys, the bishop of Bangor's domestic chaplain. Ralph Harrison in Colchester asked for a few more papers so that he might renew Wase's design with the assistance and favour of the bishop of London.[6] In June 1677 the bishop of Hereford was visiting his diocese and hoped 'to meet with those schoolmasters who' were 'behinde with their Answers'. 'If hee can prevaile with them to send 'em in,' wrote Joseph Harvey to Wase, 'you shall receive them by the next opportunity from mee: but I feare (if hee does speed) they'll come too late for *your* purpose.'[7]

Wase also had the patronage and assistance of some heads and fellows of colleges in the University of Cambridge. George Griffith, writing on 1 July 1674 describes Mr. Foxcroft, the senior proctor of the university as Wase's 'good friend' whom he had heard 'speake worthily' of him. The same letter refers to the activity of Oliver Doyley, fellow of King's College, who was making inquiries about scholarships and exhibitions in Cambridge and hoped to send an account of them.[1] Doyley's interest and support is attested by David Morton of St. John's College, Cambridge in a letter of 15 November 1675 which also shows Wase's purpose with regard to the colleges in the university:

> I did with very great approbation & content about a yeare since (or perhaps somewhat more) receive from our worthy friend Mr. Oliver Doyley an account of ye design for Collecting & Reporting ye state of ye present English Freeschools; & more particularly, so farr, as any College is concerned in their Patronage, or Inspection, or any Endowment for Scholarships or fellowships or Exhibitions.[2]

The president of Jesus College, William Cooke, applied on Wase's behalf to Mr. Matthews, president of Sidney Sussex College who promised to give him 'an account of such Schooles, as related to ym'.[3] From Ben'et College John Spencer reported on 14 August 1676: 'There is no Schole w*h*ich hath any great dependence on, or relation to our little College, beyound what this paper, here inclos'd doth mention . . . I like yo*u*r designe very well, & would gladly contribute thereunto, to my poor ability.'[4] As for those colleges in the university of which Wase had so far received no account, Robert Herne of Clare Hall believed that he would be able to obtain information from most of them with the exception of Trinity College. He suggested on 19 June 1676 that Wase should send a letter which he would deliver to Mr. Bainbridge, the bursar of the college, and he felt sure that Wase would 'meet with the same candor'.[5]

A small number of schoolmasters took the opportunity to thank Wase for his services to education in the past and to commend and encourage him in his present efforts. 'I congratulate ye age that produceth Persons of so publique a spirit as yo*u*rselfe,' wrote Nathaniel Freind on 17 May 1675. 'Your learned labours as to schooles in other Particulars, render all yt have any relation to such Imploym*ent* exceedingly obliged to you, among whom I acknowledge my selfe to bee one, & should bee glad in any thing I may to serve you. May you bee happy in bringing yo*u*r intended work to perfection it being a Subject yet untreated of (I think) by any.'[1]

The master of Oundle School, William Speed, expressed his 'hearty thanks' to Wase for his 'excellent bookes already publish'd to ye world. They are ample testimonys,' he wrote, on 28 August 1675, 'of your great abilitys & labours in ye true & old method of Didacticks; now all ye Kingdome over generally embraced, & found eminently successfull; beyond all ye deluding Quackerys of new-fangled Imposters.' Speed wholly approved of Wase's design 'to transmitt a Record to posterity of our publick Nurserys of Learning in England, with ye revenues & advantages belonging to them' since he agreed 'that ye Foundations & Endowments &c of schooles, faithfully look'd into & improved, is a principall meanes of their advancement, (for money is the encourager of other arts as well as ye military:)'. In the following April Speed wrote again of his desire to further these 'most worthy undertakings' which he trusted that Wase would 'perfect to ye great advantage of our nation'.[2] William Bland, the schoolmaster at Towcester in Northamptonshire, was another who took the opportunity to thank Wase for 'his excellent books', which had 'benefited all the officers in the commonwealth of learning'.[3] It was from Bland that Charles Griffin, schoolmaster of Blisworth in the same county, heard of these 'laudable undertakeings'. 'I forthwith made it my care & study to answer those enquiries inserted in the print,' he wrote on 3 August 1675, 'Accounting it an happinesse if my endeavours may in any wise availe to the accomodacon of a person soe compleated, or promote to the perfection of soe meritorious a work.'[4]

The readiness and efforts of schoolmasters to comply with Wase's request and to further his intention were, however, often impeded by the attitude of school governors. On 11 November 1673 Josiah Simcox, the schoolmaster at Stratford on Avon, wrote:

I have been thus long in answering the contents of your letter hoping that by this time I might have been able to give a full and infallible account of our school, for wee have in the Chamber of Stratford records concerning it, but the ignorance of our Corporation renders their owne search into them insignificant, and their Jealousies forbid another's search, soe that I am forc't to give you but a slender account thereof.[1]

When John Hunt, the schoolmaster of Ilminster in Somerset, acquainted the school feoffees with Wase's letter they refused to give him any information. On 21 May 1674 he explained that his delay in answering Wase's queries was contrary to his 'wishes and earnest desire', and gave evidence of his own readiness to help in spite of the opposition of the school authorities. 'I have used all ye means both by my self and others to inform you off what I could possibly learn of ye state off ye school,' he wrote, 'and with much intreaty I prevaild with one off ye Gentlemen to give me this accompt.'[2] On 7 February 1675–76 Thomas Leigh reported a visit to Charles James, the master at St. Albans, who had received Wase's letter but 'found it very difficult to prevaile with ye Corporacion for a search into their Writings'.[3] Leigh also had difficulty in obtaining information about the free school at King's Lynn in Norfolk which surprised him since he had employed one of his former pupils 'a native & scholar of that Towne'.

> When he began to search ye Records belonging therto, ye Magistrates there were (he tells me) highly offended, & would not give way thereto, nor suffer any account to be given forth, which might be made public: Whether from that shighnesse, usually found in Corporations, whereof you forewarn'd me; or from the difference that is at present between ye now Master of ye Schoole Mr. Edward Bell (who hath been about 30 years Master) & ye Towne, I know not.[4]

The records of Bridgnorth School in Shropshire had been 'burnt with ye town in ye late unhappy warres' as the schoolmaster, Richard Cornes, pointed out in his letter of 11 March 1676–77. 'What satisfaction I had,' he wrote, 'was from ye Town Legier Booke, & from some leases belonging to ye Town & Schoole of which to obtaine a sight was very difficult, & required much time & labour to search them.'[5]

Uncertainty about the attitude of the provost and fellows was expressed by the master and caused delay in the return from Eton

College. 'I should be willing to serve you to ye utmost in the designe you are upon,' wrote John Rosewell on 29 September 1673.

> But I cannot do it without perusall of the Bookes, which I cannot tell, whether it will be allow'd me, nor whether the Provost and Fellowes will be willing the world should know all those particulars you desire to be inform'd in. Your best way therefore will be to propose the whole matter to Mr. Provost, and if he approve the thing, and will impower me to turne over the Bookes, I will then indeavour to give you the best satisfaction that I can. But without ye leave of him and the Fellowes I can do nothing in it.[1]

Deference to the wishes of the school governors caused first a delay and finally a failure of response from Bristol Grammar School. The letter from John Rainsthorpe, dated 31 October without the year, begins by explaining the tardiness of his reply: 'Yours I received not til last night bearing date Oct: 6th, which, if sooner received had been sooner answered.' The master of Bristol Grammar School was reluctant to become involved in Wase's scheme 'having been once before frump'd by ye City upon almost ye like occasion' and a friend had advised him not to concern himself 'in this affaire without ye knowledge and consent of ye City'. 'When ye Townclarke returnes from London,' Rainsthorpe concluded, 'I wil have his opinion; for ye City in all cases adhere to his judgment.' The decision of the school governors in this matter was conveyed to Wase by William Gibbons, fellow of St. John's College, Oxford to whom Rainsthorpe wrote on 16 June 1676 about entering one of his pupils at the College. In a postscript to this letter Rainsthorpe added:

> I received a letter last week from Mr. Wase, who presseth mee (as formerly) to give him an account of ye qualification of my schoole. Present my service to him with an excuse for not writing, and tel him yt I communicated his letter to ye magistrates, ye Patrons of ye schoole; but they would not condescend (as eminent corporations are commonly stately) yt I should make ye least discovery.[2]

The schoolmaster of Newbury in Berkshire was not obstructed

by school authorities for his answer to Wase's sixth question was 'Nor Governors, Patrons, or Visitors.' But perhaps, as an editorial comment in the manuscript suggests, he was nervous about the inquiry since he added to the queries an eighth which he answered 'Nor other remark propre to the place.'[1] Not all schoolmasters were convinced that the inquiry was well-advised or likely to be to their advantage. A not surprising reaction came from the schoolmaster of St. Albans, Charles James, who had been slow to reply. The design seemed 'at least at first view so like an Inquisicon without Authority to backe it', he wrote on 3 October 1674, 'that I doubted with my selfe some while, whether I ought to propose it to the Court of Aldermen of this Towne, in whose absolute disposal the Revenue, Government, &c of this school resides, who, I suppose would not easily admit of any new Visitors, especially having received some disturbance in this kind by my predecessor'.[2]

Joseph Harvey reported on 28 May 1674 that many school-masters in the diocese of Hereford were 'very backwards' in giving any account at all to the registrar; they were prejudiced against the inquiry and entertained jealousies because they believed that 'however it may tend to the promotion of great publicke schooles, yet it may aime at the ruine of the private'. On 24 June Harvey wrote to Wase that some schoolmasters were 'strangely fearefull' that he intended them 'noe good'. Wase's account of schools in the diocese of Hereford was still incomplete when Harvey wrote to him again on 15 September 1675, 'Hee (i.e. Mr. Register) has this answer from those schooles you have heard nothinge of, that either their Records are lost, or else the account they could give is soe lame, & imperfect that tis not worth sendeinge.'[3]

Reports from friends on the progress they were making indicate a disappointingly slow response from many schoolmasters. In Derbyshire and the West Riding of Yorkshire John Matthews found 'some slackness & remisness' in those from whom he had 'requested an Answer'. 'More Readines to serve You & further You in your painful undertaking is due from those of my Calling,' he wrote. 'Your Worth & Goodness require more satisfactory Service than You have received from your affectionate Friend.'[4] On 2 February 1673–74 William Walker wrote from Grantham

in Lincolnshire: 'I have long expected the coming in of Informa-
tions from divers Schools, from whence I might promise my self
to have them, having reasons for it. But they failing, I resolve to
send you an account of such as I have, and wait for the rest.'
Walker wrote again in the following November: 'I have concerned my self verie much in your designe, using many to gain
you the best satisfaction from sundrie Schools in Lincolnshire,
indeed aiming at all, if possiblie to be by me effected. But I find
not that readiness and quickness in them to answere my desires.'[1]
Thomas Leigh, writing on 10 August 1674, was dejected because
he had met with 'such bad successe' and Samuel Frankland at
Coventry on 27 April 1674 assured Wase that he had 'never in
life laboured more with lesse successe' than he had done 'in this
busines'.[2] Frankland gave three reasons for his failure. 'Some
are suspitious that the discovery of school-meanes may be a
leading card to the discovery of other publique incomes that
have hitherto time out of mind layne dormant,' he wrote. Others
were opposed to the design because of what its author had printed
about 'the established Catechisme', and others were 'sluggish'
and treated 'workes of publique concernment' as of no importance.[3] In two letters, dated 5 June and 27 November 1676,
Robert Herne of Clare Hall, Cambridge also reported setbacks.
Part of his inquiry was about schools in the gifts of colleges and
about scholarships and exhibitions from schools to colleges in the
university. The reason for his failure to obtain 'so speedy an
account of them, as might comply' with Wase's desire was, as he
explained in the former letter, that Cambridge had 'been lately
much troubled with ye Small Pox' and that friends upon whom
he had relied for information had gone 'in to ye Country to
avoid that distemper'. In the second letter Herne informed Wase
that he had 'not as yet received any account of ye schools in
Norfolk, or this Diocesse'.

I have used my utmost Indeavours to obtain ye favour of
those friends, which I did really thinke would not have
denied it; I cannot Imagine what reason they have to be so
backward in promoting so good a design; I am very sorry
that you have not met with so great an encouragement as
you expected, or have found in other places. As for my part

I will not cease to sollicite my friends in your behalfe, and if
it be possible I will know ye reason of their silence.[1]

Stephen Newcomen in Suffolk was unable to account for 'a very
great backwardness and unwillingness in Persons hereabouts to
answer the Queries'. He had 'severall times called for the Answers'
and had received 'promises thereof'. 'But all have hitherto
failed,' he wrote on 23 April 1677, 'so that I now even dispair
of obtaining them.'[2] And finally on 13 June 1677 Thomas Leigh
wrote from Bishop's Stortford, almost a year after his last letter
to Wase, and explained his long silence by his 'ill success in ye
inquiries' for which he blamed 'ye idlenesse of those that are
sometime worse imploy'd'.[3] But already in 1676 Richard
Richardson in Lampeter had heard that Wase had abandoned
his design.[4]

There is indication that Wase had decided to publish an
account of schools in the Oxford diocese, either preliminary to
or in place of the larger work, although there is no clear evidence
that he carried out this intention. On 27 November 1676 Robert
Herne wrote to Wase: 'You are pleased to make me acquainted
with your design of drawing up a general Scheme, and first to
give a Specimen, of ye Schools in ye Diocese of Oxford,'[5] and
under some notes on Woodstock Free School Anthony Wood
added: 'See the account of Oxfordshire Schooles in Mr Xtop
Wases hands.'[6]

Such is the story of Wase's inquiry into the state of the free
grammar schools in England and Wales. But, at its close, two
questions remain to be answered. Why did he abandon his intention to publish all the material which he had collected? What
relation does the inquiry bear to the book about the grammar
schools which he eventually produced? We do not know and can
only guess the answer to the first question. Perhaps he had grown
weary of the whole project, or was preoccupied with other
matters, or was disappointed in the response to his efforts to
obtain comprehensive statistical evidence.[7] These answers are
unsatisfactory, and especially so in view of the fact that he
showed his continuing concern with the schools by the publication in 1678 of *Considerations concerning Free Schools, as settled in
England*. And, indeed, it is in the content of his book, to which

our attention is directed by the second question, that we find what seems to be the most likely reason why Wase laid aside his original design.

There is, in fact, no obvious connexion between the material which he collected and the book which later he wrote about the grammar schools. The book shows clearly its author's deep interest in and support for grammar schools and schoolmasters, but it reveals no detailed knowledge of the actual conditions which prevailed in the schools. It is difficult to understand how anyone, with the material which Wase had at his disposal, could write a book which contained no statistical and little illustrative evidence, unless he was deliberately avoiding references to particular schools and schoolmasters. Wase may have been disappointed at the support which he had received for his undertaking. But, as we shall see, the points which he made about free schools and fees, endowments, teachers' status and salaries, the constitution of governing bodies, school libraries, could all have been immeasurably strengthened by quoting from his evidence. Why, then, did he not make use of it?

It has been shown that two of his friends had misgivings about the project from the outset, that school trustees were often unwilling to help and that some schoolmasters were afraid that it would do them harm. It seems, too, that Wase's hope of widespread support from the bishops was disappointed. Mr. Falconer Madan quotes from a copy of the certificate of 1673 in which Aubrey noted that ' Mr. Chr. Wase expected to have great help and furtherance in this Designe from the Bishops; but it proved just the contrary: for they were the maine Obstructors, as being unwilling to disoblige Gentlemen who had gott the lands given to these Scholes, into their hands and possession.'[1]

Wase must surely have been impressed by the opposition shown to his scheme and by the doubts which had been expressed about its beneficial effects upon schools and schoolmasters. To publish his information, in full or in part, was to run the risk of causing further resentment and of doing more harm than good to the institutions and men he wished to benefit. All probability therefore favours the view that he abandoned his design completely because he came to the conclusion that any other course would be ill-judged.

D

III

FREE GRAMMAR SCHOOLS

In 1664 the churchwardens and sidesmen of the parish, as trustees of Cartmel Grammar School in Lancashire, paid to their schoolmaster a salary of twenty pounds a year which was made up of small charitable gifts to the school and fees paid quarterly by all the pupils except those whose parents were unable to afford them. In 1635 boys who were learning grammar paid sixpence a quarter, while the fee for the petties was fourpence. By 1711 these fees had been increased so that the grammarians paid one shilling and sixpence while those who had not yet begun Latin were charged one shilling a quarter. Three years later it appears that fees were abolished and that entrance to the school and instruction were free to all boys of the parish. But as early as the year 1619 Cartmel Grammar School was described in the parish accounts as a 'free school'.[1]

The term 'free school' has been variously interpreted as meaning a school which was open to all who wished to avail themselves of the education supplied, or as subject to no other authority and to no other control than that of the governors, or as free from tuition fees.[2] A free school might be open only to boys of a particular locality or to all boys from any part of the kingdom. The privilege of freedom from tuition fees was sometimes confined to scholars of the parish, or town, or neighbourhood, or to those whose parents were of a certain status, such as freemen of the borough, the successors of the original contributors to a fund for establishing the school, or the heirs of the private founder. This freedom did not necessarily preclude the payment of other fees such as admission fees, fines for absence without reasonable cause, occasional expenses involved in the running of the school, and gratuities to the master, which might be a customary offering from all who sent their sons or payable at the discretion of the parents. Examples are not lacking in the period 1660–1714 of schools where the fixed and inadequate

40

value of the endowments made it impossible to continue the original intentions of the founders to grant exemption from tuition fees to all or some of the scholars, and where subsequent statutes and orders introduced fees for all the scholars, with sometimes a reduced rate or special privileges for the foundation scholars. But whatever the original implication of the term 'free school', the grammar schools which claimed this title appear in their original intentions to have had this in common, that some at least of the scholars were to be taught without anything being demanded for their instruction. In the case of Cartmel Grammar School, as we have seen, exemption from payment of tuition fees was granted to the poor.

Some founders of endowed grammar schools made clear in their foundation deeds that they contemplated schools in which there should be no charge for tuition, where the master was to teach 'without taking any Stipend, wage, or other exaction of the Scholars, or of any of them resorting to the said School to learn' or 'without any after reward or benefit to be demanded or expected'.[1] The purposes for which Manchester Free Grammar School was founded were first expressed in Latin in an indenture of 20 August 1515 which witnesses to the desire

> that grace, virtue and wisdom should flower, and take root in youths during their boyhood, especially in boys of the county of Lancaster, who for a long time through the default of teaching and instruction had wanted such grace, virtue, and wisdom in their youth, as well through their father's poverty as through absence and want of any such person who could instruct and educate such children and their minds in wisdom, learning, and virtue.

It is intended 'to remove this defect', and 'a fit person, eminent for wisdom, character and virtue, and for example in his own person, shall freely, and without anything being given therefore or taken by him, teach and instruct others, as well youths as grown-up persons'.[2]

The fact that parents who were able to obtain for their sons the advantages of a grammar school at no cost to themselves might wish to give some tangible evidence of their gratitude was not overlooked by some founders who provided that the school-master might accept 'any reward . . . freely and liberally offerd'. Such provision was made at Lewes Grammar School in Sussex which was founded in 1512[1] and at Bruton Grammar School in Somerset which was founded in 1519 or 1520.[2] Other rewards recognized and accepted in some grammar schools, as at Warrington in Lancashire[3] and Hartlebury in Worcestershire,[4] and expressly forbidden in others, as at Manchester,[5] were 'cockpenny' and 'potation-penny'. These 'pretexts for perquisites', as Nicholas Carlisle described them,[6] were gratuities given by his grateful pupils to their schoolmaster when at Shrovetide he provided for them an annual cock-fight and when on this or some other occasion he gave a feast.

The freedom of the school might bear a wider interpretation as availability to boys of every locality, and some founders were explicit in their instructions that the schools were to be open to scholars from any part of the kingdom. Thus the statutes of 1525 for Manchester Grammar School ordained that 'there shall be no scollar nor infaunt, of what cuntrey or schire so ever he be of, beyng man child, be refused'[7] and Francis Rawlinson, the founder of the free grammar school at Caistor in Lincolnshire, in his will dated 20 December 1630 desired 'that the Town of Caistor, and whatsoever Towns besides that shall send, shall be free to have their Children taught in the said School'.[8] The purpose of the grammar schools to serve the whole kingdom, and not any particular neighbourhood, was expressed in Edward VI's charter of 1551 for the free grammar school at Louth in Lincolnshire:

Whereas We have always coveted, with a most exceeding, vehement, and ardent desire, that good Literature and Discipline might be diffused and propagated, through all the parts of our Kingdom, as wherein the best government and administration of affairs consists; and therefore, with no small earnestness, have We been intent on the liberal institution of Youth, that it may be brought up to Science, in places of our Kingdom most proper and suitable for such functions; it being, as it were, the Foundation and growth of our Commonwealth, and having certain and unquestionable knowledge that our Town of Louth, in our County of Lincoln, is a place most proper and fit for the teaching and instructing of children and youth, in regard it is very populous and stocked with youth, and, heretofore, a great concourse of children and youth have flocked thither, from the adjacent Towns, to acquire learning

his Majesty therefore grants that 'hereafter, there may and shall be one Grammar School, in the said Town of Louth, which shall be called "The Free Grammar School of King Edward the Sixth", for the education, institution, and instruction of boys and youth, in the Grammar, to endure for ever'.[1]

Other founders by their silence in this matter clearly had no intention of giving any preference to the boys of particular localities. In 1519 the master of Bruton School is directed to 'teche all such scolers of men children as to hym shall resorte for lernyng and noon other indifferently after their capacities as well the poore mannes child as the riche'.[2] Robert Holgate, archbishop of York, in the foundation deed of 10 January 1546–47 for his school at York, declared that he established 'one perpetual and Free School of Grammar' and 'one Schoolmaster and his Successors . . . for ever to teach Grammar and other knowledge and Godly Learnings in the same School freely without taking any Stipend Wages or other exaction of the Scholars or of any of them resorting to learn and know the same'.[3] The same provision was included by Archbishop Holgate in the foundation deeds of 4 May 1547 for the free grammar school at Old Malton, and of 24 May 1548 for the free grammar school at Hemsworth.

On the other hand some founders intended their schools for the benefit of the inhabitants of a particular neighbourhood as did Sir Edmond Shaa when he founded the grammar school at Stockport in Cheshire. By his will of 20 March 1487–88, he ordered that the schoolmaster

shall teche allman persons children and other that woll com to hym to lerne, as well of the said Towne of Stopforde as of other Townes thereabout, the science of grammer as ferre as lieth in hym for to do in to the tyme that they be convenably instruct in gramer by him after their capaciteys that God woll geve them.[1]

Sir John Percyvale in 1502 founded a free school at Macclesfield in Cheshire in order that 'Gentilmens sonns and other good mennes Children of the Towne & Contre thereabouts' might be taught grammar.[2] Richard Rands, vicar of Hartfield in Sussex, by his will of 30 June 1640 provided twenty pounds a year for a graduate to teach freely all the children of the parish who could read and came to him for instruction.[3] Similarly John Sampson by his will, dated 16 September 1691, declared that he had established a free grammar school at South Leverton in Nottinghamshire for the children of the inhabitants of that parish.[4]

While expressing a preference for boys from the vicinity of the school, founders, like Peter Blundell of Tiverton, sometimes allowed for the admission of other children. The founder of the free grammar school at Tiverton in Devon willed, on 9 June 1599, that no more than one hundred and fifty scholars should be taught there at the same time 'and those from time to time of Children born, or for the most parte before their age of Sixe yeares, broughte upp in the Towne or Parrish of Tyverton. And if the same number be not filled upp,' Peter Blundell directs, 'the wante shall be supplyed with the Children of Forreyners' who were to be admitted with the assent of ten householders of Tiverton. These were to 'make choice of the Children of such Forreyners as are of honest reputation and feare God, without regarding the riche above or more than the poore'.[5] The grammar school at Horsham in Sussex was founded by Richard Collyer, a citizen and mercer of London, who by his will of 23 January 1532–33 directed that the scholars should 'be at noo charge of their scole hire, but freely without any money paying therfor'. While Collyer willed that preference should be given to 'the poore people in especiall of the same parishe and they next about the same parishe' since 'gentilmen and other men be in better habilitie then poore men be', he also wished that none should be refused admittance who were 'likely to lerne'.[6]

In some cases, although the schools were open to boys of any locality, freedom from payment of tuition fees was specifically granted only to the boys of the parish, or town, or neighbourhood, in which the grammar school was situated, or to other privileged persons. Thus in their orders of 1639 and further orders of 1678 for Kimbolton Grammar School in Huntingdonshire, the trustees declared that instruction in the school was free to boys of Kimbolton but that others should pay a prescribed fee.[1] A similar arrangement possibly obtained at Biggleswade Free Grammar School in Bedfordshire since it was stated in evidence in 1660 before a Commission of Charitable Uses that free teaching for their sons was enjoyed by the inhabitants and also by Henry Pigott whose claim rested on his possession of a chapel in Holme.[2] In his statutes of 12 January 1677–78, for Midhurst Grammar School in Sussex, Gilbert Hannam ordered that there should be twelve free scholars who had 'been inhabitants of Midhurst or Liberty of Saint Johns Seaven Yeares before', since his 'Charity was intended chiefly for this place', and whose parents agreed to their being 'brought upp in the Protestant Religion'.[3] The free grammar school at Charlbury in Oxfordshire was founded by Ann Walker, a spinster of London, in 1667 and established in 1675. The statutes of 29 January 1674–75 modelled on those for Witney Grammar School and drawn up by the founder's uncle, Richard Eyans, declared that the school was free for the sons of inhabitants of Charlbury with preference for the children of the poorest people and of Richard and Anthony Eyans. The schoolmaster was allowed to admit as many children from other areas as the principal and fellows of Brasenose College, as visitors, considered reasonable.[4]

Whether the founders stated their intentions in precise terms or left it to be implied by the titles which they gave to their schools, the free schools as a whole were evidently meant to offer education of an advanced sort to children of all classes who wished to avail themselves of it. These schools were open to the sons of labourers no less than to the sons of the clergy, of the merchants and of the gentry. Abraham Colfe founded the free grammar school at Lewisham in Kent in 1647 'for teaching Thirty One youths or male Children of the Laity, besides the Children of the Ministers incumbent, chosen out of all the Parishes of the Hundred of Blackheath, freely'. He left no doubt as to the antecedents of the children who were to be elected 'in their respective Parishes, at a Public Meeting, in Easter Week'. They were to be 'destitute Orphans, the Children of Parish Pensioners, and of Day Labourers, Handycraft's-men, mean Tradesmen, painful Husbandmen, or of any other honest and godly poor persons, in every parish, so that the Children be of a good wit, and capacity, and apt to learn'. But if no candidates were offered for free places in the school by those who were prepared to be responsible for 'the maintaining of them with diet, and fitting apparel, sweet and clean, both linen and woollen, and for the payment of some small duties to the Schoolmaster' then the parish officers were to choose other children 'to be taught freely, without limitation of the real or personal estate of the Parents, as they, in their own conscience, shall judge and be persuaded will prove the fittest instruments to the promoting of God's Glory, the advancing of Learning, and the general benefit of the Country'.[1]

The free grammar schools were intended for children of all classes; they were not generally attended by children of both sexes. It is well to realize that in our investigation of grammar schools we are concerned with an area of education which was virtually a male monopoly. The problem is to understand why girls were excluded from these schools. Did this exclusion faithfully represent the intention of founders from the first, or was it something which came about as a result of male encroachment upon or female indifference to educational advantages? Unfortunately the foundation deeds of schools do not enable us to give a conclusive answer to these questions. Only rarely were founders explicit in their direction that the schools were for 'boys and girls'. Before the Restoration there seems to have been specific reference to girls only at Madeley in Staffordshire where in 1645 Sir John Offley founded two schools divided by a partition wall, one for boys under a master and usher, the other for girls under a mistress. In the later Stuart period co-educational schools were founded at Waitby and Smardale in Westmorland in 1682, at Haydon Bridge in Northumberland in 1685, at Kingsbury in Warwickshire in 1686, and at Over in Cheshire in 1698, though in the last-named girls were not allowed to continue after they reached the age of twelve years.[2] Often founders stated that their schools were for the education of boys only. Often, too, the language of statutes fails to indicate the sex of the children for whom the schools were intended. What are we to make of such vague expressions as 'children and youth', 'youths and children', 'scholars and children', 'children of inhabitants' and 'poor scholars'? And what of those cases in which the founders simply expressed their purpose to establish a grammar school? At Rivington in Lancashire the words 'children and youth', in the charter of foundation of 1566, and 'scholars' in the statutes, drawn up by James Pilkington, bishop of Durham, were interpreted as meaning children of both sexes. The lists of pupils in this school in the seventeenth century included a girl named Alice Shaw in 1615, two or three girls in the next two years, twelve girls in 1678 and thirteen girls in 1681. They do not appear to have stayed more than a year or two and the likelihood is that their education and school days did not normally extend beyond the time needed to acquire proficiency in reading and writing. But, as the school historian has pointed out, the fact that there were girls in the school is itself surprising and worthy of note.[1]

And yet it is reasonable to assume that, unless they expressly excluded them, founders intended that girls should share with boys the benefits of grammar school education. A writer in *The Quarterly Review* in 1878 drew attention to 'the quaint little figures of each, which stand over venerable portals in old market-places' in support of the contention that old endowed grammar schools were open to children of both sexes, and quoted Crewkerne Grammar School in Somerset as an example of a school where boys simply took possession of places intended for and left vacant by girls.[2] Similarly Professor J. W. Adamson has drawn attention to the seal of Oakham and Uppingham Schools, founded in 1587, which has on it the figures of four boys and two girls and which indicates that originally both sexes were welcome as pupils in these schools.[3] Indeed the express exclusion of girls from particular schools, as at Harrow by John Lyon's statutes of 1589–90[4] and at South Leverton in Nottinghamshire by John Sampson's will of 1691,[5] suggests that sometimes girls were to be found among the pupils in grammar schools. Probably the most satisfactory explanation of this singular situation, in which girls and young women were almost entirely excluded from the benefits of educational endowments, was provided by the royal commissioners who reported on the endowed schools in 1868.

They were of the opinion that founders had taken for granted that only those who could profit by grammar school learning would come, or stay for long, to be taught, that thus the grammar school population would be determined, as it were, by natural selection, and that since men rather than women were in a position to make good use of this sort of education in the world and in the service of Church and State, school regulations were addressed to boys rather than to girls.[1]

When fees were allowable these were normally to increase the efficiency of the schools at the expense of parents who could afford to pay while in no way barring the entrance of the children of poor parents who could attend the schools free of charge. The grammar school at Colwall Green in Herefordshire was free for poor inhabitants while 'the better sort' were required to pay ten shillings a year for the education of their children,[2] and the salary of ten pounds a year paid to the schoolmaster at Camberwell in Surrey was expected to be supplemented by fees from the sons of 'subsidye men' who 'ought not to be taught freelie'.[3]

The problem which confronted founders was whether to prohibit fees and by so doing to offer equal advantages to the children of all classes, rich and poor alike, or to allow or direct fees to be paid by those who could afford them and so to benefit the school and the schoolmaster by an increased income. John Rowland, rector of Foots Cray in Kent, who described himself as 'a Scholer of some famous free Scholes, and sometimes a Master' was in no doubt about the correct answer to this question and in a letter of 17 March 1674–75 to Christopher Wase he expressed himself forcibly in deploring the effect of the educational system upon schoolmasters.

> I undervalew not Mens Charity; yet, I think, yt most of the Founders, were unwittingly, to indulgent to many yt need it not. Free Scholes generally, are a prey for greedy Feoffees, a pretence for unthankfull Parents, a Provision for the Rich, a multiplying of beggarly Scholers, a Nursery of gibing Prentices, a bane for deserving Masters: were it not for soe many free Scholes a Scholar might live plentifully with honour, allmost every where; but now they can scarce live any where but with very small means, and less Credit. The

great and rich Town of Manchester, yt might well maintain
3 or 4 Masters, one free-schole, makes the Master tide up to
the strickt Rules of the foundation, for 20 li per annum, a
slave to them all: but in Eltham, a small Town, where is
noe free Schole there are noe fewer than 3 free Masters
receiving 200 li, or 250 li per annum, by their Scholers, with
many gratuities, and a great deal of love.[1]

When four years later Christopher Wase appealed for the increase in number and endowment of free schools, he was quite
clear about the need to augment the wages of schoolmasters and
to expect payment for tuition from those who could afford it.

If the maintenance be not competent, Masters may require
moderat consideration for their Labor: what is offer'd, they
may receive; however sufficient their allowance be. Onely
provided that they regard the poor with equal diligence,
and affection as any others what ever they pay: Charity
would not that the painful Teacher be over-burthen'd to
ease the Rich Scholar: nor that the means intended for his
relief be made a pretence to oppress him: but rather that a
Honorary be set him out according to his dignity and knowledge. The prudence as well as Piety of some Bishops hath
appear'd in deciding this controversie, where the stipend
hath been narrow, and the freedom express'd in terms not
particular; they have limited the number of such as should
enjoy it to a just proportion.[2]

The decision to introduce fees carried with it the danger which
Wase recognized that the schoolmaster might be tempted to
regard more favourably the fee-paying boys to the detriment of
the poorer children. This point is well brought out in the statutes
which were made for the free grammar school at Caistor soon
after its foundation. The schoolmaster and usher and their
successors were

not to expect, demand, exact, or require any money, salary,
reward, or wages other than the Stipends or Rents of the
lands belonging to the said School, for the teaching or instructing of any Child or Children but what shall be freely
given as a Gratuity, without requiring, exacting or expecting

they may receive, yet always regarding that they be as carefull and diligent in instructing the Poor as the Rich, and those from or by whom no gratuity or reward cometh to them, as those from or by whom they receive gratuity or reward.[1]

The statutes of 6 June 1614 for Steyning Grammar School stipulated that there should not be more than six boarders and that the total number of scholars should not exceed fifty so that the schoolmaster might not 'be oppressed with multitude, and thereby not able to set forward and further his said charge to his credit and profit of his Scholars: Provided always that no Child or Youth, which shall be dwelling within the liberty of the said town, and shall be found meet and able, shall be refused to be admitted and received a Scholar in the said School.'[2]

Instruction at Solihull Grammar School in Warwickshire was free to the children of inhabitants but other fee-paying pupils were admitted. George Long, who was master there from 1663 to 1668, was directed by the trustees 'not to admit so numerous a company of foreign children' that his attention should be diverted from the 'effectuall and conscientious improvement of the parishioners' children in school learning, and that so farr as to fitt them for the university'.[3] The possibility of preferential treatment for fee-paying pupils with which these orders for schools were concerned was clearly a real one as is evidenced by the history of Dulwich School. The condition of affairs at that school occasioned some adverse criticism during the visitation of Dr. Gilbert Sheldon, archbishop of Canterbury, between 1664 and 1667 and in the orders of 9 October 1667 the schoolmaster and usher were warned to be 'careful in performing their duty of instructing the scholars, as well forrayners as the 12 poore boys'.[4]

Small fees payable at the first entrance of the pupils were not uncommon in the endowed grammar schools, and these are found in schools which on other grounds could fairly claim to be, and did in fact describe themselves as, free schools. The custom at Oundle School was to keep a register in which were recorded 'every Schollars, & his Parents name quality, place of nativity, time of admittance & place in ye Schoole'. At this admission ceremony, according to the information supplied to Christopher Wase by the master, William Speed, on 28 August 1675, every scholar paid two shillings and sixpence which went to the usher. The boy's departure from the school was also recorded and on this occasion the master was 'gratifyed . . . of ye Free schollars'.[1] The Wase papers also contain a copy of the articles which were drawn up shortly before 1652 for a free school which it was proposed to erect at South Stoke in Oxfordshire and which was supplied by David Thomas, the vicar of the parish. They provided that 'all those scholars of ye parish of South Stoke' should 'be taught freelie giving onely admission-mony'. All others were to pay for their teaching 'as ye Schoole Master, & their parents can agree'.[2] The grammar school at Dorchester in Oxfordshire was free to scholars from Dorchester and Overy whose only charge was one shilling at their admission. The statutes of 29 September 1652 provided that other children might be admitted on payment of one shilling and sixpence at entrance and five shillings a quarter thereafter.[3] Witney Grammar School, in the same county, was free for thirty scholars who, according to the statutes of 14 December 1674, were to pay an entrance fee of two shillings and sixpence, one shilling and sixpence for the master and one shilling for the usher. The fee at admission was reduced to one shilling 'to be equally divided between the Master and Usher' in the case of children whose parents were not liable for a weekly contribution to support the poor, and preference was to be given to the children of the founder's kinsmen.[4]

Some founders were not unmindful of the fact that the free instruction which their schools offered might be abused and sought to deter would-be absentees by ordering expulsion and a further payment of the admission fee,[5] or by directing, as did the ordinances for the free grammar school founded at Chigwell in Essex by Samuel Harsnet, archbishop of York, in 1629, that if a child was kept away from school for five days together or for more than seven days in a quarter, for any reason except sickness, 'that then and from thenceforth the Scholar so absented and detained shall for ever forfeit his freedom in the said School, and shall be expelled from the School, except his Parents pay for his teaching according to the Schoolmaster's discretion'.[6] Irregular attendance of a pupil might be discouraged, as at the

free grammar school at Sandwich in Kent in 1580, by 'correccion
at his returne' and by the order that the offender should also
'paie to the common Boxe for everie daies absence a peney as the
daies come to'.[1]

As we have seen, fees at entrance and at other times were a
convenient method of augmenting the salaries of the teaching
staff. In the absence of any other provision they were also necessary to meet the expenses involved in the running of the school.
Such charges were sometimes the only revenue from which to
buy books. Thus the ordinances drawn up by Sir Roger Man-
wood for Sandwich Grammar School in 1580 provided that the
children of the inhabitants of Sandwich were 'to be frelie tawghte,
withowte any thing to be demaunded or taken, but of benevo-
lence shalbe given at the-end of everie quarter towardes buieng
and providinge of such dictionaries and other bookes as shalbe
for common use of the schollers'. 'Forreine schollers' were also
to be admitted to the school but were to pay for their instruction
a fee decided upon 'having respecte to the childe and habilitie of
his parentes'. In addition all the scholars were charged an
entrance fee, those who were resident in Sandwich paying sixpence, others paying twelvepence, 'with whiche money the
master at his descreacion shall provide necessarie bookes, as
Dictionaries or other, for the common use of the schollers'.[2]
Nearly a hundred years later similar provision was made for the
purchase of books at the free grammar school at Sherborne in
Dorset. The statutes of 10 October 1679 ordered that every boy
should be charged one shilling and sixpence on admission, and
afterwards should pay sixpence a year towards books. Of the
entrance fee fourpence went each to the schoolmaster and usher
and to the master of the almshouse who, in his capacity as warden
of the school, kept the school roll, while sixpence was towards the
fund for buying books for the library.[3]

Cleaning and sweeping, heating and lighting the schoolroom,
and the supply of birches for the schoolmaster were also reckoned
as necessary expenses which might properly be met by the
parents of free scholars who enjoyed these benefits. The statutes of
1569–70 for St. Olave's School,[4] of 1608 for Guildford Grammar
School in Surrey[5] and of Steyning School[6] provided for fees at
entrance and for quarterly charges for brooms and rods and

parents were also expected to make an annual payment for wax candles 'to keep light . . . for the scolemaster, usher and scholars to study by morning and evening in the winter time'.[1] The duties of sweeping the schoolroom and ringing the school bell might be delegated, as they were at Witney[2] and Charlbury,[3] to some poor scholar who was thereby enabled to profit from the payments of his more affluent schoolfellows. At Coventry by the orders of 1628 the scholars paid 'Quartridge to the Sweeper of that Schoole for ringing of Bell, for making of fiers there, and for roddes'[4] and the boys of Bristol Grammar School were required by the ordinances of 1666 to pay one shilling for fires in the winter and twopence a quarter towards the cost of sweeping the school.[5]

The school building also had to be kept in repair and admission fees might be directed to this purpose, as they were at St. Albans,[6] and the governors of Godmanchester Grammar School in Huntingdonshire were only fulfilling their duty and showing a proper sense of responsibility towards their school when in 1693 they determined that the cost of maintaining the schoolhouse in good repair could only be met by taking a fee at admission of one shilling from free-born children of the borough and two shillings from others, and making a quarterly charge of sixpence for all pupils of the school.[7] In the absence of such provision and of any other income the governors might be compelled to take extraordinary action in order to preserve the fabric as they did at Henley when in 1700 John Meadows was dismissed from the schoolmastership for negligence. No successor was appointed and the master's salary was used for reparations while the usher, Richard Skinner, was made responsible for all the teaching until in 1703 he was raised to the mastership as a recompense for his diligent service.[8]

When, as in so many schools, the endowment was in the form of a fixed annuity and when the terms of foundation stipulated free education for all or some of the scholars, sooner or later the fall in the value of money made it impossible to support a schoolmaster qualified to teach classics.[9] The continued existence of such schools as grammar schools depended upon increased incomes so that, in the absence of further endowments, some schools began to charge fees for tuition or to raise the existing fees for all but a limited number of scholars, while others in the course of time ceased to be free schools in all but name. The only limiting rule of any sort in the statutes of 1550 for Bury St. Edmunds Grammar School was that in admitting scholars preference should be given to the poorest sort.[1] When new statutes were drawn up in 1665 a distinction was made between townsmen and others and only the children of the former enjoyed the privilege of free tuition. The schoolmasters were allowed to receive voluntary payments from the free scholars and the usher was authorized to demand an entrance fee of not more than a shilling from every town child and two shillings and sixpence from others.[2] New statutes, drawn up in February 1674–75 for the free grammar school at Southampton, ordered that the mayor and Common Council should from time to time choose a certain number of scholars from the sons of poor men of Southampton who were to be admitted to the school and taught by the schoolmaster free of charge. For all other scholars the fees were now raised. The admission fees were five shillings for the master, two shillings and sixpence for the usher, and sixpence each for the two appositors, one of whom was responsible for the conduct of his fellows in school and the other for their behaviour in church and out of school. The gratuities, which had formerly been paid at breaking up, were replaced by quarterly fees for instruction, those under the master paying five shillings and those under the usher paying two shillings and sixpence to him and the same amount to the master.[3] In 1665 new regulations were made by the dean and chapter of Hereford Cathedral for the free grammar school.

> In regard of the smallnes of the annuall Sallary and Stypends belonging to the Schole (being £20. to the Master, and £10. to the Usher thereof annually paid out of the Revenues of the said Deane and Chapter), the Scholemaster may demand and require what he thinks fitt, not exceeding 5s. for Entrance, and 20s. per annum, to be quarterly paid for the sons of all free citizens of the said Citty, saveing only such as are poor, and unable soe to doe, who are to pay only 5s. for Entrance and to be left to theire owne will for the rest.

Any dispute which might arise in connexion with the admission of the children of poor parents was to be settled by the dean or, in his absence, by the canon in residence at the time. 'As for Forreigners', the regulations continue, 'the Scholemaster is left to his own discretion for compounding with them for his Sallary'. The entrance fees were to be divided equally between the master and the usher while the master was to receive a quarter of the tuition fees payable to the usher and also of the gratuities which might be given to the usher by poor free citizens. The master and usher were required 'to take care that those of the poorer sort be not sordidly or uncleanly habited or kept, to the offence of others of better quality, and to the scandall of the Schole'.[1] The endowment for the free grammar school at Dedham was provided by William Littlebury who in 1571 bequeathed to the school a farm then producing a rent of twenty pounds a year. When Myles Burkitt, of Sidney Sussex College, Cambridge, became master in 1694 he was authorized to admit all the boys of Dedham who wished to come and to charge them each twenty-five shillings a year tuition.[2] Restrictive measures were introduced at Warwick School when on 20 January 1701–02 the corporation decreed that for the future 'the Schoole master bee compelled to teach noe Schollers but such as were or shall be borne within the libertye of the said borough' and those whose parents had resided in the borough for the past seven years.[3]

We can therefore see that the future of the free grammar schools was largely dependent on the financial provision which had been made for their upkeep and on the areas which they had been founded to serve. In the later Stuart period some schools were attempting to solve their financial problems by introducing and increasing fees, an expedient which seemed to dishonour the founder's intention and might arouse resentment and bitterness between parents and school authorities, and which depended for its success upon the number of pupils.

In the eighteenth century some schoolmasters, having decided that the fees which could be earned from day boys were not worth considering, turned their attention to making a living from boarders. Thus for some years after Dr. John Washbourne became master of Cirencester Grammar School in Gloucestershire in 1774 parents sent their children elsewhere to be taught, not because the schoolmaster was incompetent but because he made it clear that boys of the town were not welcome.[4] The few free boys who were admitted to the school were regarded by their master with less favour than the more profitable boarders, were charged fees and not even allowed to occupy the free seats reserved for the schoolboys in the church.[1]

When the continuing existence and status of a school depended upon the support of its fee-paying pupils there was always a strong possibility that free boys would be placed in an unfavourable position and even ultimately excluded. Thus it was represented to the Commissioners to inquire concerning Charities that the people of Taunton in Somerset were not even aware that their grammar school was a free school and that they had any right to send their children to the school which in 1821 contained about eighteen boys, seven or eight of whom were boarders paying forty-three guineas a year. A gentleman of Taunton who had known the town since 1764 could recall only one instance of a free scholar who had been admitted to the school when the master's reluctance was overcome by the suggestion that if he did not accept him he would lose some of his paying pupils.[2] A similar though more lucrative situation existed in 1820 at Bath where Thomas Wilkins, who held the rectory of Charlcombe together with the mastership of the grammar school to which he had been appointed some nine years before, had never admitted and had never been asked to admit a boy on the foundation. Wilkins then had between seventy and eighty boys in the school who paid fifty-five guineas a year if they were boarders and eight guineas a year if they were day boys. 'The corporation are doubtless well acquainted with this use made of the school premises for private tuition,' commented the commissioners, 'the same having been customary with the predecessors of the present master.'[3]

If a school served a thinly populated area and if the income from its endowment was small its future as a grammar school depended on its attracting pupils as boarders from farther afield. But this saving measure might be prevented by the limit placed by the founder upon the area from which the school was permitted to draw pupils. Local schools which were poorly endowed and which continued scrupulously to observe founders' regulations prohibiting or setting a limit to fees found it increasingly difficult to attract masters of university standing. Sooner or later they became elementary schools or ceased to exist.

The authors of the article on 'Schools' in the *Victoria County History of Suffolk* have pointed to the decline in population which accompanied the change from industry to agriculture in that county as among the causes contributing to the depression of the old grammar schools[1] and Mr. A. F. Leach has described the history of these schools in Sussex as 'a remarkable illustration of the truth that education and culture vary directly with the development of wealth and industry'. He wrote: 'When in the seventeenth and eighteenth centuries commerce deserted the petty ports, silted up by the shingle banks and encroachments of the sea, and the ironworks followed the coal to the midlands and north, the schools decayed with the decay of wealth and population.'[2]

The conclusion of the matter was reported by the Schools Inquiry Commission in 1868. 'A free grammar school is an anachronism. If the school be free it is filled with a class of children who do not learn grammar; and if classics are sedulously taught, the school soon ceases to be free.'[3] The circumstances of the free grammar schools which have been considered in this chapter sufficiently explain the verdict of the commissioners upon a situation which had existed for a long time before they made their report. Other factors, as we shall see, contributed to bring about the same result. But our examination has so far suggested no reasons for the general decline in the number of pupils attending the schools, many of which were adequately and even richly endowed. The obvious explanation for this lack of support is that the grammar schools were failing to provide what men of the eighteenth century expected for their sons from secondary education. In our survey of the grammar schools in the later Stuart period we turn now to examine their educational practice which, although it may appear to be primarily of antiquarian interest, is of significance for the historian in its relation to the changing needs and demands of society.

IV

THE DAILY ROUND

1. Hours and Holidays

Scholars entered the grammar school at the age of seven or eight and continued there for six or seven years. For convenience in teaching they were divided into forms according to age and ability. The staff of a grammar school usually consisted of a master and an usher, though in the small schools all the teaching was done by one man. The demands made upon the teachers by the extensive curriculum and the various groups explain the large amount of time spent in school, on an average throughout the year not less than eight hours a day for six days a week.

The long working day began in many schools at six o'clock in the summer and seven o'clock in the winter though, in a book published in 1660, Charles Hoole wrote that in the majority of schools seven o'clock was 'the constant time, both in Winter and Summer' at which hour it was 'fit every Scholar should be ready at the Schoole'.[1] Statutory regulations sometimes made the usher responsible for meeting the boys and settling them down to their work and permitted the master, by virtue of his superior status, to approach the duties of the day more leisurely, half-an-hour or an hour later.[2] The first break in the morning's work came between eight and nine o'clock when 'some halfe an houre or three quarters at ye most' was allowed for breakfast.[3] It was the general custom that morning school should end at eleven o'clock for dinner. 'After dynner' the grammar schoolboy was required 'to returne by One of the clock, and there remaine for to be taught 'till Five of the clock at night'.[4] In some schools, like those at Dorchester, Dronfield, Houghton and Chigwell, afternoon school was prolonged in the summer months until six o'clock.[5] It was not unusual, however, for school to end before five o'clock in the winter. At Witney, for example, afternoon school continued until five o'clock or until the daylight failed since it was ordered that no candles should be used at any time for teaching or learning in school.[1]

When the hours devoted to work in school were so long it is surprising that little time was allowed for play. Schoolmasters were enjoined 'not easily' to give leave to play and not 'oftener then once in the Weeke', usually on a Tuesday or Thursday afternoon.[2] Indeed the Stuart schoolboy had reasonable ground for complaint that his elders showed little appreciation of his need for relaxation and enjoyment since on the one half-holiday each week he might be expected to use his respite from the dreary round of grammar learning to increase his proficiency in reading, writing and arithmetic.[3] Allowance was made in school statutes for extra play days at the request of 'some Honourable or Worshippfull Person' or 'Masters of Arte, or other persons of equivolente accounte' or 'some Man of Speciall worth or love unto Schoole' though the master was expected to take care that the necessary exercises had been set for the next day and it was likely that if the schoolmaster gave leave to play twice in one week then no leave would 'att all be given to the Schollers to play in the next weeke immediately following'.[4] When leave to play was given the boys were to 'play and sport together, not wandering about here and there, lest they incur loss of character, and their minds become set upon other things, and estranged from learning'. Games were to be 'of a gentlemanly appearance and free of all lowness'[5] and were confined to such activities as shooting with long bows, chess, running, wrestling, leaping, driving a top and tossing a handball.[6]

School vacations took place at Christmas, Easter and Whitsuntide and some schools, like those at Coventry, Guildford and Steyning, were given a short holiday also at Shrovetide.[7] There was no uniformity in the length of the vacations, which were normally not less than five weeks and not more than eight weeks in a year, and these were not always holidays from study or even from school. Holiday tasks might be imposed and the schoolboy might be required to attend school at the master's discretion.[8] Additional holidays were occasioned in some places by the founder's will or by necessity when local fairs associated with feast days made it impossible to conduct the work of the school because of the noise, and advisable for the pupils to remain at home in order to avoid the crowds in the streets.[1]

2. *Discipline*

It is said that King George III when meeting a schoolboy of Eton College was accustomed to ask him jokingly, 'When were you flogged last?'[2] The terrors of the rod were, no doubt, mitigated by the ability to regard it as a figure of fun, although its humorous side is more apparent in retrospect and when out of its reach than in daily or periodical contact with it. Thus in the seventeenth century even the reports of the severities which were the lot of the Eton boy proved too much for the young John Evelyn who later regretted his own 'perversenesse' and lack of foresight which deprived him of the benefit of schooling at Eton. In 1630, John Evelyn went as a scholar to Lewes Grammar School in Sussex, a school which, under its master Edward Snatt, was evidently of good reputation since it was chosen when the young man proved reluctant to go to Eton.

Evelyn was no exception to the theory that boys do not take kindly to studies and, like many others, was later sorry for the opportunities which he had missed.[3] There is no information about the inducements, if any, which were used to encourage him to learn nor is it possible to say how much he might have benefited from the severer discipline which he feared at Eton. No doubt the threat of corporal punishment proved an efficient stimulus to some unwilling pupils to acquire a knowledge of Latin and Greek which they would otherwise never have gained. It is equally certain that in many cases the fierce discipline which was frequently associated with schooling effectively destroyed a love of learning which might have blossomed under more sympathetic methods and even roused a hatred for learning not easily, if ever, overcome in later life.

The pages of educational history are plentifully supplied with schoolmasters who have attracted particular attention from writers by reason of their eccentricities or unsympathetic and sometimes even brutal behaviour towards their charges while many others, the great majority of schoolmasters, less colourful in character but perhaps more successful in their profession, have gone unrecorded. The grammar schools must have been fearful places indeed for those boys whose unhappy fortune it was to be placed under a master who took a delight in punishing them or whose severity was tempered by no humane restrictions.

An accusation of brutal violence is associated with the long mastership, beginning in 1673, of John James at Basingstoke Grammar School, the evidence for which is contained in the affidavit of Alice Kew, the mother of one of the boys who suffered at his hands. The master was charged with 'unreasonable correcting and whipping' as a result of which John Kew 'did run away from his parents and friends unknown to them and was found at Salisbury'. It was further stated 'that after he was brought home again, he the said John Kew said, that rather than he would go to school there he would be hanged up at the door, and that the said John Kew shortly after died of consumption'. The deponent's own son, Alexander Kew, had died from a bruise on the liver which he received when the master caused 'two or three boys to draw him up the end of the table to be whipped'. Four or five boys had died from consumption while others had been withdrawn from the school and sent elsewhere. The date of this affidavit is 15 July 1718, and it was sworn shortly after James's resignation from the mastership which took place early in that year or at the end of the previous year. Whatever the truth of the matter it at least appears that James was a man whose violence unfitted him for the office of a schoolmaster. Nevertheless he continued to rule the school for forty-four years and during the largest part of this time, so Alice Kew alleged, 'it was the common fame, report and complaint of a great number of the inhabitants of the said town' that the master treated the boys 'barbarously' by punishing them 'unreasonably and unmercifully'.[1]

The Basingstoke affair is exceptional in its brutality. But it is not an isolated case of cruelty[2] and in an age when the rod was generally accepted as a necessary instrument of correction it was thought advisable to take precautionary measures against the abuse of this form of punishment and against other disciplinary action which a schoolmaster might choose to adopt. Statutory regulations do not, of course, tell us what actually happened in schools but they point out what was considered to be normal and abnormal in school discipline in the seventeenth century. The schoolmaster was expected to be 'severe in his government' and to 'keep his Scholars in awe and good order'.[1] This did not mean, however, that he was to depend for his discipline upon excessive flogging or punishment dangerous to the health and character of the boys. He was to 'mix severity and lenity' and to 'be neither too indulgent in pardoneing greater faults nor too Severe in punishing lesser faults'. Indeed it was hoped that the master would be wise and experienced enough 'to discern the nature of every several child' and to deal with him according to his needs, and that when he administered punishment it would be 'out of loveing desire' to correct his pupils' faults and not from any intention to tyrannize over their bodies.[2] Correction was to be with the rod only and masters were forbidden to strike a boy on the head or face and to pull him by the hair, nose or ears.[3] A schoolmaster who was guilty of 'manifest cruelty and misusage of his Scholars' was to be dismissed.[4]

School regulations required that parents should place their children unreservedly in the charge of the schoolmasters and refrain from interfering with the conduct of their sons' schooling. Molestation of the schoolmaster by parents who refused to blame their children's faults and objected to the schoolmaster's correction was to be followed by the expulsion of their sons unless the punishment could be proved to have been excessive. Scholars were to submit to the master's authority and those who persisted in refusing his correction were to be expelled. They were also expected to be obedient and ready to help the master when he had to deal with stubborn pupils who resisted and struggled.[5]

The problems which might confront the schoolmaster are apparent in the measures which the provost of Eton College, John Meredith, was forced to take in 1665. He ordered that the doors of the school and Long Chamber should be fitted with new locks from which the keys were to be removed every night after prayers. Boys who went out of school or college in the evening without the permission of the provost or vice-provost were to be 'admonished and Registred' for the first offence, 'severely punished and Registred for the second fault, and for the third expelled'. These provisions were not unreasonable nor was Meredith's treatment of four boys whose punishment for visiting the 'Christopher' was to read in School 'a forme of Repentance'.

It is hardly surprising that when, not long after this repentance, one of the four, Curwin by name, and another boy named Baker were found guilty of 'going out of their bounds to Datchet ale-houses and beating the fishermen' their punishment was to be 'admonished and whipt and Registred'.[1] An equally difficult pupil to deal with was Charles Herbert of Monmouth School who went on a drinking expedition with 'roguish boys', quarrelled with his companions, and threw dirt into the mouth of one of them. His disorderly conduct was recorded by the usher of the school, Moor Pye, in his diary for February 1646–47.[2]

That the local ale-houses were a temptation to schoolboys is also clear from stipulations in the statutes of grammar schools which listed drunkenness as an offence for exemplary punishment and forbade the boys to enter any ale-house or tavern. Other misdemeanours which schoolmasters were expected to be vigilant to correct and suppress included filthy talking and acting, lying, gambling, stealing, carrying weapons and brawling. In the schoolroom prompting and helping one another was more reprehensible and therefore to be punished more severely than failure to do well. On the way home from school a boy was still under discipline and was ordered to go as far as possible in the company of a school-fellow 'without wandering or gadding out of Order'.[3]

To help in maintaining good discipline schoolmasters sometimes appointed monitors whose duties were to supervise their fellows in school, in church and in the streets.[4] Good and ill were obviously inherent in this system and no doubt the fear of the senior boys was added to or replaced the fear of the master in the minds of many who learned to suffer the oppression of their elders in the hope that the day would come when they themselves would be the oppressors. And yet the recurrence of family names in the lists of schools is a significant fact that, for many, school-days were not intolerable since fathers were ready to send their sons into the same joys and hardships which they had experienced.

The need for strong discipline was advocated by the Puritans and found support in the seventeenth century in the writings of John Milton, Daniel Defoe and John Locke, all of whom were concerned with the aim of education to subdue the evils inherent in human nature, and to produce Christian character by constant exhortation and firm control. Milton wrote that 'the end then of Learning is to repair the ruines of our first Parents'[1] while Defoe in his protest against the supporters of 'natural religion' concluded that 'there is something of originall depravity in nature more than those gentlemen think of'.

> What ever brightnes of parts, what ever genius, wit and capacity the man is naturally furnish'd with, it is requir'd that those jewells should be polished, that learning be apply'd to them, that rules and instruccions be layd before them, and that historys and examples of times and persons be recommended to them, and that all this be enforc'd by the authority of instructors, parents, schoolmasters, etc.[2]

John Locke maintained 'that most Children's Constitutions are either spoil'd, or at least harm'd, by Cockering and Tenderness'. He stressed the importance of 'a strong Constitution, able to endure Hardship and Fatigue' and advised that children should 'not be too warmly clad or cover'd', that they should bath in cold water, learn to swim and 'be much in the open Air, and as little as may be by the Fire, even in Winter' so that their bodies might 'be brought to bear almost any thing'. Locke considered that 'Beating is the worst, and therefore the last means to be us'd in the Correction of Children, and that only in Cases of Extremity, after all gentle Ways have been try'd, and prov'd unsuccessful'. But sheer wilfulness and stubborn obstinacy were to be met with blows 'and the Whipping (mingled with Admonition between) so continu'd, till the Impression of it on the Mind were found legible in the Face, Voice, and Submission of the Child, not so sensible of the Smart as of the Fault he has been guilty of, and melting in true Sorrow under it'.[3] The eighteenth century revealed no weakening in the theory that only good could result from constant beatings in an age when Dr. Samuel Johnson could hardly credit that flogging could be carried to excess[4] and when the influence of John Wesley, who was a lover of children, was brought to strengthen the belief that they were naturally wicked and could be formed into obedient and virtuous Christians only by the strictest discipline.[5]

A few voices were raised to protest that perpetual beating was not the only or indeed the best method of inculcating learning or of maintaining order and discipline among schoolboys. In the seventeenth century Robert South, who had been a boy at Westminster School under Dr. Richard Busby during the time of the Commonwealth Government, declared that he 'would give those pedagogical Jehus, those furious schooldrivers, the same advice which, the poet says, Phoebus gave his son Phaeton (just such another driver as themselves,) that he should parcere stimulis (the stimulus in driving being of the same use formerly that the lash is now.)' South was of the opinion that 'stripes and blows are the last and basest remedy, and scarce ever fit to be used, but upon such as carry their brains in their backs; and have souls so dull and stupid, as to serve for little else but to keep their bodies from putrefaction'.[1] In the *Spectator*, Number 157, for 30 August 1711 Richard Steele delivered a scathing attack on the practice of corporal punishment:

> The boasted liberty we talk of is but a mean reward for the long servitude, the many heart-aches and terrors, to which our childhood is exposed in going through a grammar-school. Many of these stupid tyrants exercise their cruelty without any manner of distinction of the capacities of children, or the intention of parents on their behalf.

He believed that 'the sense of shame and honour is enough to keep the world itself in order without corporal punishment, much more to train the minds of uncorrupted and innocent children' and was 'confident that no boy who will not be allured to letters without blows, will ever be brought to any thing with them'. Steele's opinion of 'those licenced tyrants the school-masters' who 'abuse the power of correction' received support from correspondents including a former pupil of Dr. Charles Roderick who was headmaster of Eton College from 1667 to 1673:

> Many a white and tender hand, which the fond mother had passionately kissed a thousand times, have I seen whipped until it was covered with blood; perhaps for smiling, or for going a yard and a half out of the gate, or for writing an O for an A, or an A for an O. These were our great faults! Many a brave and noble spirit has been there broken; others have run from thence, and were never heard of afterwards.[2]

But such views went unheeded and nothing was done to change the system that prevailed in most schools.

No doubt the Quaker Thomas Ellwood, an old boy of Thame Grammar School in Oxfordshire, was typical of many English boys who harboured no resentment for the trials of their school-days and who were able, at least in retrospect, to find an amusing side to their early sufferings. Of his schooldays at Thame he says that

> few boys in the school wore out more birch than I. For though I was never, that I remember, whipped upon the score of not having my lesson ready, or of not saying it well, yet being a little busy boy, full of spirit, of a working head and active hand, I could not easily conform myself to the grave and sober rules and, as I then thought, severe orders of the school, but was often playing one waggish prank or other among my fellow-scholars, which subjected me to correction, so that I have come under the discipline of the rod twice in a forenoon; which yet brake no bone.[1]

On the other hand to natures more sensitive and unable to bear with equanimity the cuffs and rebuffs of their masters and school-fellows, schooldays might appear, as they did to the poet Shelley, as

> one echo from a world of woes –
> The harsh and grating strife of tyrants and of foes.

Moreover, it cannot be doubted that in many minds there was fostered a distaste for learning and a tradition of hostility towards their masters which, at least on some occasions, resulted in open rebellion as it did at Manchester Grammar School in 1690. The rebellion lasted for a fortnight during which the master, William Barrow, was locked out of the school which was held by the boys who were fortified with food and beds, passed through the windows by the sympathetic townsfolk, and armed with guns and ammunition with which they shot at the legs of those who tried to force an entrance.[2]

School rebellions, foreign as they are to the educational history of the twentieth century, were still exceptional in the seventeenth and eighteenth centuries and it is likely that most schoolboys learned to grin and bear their trials which they accepted as a normal part of school routine. There was, however, one occasion in the year when an opportunity was given to the boys to vent any wrath which they may have been harbouring against their master. This was the time of the barring-out which, far from being frowned upon by the authorities, was actually encouraged by the provisions of school statutes which thus recognized the traditional enmity which was supposed to exist between master and pupils and allowed the latter to feel for a short time that they had the upper hand. Nicholas Carlisle in 1818 referred to barring-out as 'an innocent and harmless custom, which is not yet altogether relinquished in the North of England' and instanced the grammar school at Rothbury in Northumberland as one in which the practice had long continued from its foundation in 1719–20.[1]

The barrings-out were especially associated with the excitement and high spirits that accompanied breaking-up for the holiday at Christmas. In his *Lives of the Poets* Samuel Johnson mentions a barring-out at Lichfield which 'was planned and conducted by Addison'. Johnson's informant was Andrew Corbet, the nephew of a contemporary of Joseph Addison at the school to which he seems to have been sent in 1683 for a short time when his father became dean of Lichfield.

> The practice of barring-out, was a savage license, practised in many schools to the end of the last century, by which the boys, when the periodical vacation drew near, growing petulant at the approach of liberty, some days before the time of regular recess, took possession of the school, of which they barred the doors, and bade their master defiance from the windows. It is not easy to suppose that on such occasions the master would do more then laugh; yet, if tradition may be credited, he often struggled hard to force or surprise the garrison.[2]

In the period following the Restoration this ancient custom was no longer regarded with a tolerant eye by the authorities who took steps to prohibit it. The barring-out at Birmingham in 1667, recorded by the governors of the free grammar school, was doubtless exceptional; but it indicates the unbridled and dangerous behaviour which the custom might incite among disreputable persons. On 26 November some of the scholars

> being assisted by certain Townes men did presume to put in practice A violent Exclusion of theire Master to the debarring him from performing his duty in the Schoole – And not onely so, but (though they deserted the Schoole about nine of the clocke at night upon the 27th, yet about Eight of the clocke at night upon the 28th instant) by the assistance of certaine (and those more) unruly persons of the Towne (in visards and with pistolls and other Armes) gathered to them and combineing with them, did make a Second assault to enter the Schoole and then and theire did not onely threaten to Kill theire Master beeing gott into the Schoole but for the Space of neare two howers made such attempts by casting in Stones & bricks as well as breaking the Wall and Wenscote of the Saide Schoole as might endanger his Life.

The 'offending Schollars' went unpunished since the governors 'for some reasons' and probably wisely advised the master to 'pardon this present transgression'; they resolved, however, to institute legal proceedings against 'those persons which from the Towne came running into such a dangerous riott'. The governors were determined that there should be no excuse for the recurrence of such an incident and ordered

> That no Schollar whatever belonging to the Schoole shall presume to offer any violence in Excluding their Master, but shall quietly wait for theire dismission till the Tenth day of December against which Order, if any for the future shall dare to designe, or Act, hee shalbee casheered the Schoole, or else bee obnoxious to such severe punishment, as to the Governours shalbee thought meet for so grosse an offence.[1]

'The great disturbance made by the scholars shutting out their master of late years' together with 'the idleness and unfitness' of the schoolmaster caused the Coventry Corporation to order the dismissal of Samuel Frankland in 1685. Frankland was, however, able to survive this censure and discharge and continued in the mastership until his death in 1691.[2] Masters and ushers were enjoined to 'use their utmost endeavour to break' this 'mischievous custome', and, to that end, to arrange for the performance by the boys of 'some publick exercise' at the breaking-up at Christmas.[1] Nevertheless, barring-out continued to be a source of anxiety to the authorities of grammar schools in the eighteenth century and while the performance of a play at Christmas might save the person and dignity of the master it did not necessarily curb the exuberance of youth or prevent damage to the school premises.[2]

The paucity of masters inevitably meant a lack of supervision and this freedom from restraint for long periods gave scope for the roughness, turbulence and lawlessness which characterizes the histories of many schools in the seventeenth and eighteenth centuries. John Locke made the points that the schoolmaster could not be expected adequately to supervise fifty or a hundred scholars, except when they were all in school together, or to 'instruct them successfully in any thing but their Books'.[3]

On the other hand there were some who saw in the contacts with all sorts and conditions of boys a most valuable part of the training and discipline for life which the schools provided. At Thetford Grammar School, soon after the Restoration, Roger North as a boy found 'lewd company among us' but he confesses that he 'was not forward enough to be taken into their gang'. And among the advantages which a school training possessed over private teaching by a tutor North included the fact that schoolboys

> learn the pratique of the world according to their capacities. For there are several ages and conditions, as poor boys and rich, and amongst them all the characters which can be found among men, as liars, cowards, fighters, dunces, wits, debauchees, honest boys, and the rest, and the vanity of folly and false dealing, and indeed the mischiefs of immorality in general may be observed there. Besides, the boys enter into friendships, combinations, factions, and a world of intrigues, which though of small moment, yet in quality and instruction the same as among men. And further, boys certainly league with equals, which gives them a manage and confidence in dealing; teaches them to look before they leap;

being often cuffed and put to cuff again; laugh at others' follies and are laughed at themselves.

All this, North concludes, was of inestimable benefit 'to youth, in their learning to be men at little cost'. Roger North had happy recollections of his schooldays and retained the kindest memories of his Thetford schoolmaster.[1]

The solution of the disciplinary problems of the seventeenth and eighteenth centuries clearly did not lie in perpetual flogging and canings. But in those days when two men might be expected to teach a school of one hundred and forty-four boys, as at Berkhamsted, it is difficult to see how, in many cases at any rate, the schoolmasters could avoid frequent recourse to flogging and harshness in their discipline. It is perhaps a useful exercise to place oneself in the position of the master entering the schoolroom and finding himself greeted by uproar, and to consider what steps might be taken to quell it.

The problem of discipline was among the discouragements to schoolmasters and schoolmastering. Of course it is probable that the attitude of some masters and ushers towards their pupils was soured by the conditions under which they worked and by the poor financial rewards which they reaped from their labours. This consideration does not, however, sufficiently account for he fierce disciplinary measures which are associated with grammar school life. The explanation lies rather in the generally accepted belief that corporal punishment was a necessary expedient in the mental and moral training of the young.[2] Schoolmasters as well as schoolboys were the victims of this traditionally harsh system. Charles Hoole would have us remember 'how irksome it is (especially to a man of a quiet temper) to have so many unwilling provocations unto passion'.[3] It can hardly be doubted that the prospect of daily warfare with hostile pupils daunted many would-be schoolmasters and led others to abandon the profession for more peaceful pursuits at the first opportunity.

Whether the hard discipline of grammar school life damaged the reputation and hastened the decline of the schools is debatable. John Gailhard in 1678 was not opposed to the rod so long as it was used 'in measure, and with moderation, by Fathers, not by Hangmen'. But he deplored those masters of grammar schools who had 'a pernicious method, which is also too common, to affect being formidable to Scholars' and 'who would have Scholars to quake in their presence, and to fall upon their knees, and as it were, adore them'. The object of such men was to frighten their pupils into learning instead of enticing them to it. And yet 'the first rudiments of Learning are crabby, and bitter enough in themselves', said Gailhard, 'without any farther mixture of gall and wormwood'.[1]

3. Learning the Rudiments

The need to give instruction in elementary subjects placed an undue strain on the staff of a grammar school so that some of the schools insisted that boys at entrance should reach a sufficient standard in reading, or in reading and writing, and be fit to enter upon the study of the accidence.[2] This proficiency the Stuart boy might be expected to have gained from his primary training. But evidently this aim was far from being realized since Charles Hoole complained that 'the want of good Teachers of English in most places where Grammar-Schooles are erected, causeth that many Children are brought thither to learn the Latine Tongue, before they can read well'.[3]

There was by no means a uniform system of primary education in England of the Restoration period. Elementary training might be obtained at the village Dame's School or in the house of a neighbouring parson who added to his meagre stipend by giving private tuition. So the young Roger North's 'first launching' at the age of five years in 1658 was to the Reverend Ezekiel Catchpole, 'a country minister in the neighbourhood', and 'after that to the Free School at Bury St. Edmund's, though very young and small'.[4] The children of the nobility usually received their first training at home from a tutor or chaplain. Some like Henry St. John, Lord Bolingbroke, received their early instruction at 'the hands of the women' of the house before going to school and university, in his case, to Eton and Christ Church, Oxford.[5]

Lack of sufficient provision for primary education often meant that it was 'left as a work for poor women, or others, whose necessities compel them to undertake it, as a meer shelter from beggery'. Only in rare cases was there a just appreciation of the importance of the training which should be given in the petty school, 'the

F

place where indeed the first Principles of all Religion and learning ought to be taught'. Petty Schools, for the education of the 'petits', had been erected in some places by 'some nobler spirits, whom God hath enriched with an over-plus of outward means', and had been endowed with yearly salaries. But, wrote Charles Hoole, these were 'so inconsiderate towards the maintenance of a Master and his familie, or so over-cloyed with a number of Free-Scholars, to be taught for nothing, that few men of parts will daigne to accept of them, or continue at them for any while; and for this cause I have observed such weak foundations to fall to nothing'.[1] In the absence of good scholars who would 'not come down so low, as the first elementary, and to so low a recompense also', this highly important branch of teaching was 'left to the meanest, and therefore to the worst'.[2]

Some founders, more realistic than others, recognized that in the uncertain state of primary education it was necessary to make provision for training in the rudiments in the grammar schools.[3] A development in this connexion was the establishment of two schools in the same locality, sometimes on the same foundation, as at Chigwell in 1629,[4] Exeter in 1636 and Lewisham in 1647,[5] a Latin school to fulfil the function of a grammar school and an English school for the teaching of reading, writing and arithmetic. The intention behind the establishment of two schools on a single foundation, either in the same building or in separate buildings, was seemingly akin to the later development of a classical and a modern side in one school. An interesting example of a double foundation was that at Mere in Wiltshire by Sir Matthew Andrews of the East India Company, in 1667–68, 'by a vow upon a shipwrack'. The stipend of the master of the Latin school was thirty pounds a year, that of the master of the English school ten pounds and a house.[6] In the period following the Restoration provision in one foundation for a grammar school and an English school was also made at Amesbury in Wiltshire, 1677,[7] at Thrimby in Westmorland, 1681, and at Haydon Bridge in Northumberland, 1685.[8]

More usually, however, primary instruction was given in the grammar school though some founders, mindful of the demands made upon the time and labours of the master and usher by advanced pupils preparing for the university, assigned the teaching of the petties to one or more of the senior boys.[1] Such a course was unnecessary at a few fortunate schools like those at Coxwold and Drighlington in Yorkshire,[2] where provision was made for a petty schoolmaster as well as for a master and an usher, and at Christ's Hospital where in addition to the grammar master, usher and writing master there were two masters who were responsible for the teaching of the petties.[3]

The ability to write their exercises was, of course, essential for the boys of the grammar school and although some schools would not admit boys unless they could write legibly[4] provision was often made in the time-table for instruction in this art at a neighbouring writing school or by a master in the grammar school or by a visiting writing master. In London and large towns boys might go to a writing school at eleven o'clock and five o'clock, as Hoole's scholars went from his private school in Tokenhouse Gardens, Lothbury, to the writing school kept by his friend, James Hodder. In country schools it was usual 'to entertain an honest and skilful Penman, that he may constantly come and continue with them about a moneth or six weeks together every year, in which time commonly every one may learn to write legibly'.[5] In some schools the masters were authorized to strengthen their admonitions with offers of rewards so that at Durham the best writer received the pens and papers of his fellows in the same form while at Camberwell money prizes were awarded at the end of each quarter.[6] In other schools the importance of writing was emphasized by requiring, as at Clare shortly after the Restoration,[7] Deptford in 1672 and Kingsbury in 1686,[8] that the master should be able to teach this art as well as grammar. Occasionally writing was recognized as a subject which warranted the appointment of a specialist, as at Lewisham Grammar School, which was endowed with eleven pounds a year for a writing master,[9] at Shrewsbury School, where in 1656 five pounds a year was provided for a master who should 'teach poor scholars to write',[10] and at Christ's Hospital where in 1577 a writing school had been founded as a separate department within the grammar school with a master and usher.[11]

Arithmetic is rarely found in the statutes of the grammar schools before the Restoration and Charles Hoole in his survey of the grammar school system between 1637 and 1660 does not mention it as a subject of the curriculum. Nevertheless in 1655 a school-master provided a text-book in arithmetic for his scholars. The book is *An Idea of Arithmetick, at first designed for the use of the free-school at Thurlow in Suffolk, by R. Billingsley, schoolmaster there.* Arithmetic is found more frequently after 1660, but references to it show that it was still sometimes regarded as a subject unnecessary for the good scholar who would reach the standard required for entrance to Oxford and Cambridge[1] and useful especially for 'those that are less capable of learning, and fittest to be put to trades'.[2]

For the most part writing and arithmetic, if taught at all within the grammar schools in the seventeenth century, were looked upon as 'extras', as subjects for Saturdays and half-holidays,[3] for play days and after supper,[4] and for which special fees would sometimes be charged while instruction in the classics was free.[5] In the later Stuart period the majority of founders persisted in the attitude that the grammar schools were intended exclusively for instruction in the classics. The statutes of newly founded schools still stipulated that scholars should be 'such as can, at their first comeing to Schoole, well reade the Bible or Testament'[6] or 'found able to read'[7] or fitted to begin the accidence[8] and 'to learn Grammar'.[9] Nevertheless the tendency to include primary subjects in the grammar school curriculum was particularly marked after the Restoration. In forty-eight schools founded in the years 1660–1714 instruction in the rudiments was available to the scholars. Writing was included in the curriculum of twenty-nine of these schools, twenty-one of them offering also arithmetic.[10] During this period some other foundations made provision for elementary learning as at Ilminster where in 1665 the trustees of the grammar school paid three pounds for teaching English to some of the schoolboys and where in 1709 they made payments for the instruction of forty poor children in reading, writing and casting accounts.[11] In 1676 a scrivener was appointed as a full-time member of the staff of Birmingham Grammar School to teach twenty boys to write and cast accounts[12] and in 1696 an additional endowment was given by Dr. Thomas Smith, bishop of Carlisle, for Dalston Grammar School in Cumberland with provision for a schoolmaster to teach reading, writing and Latin grammar.[13] The acceptance in an increasing number of grammar schools of reading, writing and arithmetic as suitable subjects of the curriculum reflects the growing demand for a strictly utilitarian education which, as we shall see, had important consequences for these schools.

4. The Learned Languages

The proper study of the Latin language involved the memorizing of the accidence and syntax, of vocabularies and phrases, the reading of authors and the composition of sentences, epistles, themes, verses and orations. But all too often schoolmasters must have found in the prescribed Latin grammar not only the subject-matter but also the method of their instruction. In 1559 Queen Elizabeth in her Injunctions concerning both the clergy and laity enjoined 'that every schoolmaster and teacher shall teach the Grammar set forth by king Henry VIII of noble memory, and continued in the time of king Edward VI, and none other'.[1] The authorization of *Lily's Grammar* was continued by the seventy-ninth of the Canons ecclesiastical of 1604 and undoubtedly reacted unfavourably on many of the schools.[2] Grammar-learning came to be regarded as a subject in itself, and classical authors to be relegated to the position of a store-house of examples for use in the illustration of grammatical rules.[3] Charles Hoole thought 'it not good for any Master to decline' from *Lily's Grammar* which 'is yet constantly made use of in most Schools in England'. If children are made to change their grammar as often as they change their master, he says, 'they will be like those that runne from room to room in a Labyrinth, who know not whether they go backward or forward, nor which way to take towards the door; I mean, they may be long conversant in Grammar books, and never understand the Art it self'.[4]

The classical curriculum of the grammar schools in the seventeenth century is seen at its best in the account given by Hoole of his own practice at Rotherham Grammar School and at his private school in Tokenhouse Gardens in Lothbury. In the first form, at the age of seven years, the pupils received a thorough grounding in the declensions and verbs and obtained a vocabulary by reading a chapter each day from a book like the *Orbis Pictus* by John Amos Comenius and later from the *Sententiae Pueriles* by Leonard Culman.[5] In the second form the boys were introduced to the rules of the genders of nouns and of the past tenses and supines of verbs, while they were also building up their vocabularies and becoming familiar with Latin phrases. For these purposes they read Cato and were given practice in colloquies by way of *Pueriles Confabulatiunculae* both in English and Latin before going on to the more advanced *Corderii Colloquia*. The colloquies were books written in the form of dialogues which dealt with the ordinary events of everyday life. The best known in England were the works of Erasmus, J. L. Vives, Sebastian Castellion and Maturinus Corderius, and all four were among the textbooks prescribed for use in various grammar schools.[1] In the dialogues the boys exercised their memories in order to strengthen their powers of expression and increase their vocabularies, and this was the usual method for training in Latin-speaking.

After the Restoration the practice of talking Latin, always difficult to enforce,[2] was dying out although some educationists like Charles Hoole, John Locke and John Aubrey advocated that boys should learn Latin by speaking the language and hearing others speak it. Regulations for the speaking of Latin by the boys are found down to the end of the seventeenth century, as at Martock in 1662, Wigan in 1664 and Southampton in 1675.[3] Use was made of books of phrases compiled from classical authors and especially from the *Epistles* of Cicero and the *Comedies* of Terence which were considered eminently suitable for furnishing good expression in Latin-speaking. The acting of Latin plays in form and before the whole school and before visitors was another way of making the scholars fluent in the Latin tongue.

According to Hoole's curriculum Terence was studied in the fourth form where the scholars were 'to read him so thoroughly, as to make him wholly their own'. In the same form Hoole also includes Tully's *Epistles* in which the boys were to receive practice in double translation, rendering them into good English and after a while turning them back into Latin. For poetry the boys read Ovid's *de Tristibus* and learned it 'memoriter' in order to 'imprint a lively pattern of Hexameters and Pentameters in their minds' and then went on to Ovid's *Metamorphoses*. In the fifth form Hoole would have the boys 'proceed in those pithy Orations which are purposely collected out of Sallust, Livy, Tacitus, and

Quintus Curtius' and once a week 'strive amongst themselves, who can best pronounce them both in English and Latine'. Lucius Florus was an alternative to Caesar's *Commentaries* and was read in the latter half of the year after a detailed study of the historian Justin. At this stage Virgil was introduced into the syllabus. The scholars were to learn by heart the *Eclogues*, read the *Georgics* with the help of their master and the *Aeneids* with the help of a commentary, Cerda or Servius and Mr. Farnaby's *Notes on Virgil*. For the sixth and highest form of the school Hoole prescribed Horace, Juvenal, Persius, Lucan, Seneca's *Tragedies*, Martial and Plautus, Pliny's *Panegyrica* and Quintilian's *Declamationes*.[1] All the authors recommended by Hoole were among those prescribed[2] or purchased for[3] or being used in grammar schools after the Restoration.[4]

Latin composition began in the lower school. The standard expected in 1686 at the King's School, Gloucester from the boys in the lower school, probably the first three forms, was given in an entry of 28 September in the chapter books. It was decreed that

> the Antient Custome shall Constantly be observed (That is) That noe Child shall for the future be removed out of the Lower Schoole, Nor admitted de Novo into the Upper Schoole, untill he be so well grounded by ye Usher in ye Rudiments of the Latine tongue, as that he shall be able to make for his Exercise five or six Lines of plaine true Latine, and shall understand the Scanning and proving of verses, and the making of Two verses from one Nights Exercise.[5]

Elementary practice in the 'making of latyne' in the lower school led to continuous prose, usually at first in the form of letters in Latin.[6] Letter writing in Latin was preparatory to the difficult exercise of theme-writing which was entered upon in the fifth form. For theme-writing it was necessary for the scholars to collect from their authors material bearing on the subject and to arrange it under suitable headings, and 'to furnish themselves with copy of good words and phrases, besides, what they have collected weekly'.[7] Quotations on all manner of subjects useful in Latin composition were given in various books of apophthegms like that of Erasmus. Numerous phrase-books were in circulation such as *Scholae Wintoniensis Phrases Latinae The Latine Phrases of Winchester School* by Hugh Robinson.[1] The aim of the scholars was finally

> to bring their matter into handsome and plain order; and to flourish and adorne it neatly with Rhetorical Tropes and Figures, always regarding the composure of words; as to make them run in a pure and even style, according to the best of the Authours, which they must alwayes observe, as Presidents.[2]

No doubt the more capable boys under the guidance of masters like Charles Hoole and Richard Busby produced outstanding results. John Evelyn records that on 13 May 1661 he 'heard, & saw such Exercises at the Election of Scholars at Westminster Schoole, to be sent to the Universitie, both in Lat: Gr: & Heb: Arabic &c in Theames & extemporary Verses, as wonderfully astonish'd me, in such young striplings, with that readinesse, & witt, some of them not above 12 or 13 years of age'.[3]

But in the grammar schools as a whole, if the boys reached the stage of theme-writing, it is likely that in the majority of cases they had 'done it with exceeding paines and feare, and yet too-too weakly, in harsh phrase, without any invention, or judgement', and that those masters who were capable of teaching at this level would 'have been ashamed that any one should see their exercises'.[4] John Milton held that it was 'preposterous' to force 'the empty wits of Children to compose Theames, Verses and Orations, which are the acts of ripest judgment and the final work of a head fill'd by long reading and observing, with elegant maxims, and copious invention'.[5] Nevertheless it was expected that the highest scholars should be able to compose and deliver orations and on occasion their ability to do this was tested in public.[6]

The statutes of grammar schools like Southampton and Lincoln show that in the latter half of the seventeenth century the scholars were expected to reach the same standard in Greek as in Latin. At Merchant Taylors' School orations were delivered in Greek as well as in Latin at least as early as 1596. Greek was required at Merchant Taylors' School by the statutes of 1561[7] and three years earlier the founder of Witton Grammar School willed that 'there were always taught good Literature both Latin and Greek'.[1] But Greek was not taught generally in the grammar schools before the end of the sixteenth century and in the seventeenth century there must have been many schools in which the capacities of the master and scholars prevented their entrance into this subject. Greek was normally introduced into the curriculum after the scholar had been at Latin for about three years. At Harrow School after 1590 and in Charles Hoole's curriculum in 1660 Greek was studied in the fourth form.[2]

The method of study was similar to that for Latin and began with drilling in the accidence and grammar. The place occupied by *Lily's Grammar* in the learning of Latin was taken by *Camden's Grammar* in the learning of Greek, although Hoole mentions other grammars both 'ancient and modern' which he would have the boys use for reference. The *Camdeni Grammatica Institutio Graecae Grammatices Compendiaria in usum Regiae Scholae Westmonasterienis*, which was first published in 1597, was the work of William Camden who was master of Westminster School from 1593 to 1597. Charles Hoole considered that it was inferior to the grammars prepared by two other schoolmasters, Richard Busby of Westminster School whose *Graecae Grammaticae Rudimenta* was written about 1647, and William Dugard of Merchant Taylors' School whose *Rudimenta Grammaticae Graecae* was published in 1656.

Both John Brinsley at the beginning of the seventeenth century and Charles Hoole in 1660 considered that the best book with which to begin translation was the New Testament. Both writers also agree that the scholars should first read St. John's Gospel which, says Hoole addressing the master, 'you may help them to construe and parse verbatim, but after a while when they have gathered strength to do somewhat of themselves, you may let them make use of Pasors Lexicon, which they will better do, by help of the Themes, which I caused to be printed in the Margent of the Greek Testament, which will lead them to Pasor, to see the Analysis of any word in the Testament'.[3] George Pasor's *Lexicon–Graeco–Latinum. In Novum Domini Nostri Jesu Christi Testamentum* was published in London in 1621.

The classical authors recommended by Hoole for reading in the fifth and sixth forms included Isocrates, Homer, Pindar,

Lycophron, Xenophon, Euripides, Sophocles, Aristophanes and Lucian. At Wakefield Grammar School[1] at the beginning of the seventeenth century and at Southampton Grammar School after the Restoration the prescribed texts were Isocrates, Homer, Demosthenes and Hesiod.[2] In 1652 the Dorchester schoolmaster was expressly directed to teach Isocrates, Homer, Demosthenes and Aeschines.[3] About 1670 Demosthenes, Homer and Xenophon were read at Eton.[4] Johann Scapula's *Lexicon Graeco – Latinum*, which was first published at Basle in 1579 and at London in 1619, was recommended by John Brinsley and Charles Hoole for constant reference since it contained anomalies and special difficulties not otherwise found, many of them set together in alphabetical order.[5]

Reference has been made to the fact that at Westminster School in 1661 the scholars presented themes and verses not only in Latin and Greek but also in Hebrew and Arabic, and Charles Hoole drew attention to this school in support of his plea for the teaching of Hebrew composition as well as grammar. Hoole favoured the inclusion of Hebrew in the grammar school curriculum since he maintained that although many deferred learning Hebrew until they reached the university yet 'it is rarely attained there by any that have not gotten (at least) the Rudiments of it before hand, at a Grammar Schoole'. The grammar 'most used in Schooles', and which Hoole recommended for beginners was Buxtorf's *Epitome* which the student should read and get by heart and understand while learning daily the Hebrew roots from a nomenclator or lexicon. In Hoole's method construing and parsing of sentences from Scripture came next and was followed by translation of the Hebrew Psalter into Latin and out of Latin into Hebrew again, after which the scholars might attempt other books of the Old Testament for themselves.[6]

Hebrew was not generally taught in the grammar schools, but it is evident from references in school statutes and from other sources that this subject occasionally formed part of the curriculum and that it was taught in some schools to good effect. Hebrew grammar was required in the fourth form at East Retford Grammar School in 1552 and in the seventh form at Westminster School from about 1560 and Hebrew was included in the syllabus for Merchant Taylors' School when it was founded

in 1561.[1] Provision was made for instruction in Hebrew at Newport Grammar School in Essex from 1589,[2] at Blackburn Grammar School in 1597[3] and at Heath Grammar School near
Halifax from about 1600.[4] The teaching of Hebrew is also
found before the Restoration prescribed at Market Bosworth
in Leicestershire in 1601, at Hampton Lucy in Warwickshire in
1635 and at Newport in Shropshire in 1656.[5] John Wallis who
went to Felsted School in 1630 'learn'd there somewhat of
Hebrew also. So much at least, as to be able (with my Grammar
and Dictionary) to proceed further without a Teacher: which
I did afterwards prosecute to a good Degree of accuracy, as to
the Grammar of it'.[6] When John Janeway, after two years at
St. Paul's School, was elected to a scholarship at Eton in 1646
he satisfied his examiners in Hebrew.[7] Samuel Pepys went to
St. Paul's School on 4 February 1662–63 'to see the head forms
posed in Latin, Greek, and Hebrew'.[8] The purchase of a *Latin–
Hebrew Antiquities* for St. Albans School soon after the Restoration
implies that Hebrew was receiving attention there at that time.[9]
There is no evidence that Hebrew had been taught at Bristol
Grammar School before 1666, but new ordinances issued in that
year required that the master should be 'a Master of Arts of two
years standing well learned in Latin, Greek and Hebrew'.[10]

Provision for instruction in Hebrew was made by some
founders and benefactors during the later Stuart period. In
1667–68 Guilsborough School in Northamptonshire was endowed or refounded on 8 March by deed of Sir John Langham
who gave one hundred pounds a year for the teaching of boys
in Latin, Greek and Hebrew. In the following year Brigg
Grammar School in Lincolnshire was founded by Sir John
Nelthorpe who willed that Latin, Greek and Hebrew should be
taught in his grammar school and it is possible that instruction
in Hebrew was intended by George Strelley who founded Bul-
well Grammar School in Nottinghamshire in 1669, when he
ordained that the master should teach 'such of the scholars as
were capable in the Latin tongue and upwards, until they should
be fit for the university if their parents or friends should desire it,
and be able to maintain them there'. At least five other new
schools were founded between 1660 and 1714 for the teaching
of Latin, Greek and Hebrew, Martock in Somerset, 1662,

Witney in Oxfordshire about 1663, Drax in Yorkshire, 1669, and Stickney in Lincolnshire, 1678,[1] while one older school, Bideford Grammar School in Devon, which is believed to have been founded about 1598, was rebuilt in 1686 and endowed a few years later by Susannah Stucley for instruction in Latin, Greek and Hebrew.[2]

5. *Grammar School Libraries*

In the better schools and under the more competent school-masters the scholars might acquire more than the ability to speak and read Latin and a familiarity with classical authors. But for such information the scholar was largely dependent on the books of reference which might be at his disposal although, no doubt, there were schoolmasters whose qualifications and interests led them to introduce their pupils to knowledge outside their textbooks.

'The greatest benefit to Learners after the Master, is a good Library,' wrote Christopher Wase and directed the attention of his readers to the library which had been erected and replenished 'with store of choice Books' by the Company of Merchant Taylors of London and preserved in the Great Fire by the industry of the schoolmaster, John Goad, so that it remained 'a monument of the Donors munificence, still growing to the advantage of the Foundation'.[3] He might also have pointed to St. Paul's School since his manuscripts bear witness to the liberality of the Company of Mercers, the scholars and others who had restored to 'a thriving condition' the library which had been totally destroyed by the Fire.[4]

Charles Hoole desired that every school should have a library so that it might 'be furnished with all kind of Subsidiary books for the general use of all the Scholars'. In 'A note of Schoole-Authours' he gave a list of books for reference in every form amounting in all to a library of some two hundred and fifty books. He also made a plea for a small library for the master's own use, pointing out justly that every new master could not provide himself with a good library at first, or indeed at any time, without great trouble and expense especially if he lived far from London. As examples of what he had in mind Hoole mentioned Abraham Colfe at Lewisham, who 'provided a Library for the Masters use, as well as a house for him to dwell in', and William Adams at Newport in Shropshire who gave at least a hundred pounds in order to provide a library for his school.[1] What a pity material is not available to make a quantitative study of the number of libraries that existed! It is, perhaps, hardly to be expected that any but large and well-endowed schools could fully satisfy Hoole's requirements for a well-stocked library. In fact it appears from an examination of the Wase manuscripts, to which we now turn for information about school libraries, that during the latter part of the seventeenth century many schools were ill-equipped and with little expectation of improvement in this department.

Five pounds 'was once given & layd out for books' useful to Leeds Grammar School, 'but al were lost in ye troublesom times'.[2] Books belonging to Rochester Grammar School had been 'imbezled in the fanatical times' and the schoolmaster, John Edwards, in 1675 was hoping that others would follow the example of the bishop of Bath and Wells who, when he was dean of Rochester, had given to the school a Goldman's Dictionary, a Lloyd's Dictionary and a Scapula's Lexicon.[3]

The grammar schools at Cirencester, Newland and Huyton possessed only one book, a dictionary.[4] Standish Grammar School had three books, Scapula's Lexicon, Cooper's Dictionary and Goldman's Dictionary.[5] The library at Oundle Grammar School was 'very meane' while Brackley Grammar School had 'Onely some few Bookes' which had been given by the late schoolmaster, Timothy Perkins.[6] There were about forty books in the library of Diddlebury Grammar School, but most of them were 'impertinent'.[7] Kington Grammar School had 'a small Liberary of about an Hundred bookes'.[8]

Abthorpe, Boston and Hipperholme were among the grammar schools without a library.[9] Thomas Crispin whose foundation at Kingsbridge in Devon was 'finished' in 1671 had talked also of a library, but when the first schoolmaster, William Duncumbe, wrote to Wase on 2 January 1673–74 nothing had as yet been done to further the project.[10] Reading Grammar School had 'Noe Library, but a beginning for one, depending on future benevolences'.[11] Whalley Grammar School had 'six old books, too inconsiderable to be named'.[12] Ferdinand Archer, the schoolmaster at Northampton, reported that applications had 'been severall times made to the Mayors, severall of them for but Dictionaries, and Lexicons, yet None could bee obteind' and that at his first coming to the school he had found 'Onely five Old Folios'.[1]

Some schoolmasters reported failure to replace books which had formerly belonged to their schools. 'A considerable number of books kept in two presses for the use of the Scholars' at Lincoln Grammar School were 'most by tract of time worne out, or pilfered in the times of the warre'.[2] Meredith Maddy bequeathed to the school which he founded in 1643 at Dorstone in Hereford-shire 'all his Divinity books, to be a Library there forever, but they were purloynd by his Executors'.[3] Books presented to Rivington Grammar School were 'by one ill meanes or other . . . reduced to a small & inconsiderable number'.[4] The small library of old books at Houghton le Spring Grammar School was 'soe shattered' that they might 'rather be called Rudera Librorum, quam Libri' with the exception of 'some very few' which had of late years been given by old boys and by the rector of the parish.[5]

Such books of reference as there were in some schools at the time of Wase's inquiry were provided by the industry or liberality of the schoolmaster or bequeathed by one of his predecessors. 'The present Master' of Lady Chandos' School at Winchcombe had 'adapted & adorned the House & Garden' and had 'also adjoined to the School a little Library' which he had furnished 'with some Books, usefull both for the Master & Scholars'.[6] There were 'but a few ordinary bookes' at Whitchurch Grammar School in Shropshire and most of these the schoolmaster, Thomas Henshaw, had 'caused bought'.[7] After the Civil War not one book was left of the large library at Carmarthen Grammar School until the schoolmaster, Nicholas Roberts, 'procurd of severall gent a considerable number of books in order to refurnish it, & a small summe of moeny [sic]'.[8] Heskin Grammar School possessed a small library of some eighty volumes most of which 'were left to ye school by Mr. Radcliff Master thereof'. Some of these books were 'very considerable' and included Sir Walter Raleigh's *History of the World*, two folios of the works of Joest Lips (1547–1606) who from 1579 was professor of history in the university of Leyden, *Lexicon Graeco – Latinum* by Johann Scapula, a sixteenth-century German scholar, *Thesaurus Linguae Romanae*

et Britannicae by Thomas Cooper (*c.* 1517–1594) who was president
of Magdalen College, Oxford, bishop of Lincoln in 1570 and
bishop of Winchester in 1585, and commentaries on Horace, by
Denis Lambin (1521–1572), a distinguished French scholar and
professor of Greek in the Collège de France, and on Juvenal and
Persius, by Eilhard Lubin (1565–1621), a German scholar who
successively held the professorships of literature and theology at
Rostock. There were also 'severall other schoole books, & others
very useful both for ye schollers & Masters'.[1]

Wase's correspondents make it clear that the hopes and ideals
expressed by Hoole were far from realized between the years
1673 and 1678. In some schools, as we have seen,[2] provision for
acquiring reference books was made by taking fees from the
scholars for this purpose. Charles Hoole was in favour of this
procedure and suggested that every boy at admission and on
removal to another form should pay a shilling to the library
fund.[3] Such an expedient was often made impossible by the
terms of the foundation or by the need to direct fees to other
purposes so that most schools were dependent upon benefactors.
Witney Grammar School benefited considerably from the ben-
evolence of Mary Box whose concern, expressed in the statutes,
about the cataloguing and care of books there is explained by the
handsome volumes which she presented to the school shortly
after 1674 and which had probably been the library of her
husband. The founder's insistence 'that none of the books upon
any pretence whatsoever shalbe lent out of the said Library and
School' has resulted in the preservation to the present day of this
splendid collection with the loss of only one volume. An account
of the library is given by Miss Mary Fleming in her history of the
school. Among Greek authors are Homer, Sophocles, Aristophanes, Herodotus, Thucydides, Plutarch, Demosthenes and
Aeschines. The literature of Rome is represented by Plautus,
Terence, Cicero, Caesar, Virgil, Horace, Ovid, Livy, Martial,
Persius, Pliny the Elder, Juvenal, Suetonius and Tacitus. Miss
Fleming draws attention to the polyglot Bible which was edited
by Brian Walton and published in London in 1657, to Denis
Lambin's commentaries on Cicero and Horace, to Isaac Casau-
bon's annotated version of the work of the Greek historian
Diogenes Laertius, and to Joest Lips's fourth edition of Tacitus.

The advanced scholarship of some of the books shows that the library satisfied Hoole's desire for books for the master's own use. Among books in this category are Guillaume Budé's *Commentarii Linguae Graecae* and Henri Estienne's *Thesaurus Graecae Linguae*.[1] A less notable gift, but one which was commended by Christopher Wase, was that of Lord Crew who at the request of the schoolmaster, Ferdinand Archer, mediated through a friend, gave two books from his library for the use of teacher and pupils at Northampton Grammar School. The books were Henri Estienne's *Thesaurus Graecae Linguae* in four volumes and *Athenaeus his Dipnosophist* with the notes of Isaac Casaubon in two volumes.[2] A school might benefit as did Nottingham Grammar School which in 1707 welcomed a new master, Richard Johnson, and the first purchase of books for the founding of a library.[3]

To Christopher Wase improvement in libraries was inseparable from the general improvement in the condition of the grammar schools which would follow if only 'Gentlemen could once judge these publick Schools worthy to be trusted with the Education of their Children'. For then 'they would without difficulty be induc'd at the entring of their Son to bestow some useful Book, such as the Master should propose'. Thus in process of time the schools would be furnished 'at least with the more necessary helps', and the donors would 'leave a standing Treasure to the House; not to be despised by the Town'.[4]

6. The Grounds of True Religion

Every school was subject to ecclesiastical control and provision for religious instruction and worship was frequently included in school statutes. Professor Foster Watson in summing up the main influences upon the grammar schools in the latter part of the sixteenth century and the whole of the seventeenth century wrote that

> the English Grammar Schools were, indeed, classical in aim. The curriculum and text-books dealt with classical authors, Latin and Greek speech, Latin and Greek composition. Nevertheless, the main stimulus, the outstanding motive of the whole English Grammar School system, seen in the Statutes of Foundation, both in the curriculum and in the text-books employed is distinctly religious.[5]

Schoolmasters were required to 'interpret and reade those authors which may induce and lead them to vertue, to godliness, and to honest Behaviour, and to the knowledge of humanity, but not to wantoness or sauciness' and to teach such 'Books as are without taint of Athisme, Epicurisme popish Superstition, Laciviousnesse and otherlike Infections which rather poyson then profitt youth.'[1] With these objects in view such textbooks as Cato, *Aesop's Fables*, Tully's *Offices*, *De Amicitia* and *De Senectute* were prescribed in statutes and frequently found a place in the curriculum of the grammar schools.[2] The influence of the Church remained apparent in the grammar schools and is most clearly discernible in the religious observances which formed an important part of the curriculum of these schools which were themselves a monument to the good endeavours of the Church in pre-Reformation days to provide education for the people.

The daily round of the grammar schools began and ended with prayers,[3] the form and content of which were sometimes prescribed by the school statutes.[4] These might be said in the neighbouring parish church[5] or in the schoolroom.[6] In many grammar schools reading from the holy scriptures completed the corporate acts of worship,[7] a practice to which Charles Hoole gave his support.

> It is necessary for childrens more profiting in the Scriptures, to cause that an English Chapter be read every morning at the beginning, and every night at the [*gi*]ving over Teaching. And in this, every boy throughout the Schoole should take his turn, that it may be known how perfect he is in reading English readily, and distinctly. Let him that is to read, take his place at a desk in the middle of the Schoole, and be sure he speak aloud, and let every one reverently attend to what is read, the lower boyes looking upon their English, and the higher upon their Latine Bibles. Those also that are able to make use of the Septuagint in Greek, may doe well to procure them to look upon.[8]

Where boys of the grammar school were boarded in a neighbouring house they might be expected, at times when most of the household were present, to read to the others 'some piece of the Scriptures or some other godly book'.[9]

G

Schoolmasters and ushers were required to give instruction in the Catechism so that 'the Seeds of Religion' might be 'sowen in the Hearts of Children there to Grow and bringe forth fruit in their whole life followinge'.[1] Saturday morning or afternoon was a usual time for this teaching[2] which might be preparatory to further instruction or examination by the vicar or curate of the parish.[3] Such preliminary instruction was from the Catechism in the Book of Common Prayer, first published in 1549, which in some schools was the first manual of Christian instruction in the lowest forms. More advanced instruction was given from one or more of the various catechisms, the most popular being the catechisms of Alexander Nowell, dean of St. Paul's, which were published in three editions, the *Latin Catechism* and the *Middle Catechism* in 1570 and the *Smaller Catechism* in 1572.[4] An English translation of the *Latin Catechism* was prepared and published in 1570 by Thomas Norton who was responsible for the English version of the *Smaller Catechism* which was published in 1572. Greek translations were prepared by William Whitaker of the *Middle Catechism* in 1573 and of the *Smaller Catechism* in 1574. Nowell's catechisms were prescribed for use in the grammar schools, sometimes 'the greater as well as the lesser catechism', in Latin or English or Greek.[5] Other catechisms which were used 'with good success', as Christopher Wase says in 1678, were *Ursinus's Catechism*, which was published in 1563 and translated into Greek by Henry Stephens, and the *Praxis of Birket*.[6]

School books of instruction in the Christian faith were not necessarily limited to the catechism. Charles Hoole included Gerard's *Meditations*, Thomas à Kempis's *Imitation* and St. Augustine's *Soliloquies* or *Meditations*, 'or the like pious and profitable Books', for the children of the third form, aged nine and ten years, and advised the boys to carry them in their pockets to read in English and Latin in their leisure time. Hoole's intention was that the boys should improve their Latin but the books were chosen because of their religious value.[7]

It was an important part of schoolmasters' duties to see that their pupils accompanied them to church and indeed to 'command and compell their Scholars to come and hear Divine Service in the Parish Church . . . every Sunday and Holiday'.[8] The boys were expected to carry with them to church their psalm books and prayer books and statutes occasionally required that boys should have a prayer book either in Latin or in English, as the master should decide. Special places were reserved in the parish church for the schoolmaster and his pupils, and convenient seats were often found in the Long Gallery, as in the parish church at Woodbridge in Suffolk.[1] School statutes recognized that in the interest of good discipline and seemly behaviour it was necessary that the master and boys should sit all together and sometimes reminded the governors that it was their duty to arrange 'in the churche place convenient for the said schollers to be together, and not aney other boyes or children to be theare emongst them, to thend their sylence and other demeanor maie the better be seene unto and reformed'.[2] In church it was the master's responsibility to see that the boys were not 'troublesome in talkes and jingling'.[3]

On Monday morning the boys of many grammar schools were called before the master or usher or both and made 'to give account of their profiting in the hearing of the word on the Lord's day before'.[4] The younger boys would give a verbal account while the older boys who were capable were often expected to take notes of the sermon and to produce them on the following morning.[5] As a means to ensure attention to and profit from the words of the preacher the practice prescribed for the younger boys would seem to have been more useful and more testing than that for the older boys while note-taking was certainly not the way to improve writing. There is an interesting comment on the two methods in John Aubrey's account of Dr. Edward Davenant who was vicar of Gillingham in Dorset from 1626 to 1680.[6]

> He had an excellent way of improving his children's memories, which was thus: he would make one of them read a chapter or &c., and then they were (*sur le champ*) to repeate what they remembred, which did exceedingly profitt them; and so for sermons, he did not let them write notes (which jaded their memorie), but gave an account *viva voce*. When his eldest son, John, came to Winton-schoole (where the boyes were enjoyned to write sermon notes) he had not wrote; the master askt him for his notes – he had

none, but sayd, 'If I doe not give you as good an account of it as they that doe, I am much mistaken.[1]

Monday was also a day of reckoning and correcting for boys who had been absent from church or come late to church or misbehaved during the service.[2] Failure to attend church might lead, as it did in one recorded instance, to the expulsion of the offending scholars. In the period following the Restoration some grammar school authorities insisted rigidly that all the scholars should conform to the principles of the established church. At this time Abingdon School was ruled over by Robert Jennings, a former master of Reading Grammar School from which he had been ejected in January 1655–56 by the Parliamentary Committee for Scandalous Ministers and Schoolmasters, and in 1671 he expelled ten boys who, after due warning, had continued to absent themselves from divine service in the parish church.[3]

7. Method and Results

The grammar school system which appears so narrow in the eyes of modern educationists might be expected to stifle rather than encourage intellectual curiosity. The fact remains, however, that it produced a fine breed of men and eminent scholars.

Most commonly the schoolmasters were left free to devise their own methods of teaching, but the specifications in the statutes of Dorchester Grammar School may be taken as typical of the daily practice in many grammar schools in the late Stuart period. Immediately after morning prayers the master heard his scholars repeat some part of the Latin or Greek Grammar and examined their understanding of it by requiring examples composed by themselves or culled from their reading. The younger boys were likewise called upon to repeat parts of the accidence. Those who were capable had to write an exercise, in Latin or Greek, prose or verse, as translation, epistle, theme or oration. Daily, except on play days, the master gave two lectures to every form, one in the morning which the boys reproduced in the afternoon and one before supper which the boys reproduced on the following morning.[4]

The boys sat on benches, arranged against the two long walls, and faced one another across the schoolroom, those in the highest form occupying the positions nearest to the master's chair. Charles Hoole recommended that boys of the same form should sit in order of proficiency on both sides of the room and that this order should be determined once a month by the two best scholars in each form who in turn should choose the members of their teams. Thus the boys would be 'ready paired at all times for Examinations, Disputations, or Orations, or the like'. From his chair on a platform at the end of the room the master was 'able to have every Scholar in his eye, and to be heard of all' when he had 'occasion to give any common charge'.[1]

Lectures enabled the master to give instruction to a large number at one time, but although the scholars were expected to remember and later reproduce the material, this oral method placed the burden of the work on the teacher and allowed the boys to be passive and more or less receptive listeners. It is evident that for much of the time the pupils were engaged in private preparation and it is unlikely that they gave their undivided attention to their studies except when the master was dealing directly with them. No doubt Stuart schoolboys found ways and means of relieving and enlivening the tedium of school life while the restlessness engendered by long hours and a monotonous curriculum must have been a sore trial for many schoolmasters in their task of maintaining order and inducing industry among their charges.

According to Charles Hoole, local free grammar schools with one man to do all the teaching seldom advanced their pupils beyond reading, writing and a little grammar, partly because the master was overburdened with too many petty scholars and partly because parents withdrew their children in order to save the expense of keeping them at school. In more populous places where allowance was made for an usher to teach the petties Hoole says that he had 'knowne some boyes more pregnant witted then the rest, to have proved very good Grammarians, and to have profited so in the Latine and Greek Tongues, as to come to good maturity in University studies, by a Tutors guidance'. But, he adds, the task was so exacting and discouraging that

the Masters of such Schooles for the most part, either weaken their bodies by excessive toyle, and so shorten their dayes;

or (as soon as they can fit themselves for a more easie profession, or obtain a more profitable place) after a few years quit their Schoole, and leave their Scholars to anothers charge, that either hath his method to seek, or else traines them up in another, quite different from that which they had been used to.

Schools in which the master and usher were concerned only with teaching grammar happily trained up many scholars who at the age of sixteen or seventeen years were ready to be sent to the university.[1]

V

THE DEMAND AND NEED
FOR CHANGE

The grammar schools were, as their name suggests, places for the learning of Latin and Greek grammar. Education as presented in these schools was 'a mere synonym for instruction in Latin and Greek'.[1] Often the master taught in Latin and in many schools the boys were expected to use that language in their private conversations. The curriculum also included divinity and sometimes Hebrew. These subjects formed the whole curriculum of almost all the endowed schools of England and Wales in the seventeenth century.

Its supporters, as Mr. W. O. Lester Smith has reminded us, might have defended the educational practice of the grammar schools on the grounds that it provided stimulation and discipline for the mind, inculcated habits of accuracy in thought and speech, and taught boys to esteem spiritual values.[2] They might also have argued that the ability to read classical authors and to imbibe their wisdom gives a man an abiding source of inspiration and pleasure. But it is doubtful if in the seventeenth century these admirable objectives were often attained. Indeed, the mechanical method of learning grammatical rules was likely to produce an aversion to intellectual effort and to classicism which remained with a man for the rest of his life.[3] Writers on education in the seventeenth century pointed to the waste of time and little advantage to be gained from the study of languages by grammar learning and argued in favour of applying to the teaching of the ancient languages the usual method of learning modern languages, by speaking and reading.[4]

The curriculum was well-fitted to train boys in a preliminary way for the Ministry, the Law, administration and school-mastering. But there is little doubt that the main attraction of the grammar schools in the sixteenth and seventeenth centuries lay in the professedly religious basis of the whole system. The general opinion, as expressed by Hoole in 1660, was that all teaching 'was but meer trifling, unlesse withall we be carefull to instruct children in the grounds of true Religion'.[1] That theme recurs in the foundation statutes of the grammar schools, and schoolmasters and ushers were charged 'as they will answer it to God and all good men, that they bring up their Scholars in the fear of God, and reverence towards all men, that they teach them obedience to their parents, observance to their betters, gentleness and ingenuity in all their carriage'.[2] Christopher Wase maintained that it was a matter of great importance to parents 'that their Children be train'd up in the principles of Christian Religion, entire and uncorrupt: that they be built up in the fundamental points: by Catechism and other reasonable address' and that this purpose was 'best secur'd in publick Schools'.[3] The basis of the education in the grammar schools with its emphasis on Christianity and the classics was, in fact, Renaissance Christian Humanism.

At first glance the number and popularity of the grammar schools in the seventeenth century seem to justify the assumption that the curriculum sufficiently satisfied the intellectual and moral requirements of society. Nevertheless, it was failing to meet the needs of the majority who had to earn their living and wished to follow commercial pursuits when they left school. Similarly, it was felt to be out of touch with the vocational aims of the governing class who wished to be trained for positions of responsibility in the Court, in the Army and elsewhere, and to obtain some practice in those exercises which fitted a person of quality to take his proper place in society. We shall see later to what extent the grammar schools were affected by the competition of private teachers who purported to satisfy the demand for specialized training. It is the purpose of this chapter to examine in educational writings the desire for a broader type of education, embracing the 'modern subjects' and encouraging the use of the mother-tongue, and to consider the effects upon the grammar schools of the growing demand for 'practical' education.

The subject of education and its relation to the preparation of the pupil for his work in the world after he left school received treatment in *The Moderate Intelligencer* for 5 to 12 February 1646.

> Education is then like to be fruitfull, when suited to the probable after-Imployment of those instructed. We speak not of that generall ground-work laid for the first twelve or fourteen yeares, (though in the opinion of many, that is not so well done as might be) But of that which ought to relate to the particular Imployments afterward: as if to such an imployment, so; to such, so. As for those who are born to Fortunes, and so in all Kingdomes and States usually imployed in service in their Country, or in Court to attend upon the King or his children, or serve as chief Counsellors, whether in Parliament or otherway, or in Arms for defence of their Country, or offence to its Enemies, to go Ambassadors to Forraigne States, which are various. Sure it were far better for those who may expect such Imployment, to get the knowledge of, and be understood in Maximes of State, skill in Arms, get knowledge in the Rationall part of Divinity, and the Lawes of their own and other Countries, how to inrich their Country, make great their Prince; To discourse in publique places of, and act as occasion, in these; Than to trouble their brains with Hebrew roots, the Volumes of old Learning, whether of Arts, Law, or Divinity on the one side; or with frothy Pleasure, or rather pains in the end, on the other.

To the same year 1646 belong some notes of John Dury in which he deals with the need for furnishing each class with the form of education suited to its particular needs. He proposes schools which shall provide special training for young nobles and gentlemen to equip them for posts in the State and in the Army and to teach them the language of commerce; children intended for the learned professions shall be taught Hebrew, Greek and Latin; and in addition those who are to engage in trade and in servile work shall learn 'in their mother-tongue the right notions, names and expressions of things'.[1] John Dury returned to the same subject in his work *A Supplement to the Reformed-School*, which was published in 1650:

Thus then I conceiv that in a well-Reformed Common
wealth, which is to bee subordinate unto the Kingdom of
Jesus Christ, wherein the Glorie of God, the happiness of
the nature of man: and the Glorious libertie of the Sons
of God is to bee revealed; all the subjects thereof should in
their Youth bee trained up in som Schools fit for their
capacities, and that over these Schools, som Overseers
should bee appointed to look to the cours of their Education,
to see that none should bee left destitute of som benefit of
virtuous breeding, according to the several kinds of em-
ploiments, whereunto they may bee found most fit and
inclinable, whether it bee to bear som civil office in the
Commonwealth, or to bee Mechanically emploied, or to
bee bred to teach others humane Sciences, or to be imploied
in Prophetical Exercises.[1]

The ascendancy of the ancient languages did not go unchal-
lenged in the age following the Restoration and there were some
who maintained that 'a gentleman might become learned by
the onely assistance of the modern languages'. Thomas Hobbes
in his *Behemoth*, published about 1668, was of the opinion that
Latin, Greek and Hebrew might with advantage be replaced in
the universities by French, Dutch and Spanish.[2] John Evelyn
was convinced of the value of studying modern languages and
discussed the subject in an article which he wrote for the duke
of Norfolk at the request of Sir Samuel Tuke and which he
evidently intended to publish. The discourse, he told Pepys,
contained a list 'of Authors, and a method of reading them to
advantage'. Learning, he felt, would resume a more attractive
form in the eyes of the majority if it were attained through
modern languages.[3] In 1670 Dr. John Eachard set down his
'thoughts concerning the orders and customs of common Schools'.
While not wishing to disparage Greek and Latin, which there
was good reason to value since 'the best of humane Learning has
been delivered unto us in those Languages', Eachard questioned
the necessity 'to keep Lads to sixteen or seventeen years of Age,
in pure slavery to a few Latin and Greek words' and made a
plea for 'the reading of some innocent English Authors' and for
instruction in 'the principles of Arithmetick, Geometry, and such

alluring parts of Learning'.[1] John Aubrey's scheme of reform was concerned with the education of the rich, but he was in favour of saving the time and effort then devoted to learning the accidence and grammar and preferred to restrict the curriculum to English and mathematics rather than inflict such drudgery upon scholars.[2] In *A New Method of Educating Children*, published in London in 1695, Thomas Tryon proposed a school in which there should be a tutor for Latin and French, or one tutor for each language, and visiting masters for music and painting. The curriculum also included writing, arithmetic, accounting and gardening. In a year's time, said Tryon, the children who were not above five or six years of age at entrance, would learn Latin and French 'by Custom and Conversation; for there shall be nothing else spoke in the School'.

John Locke held that learning was of secondary importance and to be esteemed only in so far as it had a practical value in later life. French and Latin he considered necessary to a gentleman, though only so much Latin as suited the ability and future need of the scholar, and the tutor was expected to talk Latin since this subject, like French, was to be learned by speaking and reading. His curriculum included drawing, shorthand, geography, arithmetic, astronomy, geometry, chronology, history, civil law, the laws of England and keeping accounts. Greek was omitted since Locke was concerned not with 'the Education of a profess'd Scholar, but of a Gentleman'. As for the accomplishments he favoured dancing which gave 'graceful Motions all the Life, and above all things Manliness, and a becoming Confidence to young Children'. Music and painting were not recommended since the attainment of even a moderate skill wasted too much time while riding and fencing should probably be practised only at intervals as exercises for good health.[3] Bishop Burnet attached little value to the learning of Latin grammar, which was not necessary for an understanding and enjoyment of the Roman writers, and while admitting that an ability to read the Latin authors could bring a man entertainment throughout his life, he maintained that the teacher should not despair of his pupil if he showed an aversion to that subject. There was 'much noble Knowledge to be had in the English and French Languages', said Burnet, while the study of geography, history, nature 'and the more practical Parts of the Mathematics' might 'make a Gentleman very knowing'.[1]

These proposals, made for the most part by men of intelligence and learning, are interesting as showing that there was a feeling of dissatisfaction in some quarters with the normal educational methods and a desire to widen the scope of the prevailing curriculum. Yet there is little evidence that the theories of educational reformers had any effect in a time when the endowed schools hardly felt the impact of the movement towards modern studies. In the later Stuart period when text-books in English were available to expound every important branch of knowledge and when many of them had been simplified for school use, the doors of the grammar schools were for the most part closed to the new learning and the schools remained bound by their statutes, by the requirements of the universities, by the power of the diocesan to issue licences to teach and by the royal authority which prescribed some of the text-books to be used in schools.

It is refreshing, therefore, to meet with any indications of readiness to broaden the curriculum and to respond to the needs of the time. Such evidence is provided by an advertisement of Saffron Walden Grammar School which in 1674 appeared in *The London Gazette* for 20 to 23 April. About that time Henry Rix resigned the mastership and the advertisement may be the work of his successor, Richard Carr, in an attempt to increase the number of scholars, although Carr's mastership is stated to have begun in 1676.[2] The advertisement is as follows:

> These are to give notice, That there is a School-master now setled at the Free-School in Saffron-Walden, in the County of Essex, near unto His Majesties Palace of Audliend, who doth teech the Latine, Greek, and French Tongues. In all which, he hath already given good testimony elswhere of his Abilities, Diligence, and Success. And withal, there is taught Arithmetick, Merchants Accompts, and the Writing of Twelve several hands by his Assistant, who hath also approved himself very skilful and dexterous in the Instruction of Youth in the said Arts.

The teaching of mathematics did not come within the scope of the grammar schools and the mention of geometry in the

statutes of 1597 for Blackburn Grammar School as a subject
'proffitable' to be studied is a notable exception.[1] In the reign
of Charles II the need for officers in the mercantile marine, to
meet the increasing demands of seaborne trade, and also for
men to serve in the navy led to the establishment within
Christ's Hospital of a Mathematical School in 1673.[2] The
establishment was for the maintenance of forty poor boys,
chosen from the scholars within the school, who were considered
competent in grammar and arithmetic. The boys were to receive their further education in the Mathematical School and
there be instructed in 'the Art of Navigacon and the whole
Science of Arithmatique' until they reached the age of sixteen
years. When, in the opinion of the Master of Trinity House, the
scholars were sufficiently qualified by age and proficiency they
were to be bound apprentices to captains of ships for seven years.
A schoolmaster was appointed to be in charge of this school which
was equipped with the necessary books, globes, maps and
mathematical instruments. The master, according to the qualifications demanded in 1678, was required to be versatile as well
as worthy by reason of his good life and conversation. He was
expected to be a first-class mathematician as well as learned in
Latin and Greek, so that the boys would not lose their proficiency
in these languages, and a very good scrivener who would fulfil
the function of a writing master to the boys in his care. Such a
man did not prove easy to find and the story of the Mathematical
School down to the second half of the eighteenth century is one
of failure due largely to incompetent masters and in some
measure to inefficient control on the part of the governors.[3] A
similar vocational aim may be seen at Dartmouth Grammar
School which was founded in 1679 with provision for two masters,
one to teach Latin and the other to be responsible for the teaching
of English, the art of navigation and other mathematics.[4]

Geography and history, in so far as they obtained any recognition in school studies, were treated as providing matter for
illustration of the Latin and Greek theme, oration and verse.[5]
But towards the end of the seventeenth century it was evidently
intended that geography should form part of the curriculum at
King Edward's School, Birmingham, since the new statutes of
20 February 1684–85 required that the schoolmaster and usher

as well as being qualified in Latin should have a thorough knowledge of geography and chronology.[1] About the same time
George Hickes, dean of Worcester, was responsible for the
introduction of geography into the cathedral grammar school.
In 1686 a terrestrial globe was bought for the school at the cost
of one pound and in the following year Horn's *Accuratissima orbis
antiqua delineatio seu geographia vetus sacra et profana*, published at
Amsterdam in 1653 and 1660, and Ferrarius's *Lexicon Geographicum*, published in Milan in 1627.[2]

Evidence of any tendency towards a wider outlook in the old
endowed schools in the later Stuart period is very scant indeed
and it cannot be said that the views of educational reformers or
the demand for a 'useful' education made much impression upon
the grammar schools as a whole throughout the eighteenth
century. And here it would seem desirable to reach forward
beyond the limits of our period, firstly to make clear the continuity of educational practice in the grammar schools, and
secondly to show the vital importance for the future of these
schools of the failure of the advocates of a broader curriculum
to make any headway against the tradition of classical and
religious learning.

'One is apt to think that the Grammar School course could
not possibly have been so restricted as it is reported to have been,'
wrote Mr. W. O. Lester Smith; 'but an examination of the time-
tables shows that right up to the nineteenth century, it is per-
fectly true to say that the basis was Latin, and that if you add a
little Greek, nothing else was taught except divinity, including
occasionally some Hebrew.'[3] In 1622 a private schoolmaster,
Dr. Joseph Webbe, protested that grammar 'is become a full-
swolne, and overflowing Sea, which by a strong hand arrogates
unto it selfe (and hath well neere gotten) the whole traffick in
learning, but especially for languages'.[4] In the middle of the
eighteenth century Robert Lloyd who was usher for a short time
at Westminster School complained of being

> pinion'd down to teach
> The syntax and the parts of speech;
> Or, what perhaps is drudging worse,
> The links, and joints, and rules of verse.[5]

The new statutes of 1809 for Bury St. Edmunds Grammar School show that so far as the curriculum was concerned there had been no advance since the beginning of the seventeenth century. By a repetition of the clause of 1665 it was decreed that 'nothing should be taught in the school but the best Greek and Latin classics, except that the head master might teach those who would desire it, the rudiments of Hebrew'.[1] During the high mastership of Dr. John Sleath, which lasted from 1814 to 1837, he is reported to have answered a parent's question by saying, 'At St. Paul's we teach nothing but the classics, nothing but Latin and Greek. If you want your son to learn anything else you must have him taught at home, and for this purpose we give him three half-holidays a week.'[2]

Lord Eldon's judgement on 22 July 1805 in the Leeds Grammar School case has been taken to mean that at the beginning of the nineteenth century the endowed grammar schools were fettered to a purely classical curriculum not only by tradition but also by law. The Lord Chancellor's decision does not seem to warrant this interpretation and Dr. S. J. Curtis doubts the justifiability of Mr. A. F. Leach's assertion that it 'carried dismay to all interested in the advancement of education and nearly killed half the schools in the country'. It may well be, however, that other schools contemplating the possibility of change were discouraged by the facts that the Leeds case dragged on for ten years and involved considerable expense. In accepting Dr. Johnson's definition of a grammar school as one 'for the teaching grammatically the learned Languages' Lord Eldon's concern was to ensure that the founder's intention should be honoured and that the charitable foundation should not be diverted from its original purpose by becoming the means to support a commercial school. He was not opposed to modern studies but to their displacing the classical learning which the school had been founded to give. Indeed he suggested as a form of compromise that 'if according to the Plan every boy to be brought to the School was to be taught the learned Languages and the circumstances that these other Sciences were to be taught would induce persons to send Boys to the School to learn Greek and Latin also that purpose might have a tendency to promote the object of the Foundation'. As Dr. Curtis wrote, 'The introduction of modern subjects in the very school in which the dispute has arisen makes his point of view sufficiently clear.' In 1806 the governors resolved that the boys coming to the school to learn Greek and Latin would increase in number if they were also offered the opportunity to learn some mathematics, that 'other sciences' should not be taught except to those who were following the normal course in classics and only when they had reached the stage of being able to 'construe the Latin Testament'.[1]

It is true that the grammar schools were fettered by the terms of their charters which did not readily lend themselves to modification or reinterpretation. Yet the histories of these schools lend support to the contention that in general trustees of schools and teachers 'are by nature almost obstinately loyal to the past'.[2] And such loyalty to traditional methods may sometimes be an excuse for inability as well as unwillingness to use new methods and material. It was evidently not impossible to introduce new subjects of study and still to maintain the classical tradition for which the schools were founded, as the experience of some more venturesome schools in the eighteenth century shows. Thus Rugby School under Dr. Thomas James, who was elected in 1778 and was the first to hold the title of headmaster, flourished and grew in number from sixty-six in James's first year to two hundred and forty-five in 1794 when he retired. The curriculum of the school was still mainly classical but time was found in the normal programme for the fifth and sixth forms, which the headmaster taught, for biblical, Roman and English history, for the reading of Milton and for modern geography. James was a keen mathematician and sometimes lectured on this subject to his boys in the top two forms. In 1781 an assistant master was appointed to teach writing and arithmetic and the boys were encouraged to learn French.[3] An enlargement of the curriculum took place at Bolton-le-Moors Grammar School in 1784 when by a Private Act of Parliament it was decreed that the master and usher should teach not only classics but also writing, arithmetic, geography, navigation, mathematics and modern languages.[4] In 1791, the first year of Thomas Henry Bullen's mastership at Oundle School, there were no boys in the school. In the following year there were forty-five boys, of whom twenty-one were boarders, and they received instruction not only in the classics but also in geography, surveying, merchants' accounts and drawing.[1] The figures collected by Mr. A. A. Mumford suggest strongly that in the eighteenth century Manchester Grammar School was keeping abreast of modern tendencies and providing an education suited to the needs of its pupils, the majority of whom were the sons of merchants and artisans. Between 1740 and 1765 there were one hundred and ninety-six boarders and four hundred and seventy-seven day boys in the school of whom a hundred, including only sixteen day boys, proceeded to the universities. From 1764 to 1807 the high master, Charles Lawson, encouraged the study of mathematics and sent boys to two mathematical schools which were taught by his former pupils, Henry Clarke and Jeremiah Ainsworth. Mr. Mumford's list shows also that the majority of boys who were at the school during the last sixty years of the eighteenth century left to go into industry and commerce and that only about fourteen per cent went on to the universities.[2]

The eighteenth century was doubtless 'a period of actual realisation of modern education' as Dr. N. Hans has shown in his valuable survey of educational establishments and movements. Yet his thesis is not substantially strengthened by evidence of what few new tendencies were to be found in old foundation schools and, though we may endorse his enthusiastic refutation of the notion that all the grammar schools were somnolent, the conclusion is still only that 'some of them, at any rate, fully participated in the general movement of reform'.[3] Indeed, so far as these schools are concerned the great weight of evidence is in favour of Dr. Cyril Norwood's description of the seventeenth and eighteenth centuries as 'a dark period in the history of English education' when, in spite of the views of educational theorists, 'the inside of the schools of the nation was given over to a narrow curriculum of much Latin and a little Greek, handled with increasing stupidity by clerical pedagogues of low status'.[4] We shall turn to a consideration of some of the men who undertook the responsible and arduous task of teaching in the next chapter.

To the economic historian the eighteenth century 'was an age when interests were directed largely to things that could be measured and weighed and calculated'. Professor T. S. Ashton wrote:

> If men may be judged by their utterances the educated no longer troubled their minds over-much with high matters of doctrine and polity: they were exercised less with the purpose of life than with the art of getting a living, less with the nature of the state than with the means of increasing its opulence. In 1700 there were fewer men searching the Scriptures and bearing arms than there had been fifty years earlier, and more men bent over ledgers and busying themselves with cargoes. There were fewer prophets and more projectors, fewer saints and more political economists. And these economists were concerned less with principles of universal application than with precepts derived from experience, less with what was ultimately to be wished for than with what was immediately expedient.[1]

In this utilitarian age many parents who wanted for their sons an education adapted to the needs of the modern world and who could afford the expense of such a training sent them to academies which claimed to prepare their pupils for commerce and the professions, for the Army, the Navy, and the Mercantile Marine. At the same time parents who were poorer saw little to be gained from the study of grammar which so many founders and benefactors offered gratuitously. To them an elementary education seemed all that was necessary before boys were set to apprenticeship at the earliest possible moment.

The falling demand for a classical education was already apparent in some areas in the seventeenth century. Thus the school at Aldenham does not appear to have flourished as a grammar school and in 1653 the parishioners obtained the dismissal of the master, Jeremie Collier, because he had shut the school when the number of boys learning grammar was reduced to two. His successor, William Elliot, was reproved in 1660 for being negligent and three years later was discharged. The next master, Andrew Champion, was likewise reprimanded and asked to leave in 1671. In 1673 the school was without a master. The company of Brewers decided that there was no demand for anything but reading and writing and planned to abandon the school at Aldenham and establish it at Watford. But opposition from Lord Holles, lord of the manor, prevented their obtaining the necessary Act of Parliament to do this.[1] At Colchester the failure of Richard Reynolds is presumably to be attributed to a lack of demand for classical teaching since he came from Great Yarmouth Grammar School with the approval of the bishop of London and was described as 'a good and diligent master'. Reynolds was master at Colchester from 1691 to 1702 and during that time only one name was entered on the admission register.[2] An interesting letter, dated only 17 March, which was written by William Bishop to Christopher Wase testifies generally to the distaste for Latin learning after the Restoration and specifically to the effect on the grammar school at Brailes in Warwickshire when the vicar of the parish chose not to accept the mastership at a salary of £8 1s. 8d. a year.

> This Free Schoole was formerly a grammar Schoole or for Latin, but since the warres learning declining and mens inclinations to Latin, English is most taught and nothing above the Accidence. The Schoolmaster heretofore was either the Vicar or Vicars deputy, but since the tyme of the present Vicar who officiates himselfe but undertakes not for the Schoole either the Clarke of the Parish or one but meanely qualified for learning hath performed it; the salary being too small to invite any one of parts to court the place.[3]

Where an English department already existed or where it was introduced to satisfy popular demand it almost inevitably led to the reduction or disappearance of grammar teaching. The encroachment of elementary subjects led, too, to a change in the social status of schools. The nobility and gentry who had been content to allow their sons to mingle with the sons of trades-men and farmers so long as they were all receiving the same higher learning and might be regarded as equals intellectually, were not so disposed to let them go to the same school as a large number of boys whose education did not proceed beyond the elementary stage and whose needs deprived the classical scholars of attention in the important early stages of their training and whose presence probably meant a deterioration in standards of behaviour.[1] 'Master Sparks' who was master at Harsnett's School, Chigwell from 1724 to 1729 had few scholars in the Latin school so that he was able to find time to help with the teaching of the boys in the English school under the master, Ambrose Halling.[2] The number of scholars at Maldon Grammar School in 1768 was so small that the master, Robert Hay, allowed an English school to be taught by its master, a Mr. Shinglewood, in the same room, keeping the seats nearest the fire for his own boys. When Hay died about 1770 no master was appointed to the grammar school and the boys of the English school continued to use the room while for a time their master received the profits from the lands belonging to the grammar school. The room, but not the rents, was allowed for the use of Shinglewood's successor and in 1810 the town of Maldon had no grammar school.[3] When Carlisle made his inquiry the school at Higham Ferrers had 'for ages ceased to be a Grammar School' while Nottingham Grammar School might 'now . . . be regarded as a useful Seminary for teaching boys English Grammar, reading, writing, and arithmetic'.[4]

Some grammar schools succeeded in maintaining their status by deliberately limiting the number of boys who were accepted for instruction in the rudiments and by charging fees which, as we have seen,[5] had the effect of making these schools the exclusive preserve of those who could afford to pay for their children's education. In 1770 Blackburn Grammar School was overcrowded with petty boys and thereafter elementary instruction was given only by the usher who charged five shillings for entrance to his department.[6] Another school which continued to give secondary education was St. Saviour's, Southwark. The Commissioners to inquire concerning Charities found in 1819 that although writing and arithmetic were taught the emphasis was on a classical education and that this had 'operated to deter the poor persons who might be entitled to send their children there from so doing'. There were then sixty-eight boys on the foundation and two private pupils and all scholars were charged a pound at admission and five shillings a quarter.[7]

What was likely to happen unless such precautions were taken and continued to ensure secondary education is well illustrated in the history of Stourbridge Grammar School in Worcestershire.

Efforts to restrict the teaching in this grammar school to elementary subjects were firmly resisted in 1700 when a new clause in the statutes stipulated that no girls were to be educated in the school, that boys were not to be admitted until they reached the age of five years, that instruction was not to be confined to one or both of the subjects of writing and arithmetic, and that no pupil was to be accepted who wanted to be taught only these subjects. The school was therefore essentially a grammar school in which writing and arithmetic were allowed merely as additional subjects. Nevertheless, those who wished were able at a later date to interpret this firm assertion of its status as an acknowledgement that the school offered education in elementary subjects. In 1809 there were about fifty boys in the school, of whom half were under the master and six or seven were boarders. A quarterly fee was charged for elementary instruction which was given to the usher who also taught grammar. Objections to payment for elementary education and to direct entry by pupils into the master's department, voiced by one of the governors, caused the relinquishment of boarders and fees with the disastrous results that classical scholars withdrew from the school and those for whom the changes had been made did not avail themselves of the opportunity which was now offered for free elementary learning.[1] In 1818 Carlisle found that the master, Joseph Taylor, was paid a hundred and fifty pounds a year and sometimes had no pupils to teach while the usher was giving primary instruction to two or three boys in return for his salary of ninety pounds a year.[2]

'Utilitarianism had become the watchword of a new age,' wrote Professor Foster Watson, and the decline of the grammar schools was in large part attributable to their unwillingness or inability to move with the times and to bring about a radical change in their outlook and practice.[3] The eighteenth century was also, judging by the utterances of ecclesiastics, an unspiritual age which witnessed 'the general Decay of Religion',[4] was characterized by 'an open and professed Disregard to religion', in which Christianity was 'ridiculed and railed at, with very little Reserve'[5] and there was a lowering of religious and moral standards 'to a Degree that was never known in any Christian country'.[6]

In the past grammar schools had owed much of their popularity to the religious element which was 'not a separate compartment of the curriculum, but *in omnibus totus*'. Mr. W. O. Lester Smith therefore sees in the decline of religion a major cause of the decline of the grammar schools in the eighteenth and nineteenth centuries.[1] But perhaps this is to oversimplify the situation. Complaints about irreligion and immorality have not been confined to ecclesiastics of the eighteenth century. Christianity was still accepted by the majority of people as the true religion and, as Dr. S. C. Carpenter has reminded us, 'it was in fact counted to be part of the law of the land, and therefore a thing to be maintained'.[2] It seems unlikely that many parents, through lack of interest in religion, deliberately boycotted the grammar schools because they were founded and maintained on a religious basis. Indeed, parents who are themselves lukewarm towards religion or even reject it are often willing to allow their children to be instructed in religious beliefs or at least appear strangely reluctant to withdraw them from such teaching. Nevertheless when the curriculum was found wanting in other respects the religious basis of the grammar schools may well not have been any longer a compensatory attraction in an unspiritual age.

Moreover, religious instruction and worship in the grammar schools were an offence to many whose deep religious convictions, given legal recognition after the Toleration Act of 1689, were opposed to those of the Established Church. The grammar schools were the monopoly of the Church and where the master did not hold in addition an ecclesiastical office the fact that he was a member of the Anglican Church, whether in holy orders or not, and presided over an Anglican foundation deprived him of support and sympathy from some neighbouring nonconformist families. The religious test closed the schools to the children of parents who were offended by their Anglican character and, as we shall now see, debarred from teaching in the grammar schools and deprived them of men who were admirably suited to serve them.

VI

SCHOOLMASTERS

1. Politics and Prescriptions

The office of a schoolmaster is one of responsibility and trust. It was also in the seventeenth century one of hazards and oaths. Since 'from the ordinary Schools all Magistrates, and Ministers, and Officers of State are taken throughout the Nations of the World, to be set over others'[1] the influence which a schoolmaster might exercise over his pupils was of interest to the authorities in Church and State and qualifications which were acceptable in one decade might be wholly unacceptable in another. During the Commonwealth period the steps taken to ensure that schoolmasters should be well-affected to the government then established are of interest as examples of State interference with the teacher and testify to the importance which attached to a schoolmastership. The policy of ejecting schoolmasters who were scandalous in their lives and doctrines and disaffected to the government, begun by the Long Parliament, was continued by Cromwell and the council. Inquiries into the fitness of schoolmasters were made by the major-generals and county commissioners who were authorized to grant licences to teach. Thus in 1656 Thomas Chaloner was confirmed in the mastership of Ruthin Grammar School by the decision of Major-General Berry.[2] In January 1655–56 the major-general and county commissioners were ordered to inquire into and report on the case of Robert Mossom who had been sequestered from the living of Teddington in Middlesex in 1650 and who had petitioned the council for a licence to teach. In the same month Francis Neves, another sequestered minister, presented a certificate from the commissioners of Surrey in support of his application to the council for leave to keep a private school at Lambeth.[3]

With the Restoration settlement schoolmasters who had been appointed by the officers of the Puritan Government were deprived of their source of income and those who continued to teach were dependent for a precarious living upon voluntary contributions. By the Act of Uniformity all schoolmasters and tutors were required, before 24 August 1662, to subscribe a declaration expressing abhorrence of armed resistance to the king or those in authority and readiness to conform to the Book of Common Prayer, and renouncing the Solemn League and Covenant as unlawful. Those who refused to subscribe were to be deprived of their places. Any schoolmaster or tutor who continued to teach without making the subscription and without obtaining the necessary licence from the archbishop, bishop or ordinary of the diocese was to suffer three months' imprisonment for the first offence and three months' imprisonment and a fine of five pounds for the second and subsequent offences.[1] But apart from the practical necessity of earning a living dissenters were not willing to abandon without a struggle all that they valued most. The government's attempt to deprive them of their right to spiritual freedom and liberty of judgement served in many cases only to increase their determination to resist. It is not therefore surprising that in 1665 the government felt it necessary to pass 'An Act for restraining Non-Conformists from Inhabiting in Corporations' which forbade dissenters to teach in public or private schools under a penalty of forty pounds.[2] In the same year Gilbert Sheldon, archbishop of Canterbury, issued to his bishops a letter 'concerning schoolmasters and instructors of youth' in which he requested them to furnish him with particulars of the masters and ushers in free schools and of all other teachers in public and private schools within their dioceses. The bishops were further directed to find out if teachers regularly attended church and caused their pupils to do the same and if they appeared to be well-affected to his majesty's government and to the doctrine and discipline of the Established Church. In a letter of 6 February 1672 the archbishop enjoined his suffragans to take action 'according to such rules as are prescribed unto us for their restraint' against any unlicensed teachers in public or private schools within their or the bishops' jurisdiction and ordered that only those who had given the necessary subscription, oaths and declaration should be admitted to the office of teacher.[3]

The severity of this repressive policy was somewhat mitigated in 1670 by the judgement in the case of William Bates to the effect that a schoolmaster might teach without a bishop's licence so long as he was appointed by the founder or lay patron of the school.[1] It was not, however, until 1779 that dissenters were relieved from legal disqualification to teach and even then they were not allowed to teach in endowed grammar schools unless they had been founded for the education of Protestant dissenters since the year 1689.[2] But in the eighteenth century, after the short-lived Schism Act of 1714 and its repeal in 1719, though the Act of Uniformity of 1662 and the Five Mile Act of 1665 remained, the general tendency towards toleration enabled dissenting schoolmasters to open and maintain undisturbed their schools.

A matter which is very difficult to ascertain is the extent to which masters of grammar schools actually changed at the Restoration. We shall presently see that some schoolmasters were forced to leave their schools on account of their non-conformity or support of the parliamentary cause, that in some instances they found employment in other schools or set up private schools and that efforts to retain the services of good masters who had supported the defeated causes were sometimes successful. According to Edmund Calamy thirty-nine school-masters were ejected 'by, or before the Act for Uniformity'. He did not know the names of four of these men, but their schools were at Wallingford in Berkshire and at Mashbury, Chigwell and Langdon Hills in Essex. In his revision of Calamy's list Mr. A. G. Matthews reduced the number of ejected school-masters to thirty.[3] To this number must be added ten who were not mentioned by Calamy and who are known to have been dismissed from their schools. It may be, as Calamy wrote, 'that there were many others, who are not now to be recover'd'.[4] We can only conjecture here, but it seems unlikely that there was any drastic uprooting of grammar schoolmasters. The Restoration and the Act of Uniformity had little or no effect upon the lives and careers of some of the best schoolmasters, who found compliance with the new conditions in the state not altogether and in all circumstances impossible.

But before we consider this problem in detail there are

questions to be asked about the qualifications required of a schoolmaster, about whether he was in holy orders or not, about the working span of a man's life. Schoolmasters were expected 'Conscionably and Carefully' to bring up their scholars 'equally in Religion and in all good learning and manners and to walke before them in all Sobrietie and Decent Conversation as a patterne of Godlyness and Conscionablenesse'.[1] Selection committees therefore looked for men of good academic standing who conformed to the doctrine of the Church of England and were deemed to be blameless in their conduct.

On the academic side insistence was frequently laid on the possession of a university degree though on occasions this statutory requirement might be waived, presumably because the man had displayed qualities which were too good to be overlooked. Such was certainly the case at Martock in Somerset where William Strode of Barrington who endowed the free school in 1661 relaxed his own order that the schoolmaster should 'be a Master of Art in some University' when he made his first appointment to the mastership. Charles Darby who had been denied 'ye advantage of being graduate in ye University' but had 'bin very prosperous there before, and elsewhere also' described for Christopher Wase the circumstances of his election in a letter of 21 April 1674:

> I had formerly receded for 10 yeares or thereabouts, when ye Gentleman declaring his mind to me, would needs oblige me to be ye first Master there: wch I did, and have continued ever since. And though I have laboured under much envy, yet God hath so blessed me, yt for 12 yeares or more, ye schoole though in a Countrey-towne, hath bin one of ye most eminent in this diocesse of Bath and Wells, and hath transmitted yearly some number of scholars to both Universityes, and many to be Clarked at London &c.[2]

Another master who overcame the lack of a university qualification was William Weston who was raised from the ushership to be master at Hartfield Grammar School in Sussex when in 1662 Edward Oliver was ejected. In order to satisfy the words of the founder, Richard Rands, rector of Hartfield, who by his will of

30 June 1640 directed that the schoolmaster should be a graduate, George Shaw, vicar of the parish, was persuaded to bear the title of master while Weston, nominally his usher, performed the duties and received the reward of the higher office. Weston was at a disadvantage and instead of the statutory stipend of twenty pounds he was paid seventeen pounds and ten shillings and given lands which were of no value to him since the tenants refused to pay the rents.[1] There was no attempt at subterfuge when William Ball, who had been elected usher of Bristol Grammar School under a special dispensation in 1658, since he was not a graduate, was further raised to the mastership in the room of John Stephens, whose Puritan tendencies were no doubt responsible for his removal in 1662, and in the face of the ordinance which required that both master and usher should have university degrees.[2]

An unusual requirement in school statutes is that of celibacy. It is found in 1658 at Houghton in Durham where the school-master was allowed to marry only if he had received 'the consent of both the governors in writing under their hands, and the common seale of the schoole, with two justices besides of this county named by the governors'.[3] A similar provision appears in the articles which were drawn up in the second half of the seventeenth century for a free school at South Stoke in Oxfordshire. The master appointed by the warden and five seniors of Merton College, Oxford was to be a single man who, if he decided to marry, was to give up his place, unless he had previously obtained dispensation from the warden and five seniors and also the consent of the parishioners.[4]

In the seventeenth and eighteenth centuries most school-masters were in holy orders and it was not until the nineteenth century that there was a differentiation between the professions of schoolmaster and cleric.* It was, therefore, not unusual for the vicar of the parish to be also the schoolmaster.[5] And, given the structure of a small village, in theory the combination of schoolmastership and cure of the parish seems a sensible practice and there can be no doubt that often the system worked well to

---

*For a table showing the percentage of schoolmasters in holy orders at varying periods, derived from as representative a sample as can be gathered, see p. 121 below.

the advantage both of the parish and of the school. A diligent parish priest would welcome the opportunity to reach many children and for a long period of time which his schoolmastership provided.

In practice, of course, the successful working of the system could be weakened by the character of the master as it certainly was for a time at Steeple Aston in Oxfordshire. The rector of Steeple Aston was by custom also the master of the grammar school until the beginning of the nineteenth century. In 1679 the two offices were occupied by Richard Duckworth, formerly a fellow of Brasenose College, Oxford, whose interest in the school was evidenced by his care in restoring the buildings in 1688. Duckworth evidently conducted the school efficiently although he 'was severe to his Scholars, some of wch were Boys of good Birth', and his 'sower, harsh disposicion, & almost intolerable', was unfortunate in one who had the charge of children. Disagreement with his parishioners over the payment of tithes caused him to depart about the year 1692.[1] The next rector-schoolmaster of whom there is any record was Thomas Beconsal who also had been a fellow of Brasenose College and who came in 1706. His short tenure of the two offices at Steeple Aston seems to have been an unhappy time. Hearne describes him as 'a strange Hypochondriacal Person' and suggests that this 'may be a reason why he was so great an Admirer of King William, & ye Ministers of Queen Anne'. Beconsal died in 1709 'having been for a great while in a Melancholy, hippish Condition'. His successor as rector and schoolmaster, George Freeman, held those offices for thirty-six years.[2]

The practice of holding benefices outside the parish in which the school was situated had obvious drawbacks. Preaching might mean absence from school duty for several days in view of the travelling arrangements. Even so pluralism of this sort was acceptable to some school authorities and evidently could be made to work satisfactorily.[3] John Price who held the mastership of Thetford School in Suffolk from about 1681 to 1736 was at the same time 'sequestrator' of St. Peter's and curate of St. Cuthbert's in Thetford, rector of Santon in Norfolk and of Honnington in Suffolk. One of his pupils who was 'brought up under him above 10 years' described him as 'a man of sound learning and great eloquence, an excellent preacher, discreet master, agreeable companion and true friend'.[1] And the trustees of Rugby School saw nothing wrong in allowing Henry Holyoake to hold successively the livings of Bourton-on-Dunsmore, Bilton and Harborough. Indeed the trustees considered that permission to hold these livings was a fitting recognition of his notable services to the school and sufficient indication of their high regard for the master whose continued success does not seem to have been affected by these additional responsibilities. No doubt, as Mr. H. C. Bradby suggests, Holyoake's assistants in the school were also able to help him in the discharge of duties in the parishes.[2]

In many schools, when the stipends of the master and usher were by no means adequate, it was a necessary and convenient arrangement that the schoolmaster should augment his salary by some ecclesiastical employment and this was indeed encouraged by penurious governors. The practice of appointing the master at Southwell Minster Grammar School to a vicar-choralship was reckoned to be expedient because it augmented the master's low salary of fourteen pounds a year with the nine pounds paid to a vicar-choral and provided for the singing of the services on Sundays and holy days when other vicars-choral could be expected to be ministering in their parishes. The performance of duties in the choir necessitated absence from school and at a visitation in 1693 John Sharp, archbishop of York, took notice of complaints of neglect against the school-master and enjoined 'that from henceforward the Master of the Grammar School strictly and constantly attend his school on all school days, and at all school hours, as much as any former Master of the school that was no Vicar Choral was accustomed to do, or so much as he himself, if he was no Vicar Choral, is in duty bound to do'. The situation at Southwell had been aggravated when Thomas Hesildon (or Hasildon or Hesleden) became master in 1685 and added the cure of the parish to the responsibilities of schoolmaster and vicar-choral at a combined salary of forty-three pounds a year. The chapter at its meeting on 30 June 1692 thought that this plurality of offices was 'inconvenient if they can be legally separated', but seems to have done nothing about it, and there is no reference to the cure of the parish in the injunction of 1693. The archbishop was not unmindful of the advantages of combining the schoolmastership and a vicar-choralship and virtually gave his approval to the continuation of this practice on condition that the chapter found someone to fill the master's 'place in the quire at all times when his presence is required in the school; provided that he himself do in person perform the duties of his Vicar Chorals' place on Sundays and Holidays'.[1]

Only by some such arrangement could a good man be persuaded to undertake the mastership of a school the endowment of which made it impossible to offer a salary on which the master and his family could live. Nevertheless it is understandable that founders and feoffees should seek to safeguard their schools against possible insufficiency on the part of the schoolmasters occasioned by conflicting calls upon their time and attention. So John Sampson, who founded South Leverton Grammar School in Nottinghamshire by deed of 26 March 1688–89, was clearly aware of the danger of absenteeism which would almost certainly arise if the master performed duties at any distance from South Leverton and accordingly stipulated that the master should not hold any ecclesiastical benefit except within the parish.[2] Some schoolmasters while not forbidden to undertake ecclesiastical work were warned that this should not be regular or frequent. The master of Needham Market Grammar School in Suffolk was allowed by the statutes only to give occasional help to the minister of Barking[3] and when Thomas Coton founded the grammar school at Kingsbury in Warwickshire in 1686 he instructed his schoolmaster 'to exercise the ministry but very seldom'.[4]

Not a few founders, like John Royse at Abingdon, Christopher Rawlins at Adderbury and William Parker at Hastings, were convinced that one man could not execute two offices and forbade the school governors to nominate a master who held a benefice either within or outside the parish.[5] Others like William Strode at Martock further expressly stated that if after his appointment the schoolmaster 'should undertake any parsonage, vicarage or care of souls, he was then to be dismissed from the school office, and profits of the school, and another to be chosen in his room'.[6] They might even take the unusual course of insisting, as did Archbishop Harsnet in his statutes of 1629 for Chigwell School, that the schoolmaster should be a layman and that as soon as he took holy orders his place should 'become void *ipso facto*, as if he were Dead'.[1] Such an insistence commended itself to the governors of Preston Grammar School who, in November 1680, demanded the resignation of George Walmesley who had expressed his intention to take holy orders. Unless Walmesley had also intimated that he wished to add the cure of a parish to his mastership the decision seems to have been a hard one since his successor, Richard Croston of Emmanuel College, Cambridge, was required 'to apply himself wholly to the duties of his office but not to be obliged to renounce his function in the ministry'.[2]

In schools which provided a good living for the master the governors could, if they wished and if it was necessary, insist that the schoolmaster should confine his attention to his schoolmastering. Institution to a benefice was held to be incompatible with the high mastership of Bury St. Edmunds so that Dr. Thomas Stevens having been given time to decide if he would 'hold to his lyveing and leave the schoole' resigned on 12 September 1663 to devote himself to the ministry.[3] And when the corporation of Kingston upon Hull appointed Robert Steel to the mastership of the grammar school in 1647 it was agreed that he 'should not undertake any Church duty, lest it should be a hindrance to his School'.[4] But statutes might be evaded as Lewis Griffin showed when he was master at Colchester Grammar School. This 'injenious, but not a very regular man' was appointed on 7 June 1664 and from 16 January 1666–67 until 17 July 1671 held, in addition, the rectory of Greensted although, according to the statutes of 1587, the bailiffs should have replaced him within six weeks of their learning of his acceptance of a benefice.[5]

In poorer schools, whether they liked the arrangement or not, if they wanted to keep their schoolmaster the governors had to allow him to eke out his salary from the school with any increment that he might obtain by performing ecclesiastical duties. Perhaps the corporation's decision in 1679 'that whosoever hereafter is elected schoolmaster shall, while he continues in that office, not accept of any parsonages, curacy, or employment whatsoever, or preach without licence from the mayor' explains why Edward Emerson of Lincoln College, Oxford, appointed in 1679 stayed for only one year at Boston Grammar School in Lincolnshire.[1]

The fact that in many cases the master of the grammar school was also the vicar of the parish no doubt made for longer tenure of office since the man was interested in two positions and, moreover, the two stipends were an inducement to him to remain. In this period and in the two following centuries long masterships are not uncommon and there is nothing unusual in a man's continuing in the same school for forty years or more. Thus William Barrow was in charge of Manchester Grammar School from 1677 until 1721[2] and Henry Allen remained at Charlbury Grammar School for fifty-three years after his appointment in 1680.[3] Tetbury Grammar School had three masters between 1698 and 1721 and then one master, Henry Wightwick, for the next forty-two years[4] while Stockport Grammar School had twenty-three masters in the seventeenth century and only four in the eighteenth century, Joseph Dale in 1703, William Jackson in 1752, George Porter in January and Elkanah Hoyle in December, 1792.[5]

Long masterships did not necessarily indicate that the man had passed the modern age of retirement. John Twells who became master at Newark Grammar School in 1674 and held office for forty years was still only sixty-one years of age when he died. Nevertheless in the seventeenth century, a man like Twells, who began his teaching career at the age of twenty-one, was young to have charge of a school. Twenty-three or twenty-four was a more usual age at which a man might expect a mastership though statutes indicate that governors hoped that candidates would be not less than twenty-seven years of age and would have had experience and proved their ability in teaching children.[6] A man could be elected to a mastership at the age of sixty-five years as was William Turner who came to Colchester Grammar School in 1723 after being master at Stamford Grammar School for thirty-two years.[7]

But in an age when few schoolmasters could look forward to the prospect of retirement on a pension, many were compelled to stay at their posts until they died or until old age and infirmity made it impossible for them to continue. The first master appointed to Mottram Grammar School in Cheshire was John Etcholls who, according to Christopher Wase's information, 'continued in ye office att ye same place about 62 yeares . . . going about ye 88th yeare of his Age being soe lately deceased as feb: 14: 1670.'[1] John Graile died on 4 January 1697–98 at the age of eighty-eight years after presiding over Guildford Grammar School for the past fifty-two years.[2] It is therefore surprising to find a school at which long masterships were not welcomed and where the compulsory retiring age suggested that a schoolmaster was too old at forty-five. At that age the master was to be removed from his office at Brigg Grammar School in Lincolnshire according to the stipulation made by the founder, Sir John Nelthorpe, in his will of 11 September 1669.[3]

It would be valuable if questions about the training, status and conditions of service of these schoolmasters could be answered statistically. But the problem is to obtain figures which can safely be used to guide us to conclusions about the quality and quantity of schoolmasters in the seventeenth and eighteenth centuries. Unfortunately, it is impossible to assess with confidence and precision the number of graduates, clergymen and pluralists among schoolmasters, their length of service, or even the total number of men who were masters of schools. The quality of the records varies widely and there are considerable gaps in our present knowledge. To assemble anything like comprehensive statistical information, not only about schoolmasters but also, in the first place, about schools, will require many researchers. Nevertheless it is worth while to set out what quantitative evidence we can, in the hope that this will throw fuller light upon these schoolmasters.

To this end an investigation was made of one hundred and twenty-one schools which existed between 1660 and 1770 and which are mentioned in the articles on schools in the *Victoria County Histories* (Sample A). The schools were selected because the available material about their schoolmasters, though not necessarily complete, promised to yield something of value. Among the nine great public schools only Rugby was included in the list. Further reference was made to the individual history

I

of a school, where this exists, and the schoolmasters were checked in the volumes of *Alumni Oxonienses* and *Alumni Cantabrigienses*.

This survey of schools' histories, which vary in the completeness of their records, produced the names of six hundred and seventeen schoolmasters. Fifty-eight of these men are remembered only by their names, and sometimes the dates of their masterships, and could not be further identified. Of the remaining five hundred and fifty-nine men, four hundred and nineteen were graduates of Oxford or Cambridge. In the two universities eleven of these schoolmasters had proceeded to the degree of B.D., fourteen others to doctorates in divinity and one to a doctorate in civil law. From Dublin came one schoolmaster and from St. Andrews two schoolmasters who had taken the degree of master of arts. Fifty-four others left Oxford and Cambridge without taking degrees. Of our total number of five hundred and fifty-nine schoolmasters who can be identified, four hundred and eighty-one were university men. At least four hundred and forty-nine men were in holy orders and of these two hundred and twenty-two were pluralists. As for tenure of office, masterships lasting more than twenty years in one school are recorded in one hundred and eighty-four cases, fourteen of these continuing for more than fifty years, thirty-five for more than forty years, fifty-seven for more than thirty years.

A further set of figures was obtained by examining information about these schools in the period 1660–1714 and then, for comparison, in the period 1714–1770 (Samples B and C). Of the total number of one hundred and twenty-one schools, one hundred and seven provided material for the earlier period and one hundred and eight for the later period. For the years before 1714 the names of three hundred and fifty schoolmasters were recovered, including two hundred and fifty-seven graduates and thirty-one non-graduates of Oxford and Cambridge, two hundred and thirty-two clergymen, one hundred and fourteen pluralists, and thirty-five men who could not be identified. The figures for the years from 1714 to 1770 are three hundred and thirty-nine schoolmasters, two hundred and twenty-six graduates, twenty-eight Oxford and Cambridge men who did not take a degree, two hundred and sixty-seven

Sample	Period covered	Number of schools	Number of schoolmasters	Number of schoolmasters identified	Oxford and Cambridge graduates	Other graduates	Matriculated but not graduates	Percentage of graduate schoolmasters	Percentage of matriculated schoolmasters	Number in orders	Percentage in orders	Number of known pluralists	Percentage of known pluralists
A	1660–1770	121	617	559	424	3	54	76%	86%	449	80%	222	40%
B	1660–1714	107	350	315	257		31	81%	91%	232	74%	114	36%
C	1714–1770	108	339	313	226		28	72%	81%	267	85%	132	42%
D	1660–1714	60	255	238	168	3	29	72%	84%	179	75%	84	35%
E	1714–1770	60	251	244	162		19	66%	74%	201	82%	84	34%

clergymen, one hundred and thirty-two pluralists, and twenty-six men who were unidentifiable.

Less than half the number of selected schools provided complete records of schoolmasters and their years of mastership between 1660 and 1770. With the evidence from sixty schools it was possible to make another comparison for the periods from 1660 to 1714 and from 1714 to 1770 (Samples D and E). In the later Stuart period the number of schoolmasters in these schools was two hundred and fifty-five, seventeen of them unidentifiable, and in the following fifty-six years the number was four less, seven of them unidentifiable. The figures for graduates of Oxford and Cambridge in the two periods was one hundred and sixty-eight and one hundred and sixty-two. Twenty-nine men who were schoolmasters between 1660 and 1714 and nineteen between 1714 and 1770 left the two universities without taking degrees. The company of schoolmasters in the earlier period included the three men, already mentioned, who came from Dublin and St. Andrews. The number of those who were certainly in holy orders rose from one hundred and seventy-nine before 1714 to two hundred and one after 1714, but the figure for pluralists remained at eighty-four throughout the period 1660 to 1770.

The findings have necessarily to remain somewhat inconclusive since the schools represent only a sample and the figures are based on incomplete data. Even so they provide some illumination and there is no good reason to think that they do not give an overall picture of a profession in which the number of graduates was always high and a substantial proportion always in orders. The table on p. 121 shows how the five samples investigated have produced very similar results. It is noticeable that the proportion of graduates among the schoolmasters remains at about three-quarters in all the samples, while the number who had experienced at least something of a university education is even higher. So far as the proportion of schoolmasters in orders is concerned, the rather higher percentages in the two samples covering the years 1714–70 over those in the two equivalent samples for the period 1660–1714 might suggest statistical support for the contention that, with schoolmasters' salaries increasingly uncompetitive, slightly more men, in the eighteenth century, were supplementing their incomes with additional duties as incumbents or curates. But the figures for the number of known pluralists does not wholly confirm this, so that we cannot draw any firm conclusions; changing conventions as well as economic need may have led to such a trend.

A schoolmaster might satisfy his examiners and the bishop of the diocese of his fitness to teach. It remained to be seen whether or not his practice matched the prescription presented in the school statutes and the faith placed in him by the governors. In the seventeenth and eighteenth centuries it was in the power of one man to make or mar a school. The most important question about schoolmasters is, therefore, whether they operated for the good of their schools or not.

2. People and Practice

The retirement of a master soon after the Restoration cannot, of course, be taken as an indication that the return of the monarchy was the cause of his leaving his school, although the historian is tempted to assume some connexion between the two events. There is no proof, for example, that one Mr. Kerridge, who was master of Abingdon School on 8 December 1655 when it was ordered that his stipend should be increased to thirty pounds a year, was ejected at the Restoration. It is clear that he left the school soon after the Restoration and he may possibly have had to make room for Robert Jennings whose loyalty to the royalist cause had been proved by his removal from Reading School in 1655–56.[1] Certainly Jennings was in the possession of the school on 11 March 1663, when a new pump was provided for him on condition that he kept it in order so long as he remained master.[2] Nor can it be taken for granted that when Richard Palfreyman left the mastership of Boston Grammar School to which he had been elected in 1657, he was influenced by any other consideration than his own desire to relinquish a post which had apparently proved uncongenial to his predecessors. At the time of his appointment the town corporation made an effort to ensure some continuity in the teaching by insisting that the new master should 'engage to this house that he would keep the said School for five years at least' and would give a year's warning that he intended to leave. It may be that the stipulated term of office was enough for Palfreyman who retired from the school in 1662 although the date of his resignation suggests the influence of the religious and political reaction of the Restoration.[3]

But nevertheless the simple fact that the man had been appointed in the time of the Commonwealth Government seems to have been in some cases sufficient reason for his dismissal with the end of that regime. He was the product of the Interregnum and sympathetic to the late rulers, therefore he must go. Such may have been the fate of men like Thomas Gerrard of Reading Grammar School,[4] Edward Norris of Wellingborough Grammar School,[5] Benjamin Masters of Newark Grammar School[6] and Francis Hanslope of St. Albans Grammar School.[7] No other reason for their removal can be discovered except that they had received their appointments during the Commonwealth period and therefore, seemingly, and in the case of Gerrard directly, with the approval of those in authority in the state, an evidence that they were in sympathy with Puritanism or Parliamentarianism or both. At Canterbury the reinstatement of the dean and chapter meant the overthrow of all who were connected with their former humiliation and carried with it the headmaster, Henry Montagu, who gave way to John Harris, an old boy of Ashford Grammar School and graduate of St. John's College, Cambridge.[1] On 23 May 1661 Roger Holmes resigned 'freely and voluntarily' the mastership of Ripon Grammar School in Yorkshire which he had held since 1650 so that he was seemingly less able to adapt himself to the changed conditions at the Restoration than Thomas Thompson who continued as usher under the new master, Charles Oxley.[2]

These dismissals coincided with the downfall of the late government, but some at least who survived the immediate re-establishment of kingship soon fell victims to the religious policy of the parliament. Under the terms of the Act of Uniformity John Woodbridge, master of Newbury Grammar School, was displaced by Samuel Sprint.[3] Both the master, Mr. Twigg, and the usher, Mr. Smith, of Ashbourne Grammar School, were ejected in 1662 and it is difficult to attribute their dismissal at that time to any other cause than the Act of Uniformity.[4]

Among the dispossessed men were good schoolmasters whose merits had not gone unnoticed and who were not allowed to depart without some protest or appeal from influential quarters. Richard Pigott had followed an outstanding schoolmaster at Shrewsbury School from which Thomas Chaloner was ejected when the town fell to the parliamentary forces in 1645. It is not surprising that Chaloner should be invited to resume the mastership when the monarchy was restored. Nevertheless the annual number of entries to the school during Pigott's time averaged seventy-four and his success was such that at the Restoration the fellows of St. John's College, Cambridge felt justified in confirming his appointment. Their support was not sufficient to prevent Pigott's dismissal and the reinstatement of Chaloner as master for the one remaining year of his life.[5] Charles Butler's ejection from Bedford School did not go unopposed and the re-appointment of William Verney had not the same amount of justification as that of Chaloner. Verney had been removed from the mastership in January 1655–56 by the commissioners named by the Lord Protector and his council by the ordinance of 28 August 1654, to examine all schoolmasters who were ignorant, scandalous, insufficient or negligent.[1] Bedford School evidently had reason to be grateful for this release at the hands of the commissioners since efforts had already been made to obtain Verney's dismissal in 1648–49 when his scandalous neglect of his duties had caused parents to withdraw their children from the school. Butler had proved himself an able man and it is difficult now to understand the reaction which could call back Verney to replace him, while it is to the credit of the Bedford Town Council that they made efforts to keep Butler by writing to the town's representatives in parliament and to New College, Oxford on his behalf.[2]

The removal even of good schoolmasters who had been appointed in the time of the Commonwealth Government, and especially of men of professed Presbyterian tendencies, is explained by the enthusiasm of the reaction against all things Puritan and Parliamentarian. Less easy to understand is the appointment of men in similar straits to other notable schools which might equally have been expected to wish to avoid any connexion with the defeated causes. Two men who had been associated with Eton College during their schoolmastering careers in the Commonwealth period and who lost their offices at the Restoration as a result of their nonconformity and allegiance to the parliamentary cause were shortly elected to masterships in grammar schools. One was John Boncle whose name, according to Anthony Wood, was pronounced Bunkley.[3] After acting as tutor to the children of Charles I he had supported the parliamentary side and was appointed master of Charterhouse in 1651. Three years later Boncle moved from Charterhouse to Eton College as master, an appointment which he held for only one year before becoming a fellow of the college. At the Restoration he was ejected from his fellowship. Soon after his ejection Boncle was appointed master of the Mercers' School, on 3 April 1661, and he continued there for the next fifteen

years. It can only be assumed that the qualifications of a man
who had been tutor to the king's children and master of two
great schools outweighed the disadvantages of his former sympathy with the parliamentary cause and carried the selection
committee in his favour. The decision proved a good one and
the demands of the Act of Uniformity evidently gave Boncle
little or no inconvenience.[1] Probably the same or similar considerations obtained the mastership of Reading Grammar
School on 29 October 1660 for Thomas Singleton who had
relinquished the mastership of Eton at the Restoration, presumably on account of his Presbyterianism. Singleton apparently
soon shattered any hope which the governors may have had
when they appointed him that he would show himself submis-
sive to the restored order in Church and State. The Presbyterianism which occasioned his leaving Eton proved equally
objectionable at Reading where his mastership lasted for no
more than a year.

Thomas Singleton's short mastership at Reading Grammar
School was not begun without some embarrassment and the
history of that school affords an interesting example of the
difficulties which might be caused by the change in teaching
staff brought about by the Restoration reaction. The ejected
man was Thomas Gerrard, M.A., formerly a fellow of St.
John's College, Oxford, who had been admitted to the office of
master on 2 January 1655–56 as the result of direct intervention
on the part of the Lord Protector in the form of a letter directing
his appointment. Robert Jennings was therefore removed in
favour of Thomas Gerrard who held the mastership until, on 19
September 1659, he was 'summoned to show by what title he
holds the school'. On 3 October Gerrard was 'disowned' as
schoolmaster after begging to be excused the interrogation on
the ground that no man is 'bound to accuse himself'. Nine days
later it was decided to reinstate Robert Jennings, and when, as
it would appear, Jennings declined this honour, one Mr.
Edwards was elected as the new master. The town council had,
however, reckoned without Gerrard's tenacity; he had excused
himself from the summons to prove his title to the mastership
but he showed no sign of willingness to relinquish his position.
On 29 November Gerrard was still in possession and was in-

formed that if he continued he would receive no more payment. It was not until the following September that Edwards was again invited to begin his duties since now Gerrard was said to have been finally evicted by law. The period of waiting had proved too much for Edwards who in the result never came at all. It was at this point in the proceedings that Thomas Singleton was appointed on 29 October 1660, but the arrival of a recognized master was still further to be postponed. Singleton is said to have officiated by deputy until the next spring, a course no doubt forced upon him by the fact that Gerrard was in possession and was indeed paid his stipend up to 1 April 1661 with deduction for the cost of law processes. Meanwhile the situation had become more complicated by the claim of Dr. William Page to be reinstated as master. Page who had been master of the school in the days before the outbreak of the Civil War reinforced his demand by a writ of restitution and only agreed to withdraw his claim on 6 March 1660–61. Singleton's appointment was finally ratified on 7 October 1661, two years after the Lord Protector's letter in favour of Gerrard had been declared illegal.[1]

It is necessary to follow Singleton's career as a schoolmaster a little further. From Reading he departed to London where he set up a private school at St. Mary Axe with good success, attracting to himself the sons of dissenters and having in his school at one time as many as three hundred pupils.[2] Other dispossessed schoolmasters were also able to continue their teaching careers in spite of the persecution of the Clarendon Code. Among these was William Dugard who was dismissed from the mastership of Merchant Taylors' School on 27 December 1660. Not that Dugard had always shown himself a loyal supporter of the parliamentary cause. Indeed he had given offence to the parliamentary party by publishing from his private printing press Claudius Salmasius's pamphlet in defence of King Charles I and had been accused in 1650 of showing himself 'an enemy to the State by printing seditious and scandalous pamphlets' and of being 'therefore unfit to have charge of the education of youths'. Dugard suffered a month's imprisonment in Newgate as a result of his rashness but was then reinstated as master of Merchant Taylors' School and became chief

printer for the Commonwealth. Such a remarkable transformation is hard to follow without further explanation. This is forthcoming in the story, told after the Restoration 'by a person who
had been Dugard's corrector of the press before his arrest', that
Dugard's wife asked John Bradshaw to obtain her husband's
release, that John Milton reasoned with the man in prison, and
that finally Dugard was unable to withstand the wiles of the
three of them. 'Legendary in particulars', wrote Mr. D. Masson, 'the story is quite credible as to the main fact. The reconciliation to the Commonwealth of a scholarly man like Dugard
must have seemed to Milton worth an effort'.[1] Among the
reasons which prompted his dismissal in 1660 was, no doubt,
the reluctance of the Company of Merchant Taylors to be
associated with a man who had printed on his private press John
Milton's reply to Claudius Salmasius's defence of the martyred
monarch, Charles I. It was further alleged that the master and
wardens and court of the company had received frequent
complaints from parents and friends of Dugard's scholars that
the master neglected his duties and had broken the company's
orders and ordinances for the school, apparently by admitting
boys above the statutory number.[2] Dugard now opened a
private school in Coleman Street, London, and continued as a
schoolmaster there until his death in December 1662.[3] Owen
Price who had been master of Magdalen College School,
Oxford, since 1657 was ejected in 1660 on the ground of his
nonconformity,[4] but it is clear from Anthony Wood's information
that his career as a schoolmaster did not end there since he
'taught school, in which he much delighted, in several places,
as in Devonshire, Bessills-Les near Abingdon, etc.'[5]

The Restoration caused no change in the masterships of
some schools for the simple reason that the masters were
Anglicans and Royalists. The only matter for surprise is that
they had been allowed to continue their masterships in the time
of the Commonwealth in spite of their known allegiance to the
Church and King. On 15 June 1662 Dr. Thomas Stevens
resigned the high mastership of Bury St. Edmunds Grammar
School 'intending for the future to imploy himself in the work of
the ministry'. The staunch devotion to the monarchy of this
'cavalier master' and the semblance of conformity which en-

abled him to retain the high mastership during the Commonwealth period were attested by Roger North in an account of
the schooldays of his elder brother, the Honourable John North,
whose 'scholastic education was altogether at St. Edmund's
Bury, in Suffolk, under Dr. Stephens'. The schoolmaster

> being reputed little better than a malignant, he was forced
> to use outwardly an occasional conformity by observing
> the church duties and days of super-hypocritical fastings
> and seekings, wherewith the people in those days were
> tormented, though now worn out of almost all credibility;
> and he walked to church after his brigade of boys, there to
> endure the infliction of divers holders forth tiring them-
> selves and everybody else: and by these means he made a
> shift to hold his school. It happened that in the dawning of
> the Restoration the cancer of the times mitigated; and one
> Dr. Boldero . . . kept a Church of England conventicle in
> Bury, using the common-prayer; and our master often went
> to his congregation, and ordinarily took some of his
> boarders with him of whom our doctor was, for the most
> part, one . . . After the happy Restoration and while our
> doctor was yet at school, the master took occasion to publish
> his cavaliership by all the ways he could contrive; and one
> was putting all the boarders who were of the chief families
> in the country, into red cloaks, because the cavaliers
> about the court usually wore such; and scarlet was com-
> monly called the king's colour. Of these he had near thirty
> to parade before him through that observing town to church;
> which made no vulgar appearance . . . I may remember,
> for the credit of that scarlet troop and their scholastic
> education, that not above one or two of the whole com-
> pany, after they came to act in their country ministrations,
> proved anti-monarchic or fanatic.[1]

The outstanding instance is that of Dr. Richard Busby who had
been appointed to the mastership of Westminster School in
1638. Throughout the Commonwealth period Busby made no
effort to disguise his loyalty and an old boy has testified to the
royalist tendencies of the school at this time. Robert South
declared that the school was

so untaintedly loyal, that I can truly and knowingly aver, that in the very worst of times (in which it was my lot to be a member of it) we really were King's scholars, as well as called so. Nay, upon that very day, that black and eternally infamous day of the King's murder, I myself heard, and am now a witness, that the King was publicly prayed for in this school but an hour or two (at most) before his sacred head was struck off.[1]

It can only be supposed that the parliament in its zeal for education was prepared to overlook Busby's royalist leanings rather than lose the services of such an excellent schoolmaster.

The charge was inevitably levelled against Busby that he 'must have been a pretty fair time-server'. The same characteristic could no doubt with no less justification be attributed to men like Mr. Umfreville of Lincoln Grammar School, Rayner Herman of Stamford Grammar School, George Griffith of the Perse School, Cambridge, Ferdinand Archer of Northampton Grammar School and Paul Greenwood of the Grammar School of Queen Elizabeth at Heath, near Halifax.[2] But it is fairer and probably nearer the truth to accept for them Mr. W. E. Gladstone's defence of Busby that 'he made the times serve him' and to believe that their schools and their scholars meant more to them than politics in Church and State.[3]

But even for men of pronounced and professed Puritan views, if they were good schoolmasters, it was possible for exceptions to be made. John Wickens of Manchester Grammar School was clearly a man of first-class abilities, 'the famous Mr. Wickers (*sic*) of Manchester' as he was described in an account of the Reverend Thomas Cotton which was published in 1730.[4] While he was master of Rochdale Grammar School, a post for which he had been chosen by Archbishop Laud in 1638, he became a staunch follower of Presbyterianism and took the Covenant. In 1648 he left Rochdale on his appointment to the high mastership of Manchester Grammar School and at the Restoration he was allowed to remain in office. Wickens probably owed his continuance to William Butterworth, his friend and former pupil and one of the new governors of the school, who used his influence at Court on behalf of the high master. And there can be no doubt that it was to the great benefit of the school to retain the services of such an excellent schoolmaster of whom it has been written that 'he was not only possessed of exceptional learning and piety, but his interests were wide and his views on education were liberal'. His merits were recognized by the company of Haberdashers who in 1663 invited him to take charge of their grammar school at Newport in Shropshire. Such a loss to the educational life of the town was not easily to be suffered and every effort, which included the calling of a public meeting, was made to prevent his leaving. As a result of these exertions Wickens was persuaded to remain and he continued as high master at Manchester until his death in 1676.[1] Similarly at Felsted School a man who had earned a reputation as a Puritan preacher as well as for being a worthy successor to Dr. Martin Holbeach, who had resigned in 1649, was allowed to continue a mastership which lasted forty years. Christopher Glascock, a former pupil of Dr. Holbeach, graduated B.A. at St. Catharine Hall, Cambridge, in 1634 and had been master of Ipswich Grammar School from 1644 to 1650 before his appointment to Felsted at the age of about thirty-three years.[2] He enjoyed the patronage of the devout Mary Rich, countess of Warwick in whose private chapel he was accustomed to preach from time to time, and attracted to his school the sons of the Essex divines. Among his pupils were William and Thomas Bramston, John Gurdon, Joseph Creffield, John Sparrow, Anthony Thomas Abdy and Sir John Comyns, who sat in three parliaments 1701–8, 1710–15 and 1722–26 as member for Maldon and who in 1726 became Lord Chief Baron of the Exchequer.[3]

Even while the Restoration reaction continued it was possible that religious opinions might cause at least severe embarrassment to a schoolmaster who supported the party in power. This is evident from the experience of Thomas Thackham, the master of Reading Grammar School, who in 1670 was the centre of a storm raised by one of the aldermen of the borough, a certain Samuel House, a man of nonconformist views. House approached the master, declaring that he did so with the approval and support of the mayor and other aldermen, and threatened that Thackham would be removed from his position unless he agreed to accept a nonconformist, named Singleton, as his assistant master. This matter was brought before the corporation who decided unanimously to expel House and later proceeded to prosecute him, possibly on the ground of nonconformity.[1]

Schools and schoolmasters were on the whole little affected by the Romanizing campaign during the reign of James II or by the events of 1688 although attempts were made to win some masterships for Roman Catholics, and opposition to the Revolution settlement and the accession of William III on the part of a master was sufficient to cause his ejection as the case of Richard Croston shows. Croston was elected master of Preston Grammar School in 1680 and nine years later dismissed on the ground that he was a nonjuror.[2] Another schoolmaster who was dismissed from his office in 1689 for refusing to take the oath of allegiance to William III was Richard Johnson, master of the King's School, Canterbury, who had received his education at Market Harborough Grammar School in Leicestershire and St. John's College, Cambridge. In 1681 Johnson obtained the second mastership at the King's School, Canterbury and three years later became master.[3] After his dismissal he set up in a private school at Kensington until in 1707 Dr. John Sharpe, archbishop of York, commended him to the wardens of Nottingham Grammar School who were happy to offer the mastership to 'a Worthy and Able Schoolmaster'.[4]

His resignation from an Oxford college led Henry Holyoake, 'the first great name among the Masters at Rugby', into an outstandingly successful career as a schoolmaster. Holyoake resigned his position as chaplain of Magdalen College, Oxford as an act of protest against the ejection of fellows of the college which accompanied the attempt of James II to fill it with Roman Catholics, and although he was later reinstated he chose to give up the chaplaincy and retain the schoolmastership which he had accepted in 1688. The fame of this master and the good reputation of the school are shown by the facts that the number of boys at any time during his mastership has been estimated as between ninety and a hundred, of whom about a fifth were on the foundation, and that he was drawing scholars not only from the county of Warwickshire but also from the neighbouring counties. The contingency had now arisen for which a Commission of Charitable Uses had provided in 1653 when it was ordered that if the numbers of the school should grow beyond the power of one man to manage the governors should supply an usher.[1] Holyoake's assistant may well have taken boarders for it seems unlikely that room on the school premises could have been found for all the boys.[2]

The mastership of Shrewsbury School was the object of religious intrigue and efforts were made to win this office for the Roman Catholics in the town during the reign of James II, which promised so well for that party. In 1686 the health of the master, Andrew Taylor, who had held that office since January 1664–65, was failing and it was clear that a new appointment would shortly have to be made. The Roman Catholic candidate was a Jesuit, named Sebrand, who on 30 June 1686 became a burgess of the town as the first step in obtaining the succession to the mastership. In August 1687 the king visited Shrewsbury and it is probable, as the historian of Shrewsbury School has suggested, that the opportunity was taken on this occasion to complete the plans for the appointment of Sebrand as soon as the vacancy occurred in the mastership. But before the Roman Catholics could bring into use the royal mandate which they had obtained authorizing Sebrand's appointment the necessary steps had been taken by their opponents to secure a master acceptable to the Anglican party. In November Taylor secretly resigned the mastership and on receipt of the news the fellows of St. John's College, Cambridge, proceeded at once to elect one of their own number, Richard Lloyd. The election was approved by the bishop of Lichfield and the new master admitted to his place by the mayor of Shrewsbury in the shortest possible time.[3]

According to John Bridges in his *History of Northamptonshire* Thomas Dominell was a Jesuit from Saint-Omer who received special dispensation from King James the Second to enter into the mastership of Wellingborough Grammar School in 1687 without the customary licence to teach. 'His election being declared void by three neighbouring justices,' wrote Bridges, 'he applied by petition to the king; and after several altercations between him, the inhabitants, and justices about the time of his majesty's abdication he thought fit to disappear'.[4] Mr. A. F.

Leach has shown reasons to doubt the truth of this story since the school records expressly declare that a licence to teach Latin was a necessary condition of Dominell's appointment and his mastership continued until Christmas, 1695.[1]

Religious and political intrigue entered the sphere of education at Warwick and Birmingham during the reign of James the Second who seemed determined to extend his Romanizing campaign from Magdalen College, Oxford to the grammar schools in these two cities. The appointment of William Eades to the living of St. Mary's and to the mastership of Warwick School was almost certainly a move to increase the influence of the Roman Catholic party. It was seemingly interpreted as such by the corporation of Warwick who immediately revealed their opposition to the new vicar-schoolmaster by paying him according to the term of the charter of 1545, which allowed twenty-two pounds to the vicar and ten pounds to the schoolmaster, while Eades claimed the sums authorized in 1636 of seventy pounds for the benefice and thirty pounds for the school. The conflict resulted in a suit in Chancery in which evidence was given that Eades' name was inscribed at his own request on a corner-stone which he had placed over the doorway of a papist chapel which was being built in September 1687, that the vicar-schoolmaster had been present at the consecration of the chapel and that after the ceremony he had entertained in his house the Roman Catholic Bishop Gifford. Eades' denial of these accusations appeared false in view of the statements of the stone-mason, Humphrey Shaksheafe, and of a former mayor of Warwick, William Tarve, who declared that Eades had told him about the stone and its inscription. The schoolmaster appeared victorious for a short time when in 1688 the dissolution of the corporation was ordered by the king. The abdication of James the Second was shortly followed by the reconstitution of the corporation and resolutions, on 1 June 1689, to remove Eades from the vicarage and the school and, on 20 August, to offer a quarterly stipend, equal to that paid annually to any schoolmaster in the town, to an approved candidate who would open a grammar school in the borough. The matter was finally settled on 2 October by concessions on both sides so that Eades was allowed the arrears of his pay to the amount of two hundred and

fifty pounds and also sixty-five pounds a year for the future as
vicar-schoolmaster. It was agreed that he was to be master in
name only and that the conduct of the school should be in the
hands of an usher or ushers appointed by the corporation.[1]

The newly appointed governing body of Birmingham Grammar School expressed their subservience in a humble address to
James the Second who had granted a charter to the school on
20 February 1684–85. Part of the business of the governors at
their first meeting on 22 April 1685 was to receive the written
promise of Nathaniel Brokesby that he would 'peaceably &
quietyly leave' the mastership 'on or before the 29th day of
September next'. Brokesby who had been chief schoolmaster
since 1654 was offered some recompense for this summary dismissal and chose an allowance of forty pounds to be paid
immediately rather than twenty pounds for the first year after
his surrender of the mastership and thereafter ten pounds a year
for life. The appointment of John Hickes on 1 September 1685
suggests the intention to encourage Roman Catholic influence
in the school since the new master was one of those who retained
their fellowships at Magdalen College, Oxford when, by the
king's command, those who refused to profess that faith were
ejected. The governors showed their desire to ensure the continuation of existing conditions when, in September 1691, they
agreed that Hickes should hold the schoolmastership at
Birmingham during his lifetime. The resignation of Hickes was
almost certainly connected with the restoration of the original
charter of Edward the Sixth and the reinstatement of the former
governors whose first recorded meeting was held on 6 November
1694. The name of his successor, James Parkinson, first appears
in the minutes of the meeting of the governors on 4 January
1694–95.[2]

It has been suggested that James Carkesse who became
master of Chelmsford Grammar School about 1663 was con-
verted to the Roman Catholic faith about the time of his
appointment. But the fact that he was still in possession of the
mastership in 1684 is strong evidence to the contrary. Carkesse
was an Old Westminster and had previously held the mastership of Magdalen College School, Oxford.[3] His continuance in
office until at least 1684 is proved by two entries in the

K

admission register of St. John's College, Cambridge, which
states that Eleazar Bownd, who was admitted pensioner on 10
September 1683 aged seventeen years, was educated at 'Chans-
ford' under 'Mr. Carkiss' and that Justinian Ailmer, who was
admitted pensioner on 4 July 1684 at the age of sixteen years,
was also at school at 'Chalmesford' under 'Mr. Carkess'.[1]

3. Literary Pursuits

James Carkesse was the author of *Lucida Intervalla,* a book of
Latin verse which was published in 1679. Some other schoolmasters there were who occasionally satisfied their own need
for greater expression or found relaxation in literary composition. A poet of greater merit than Carkesse was John Jones,
a Welshman who was usher of St. Albans School during the
mastership of Dr. Charles James. In 1684 restoration work was
being carried out in the abbey and it was in this connexion that
Jones wrote his poem, *The Fane of St. Alban* which is commemor-
ated by a tablet in the abbey as *Poema Carmine Heroico Hoc
lapide, hoc etiam aede, aevoque perennius omni.*[2] Lewis Griffin, who
came to Colchester Grammar School in 1664,[3] was the author of
two books which appeared before he began his mastership, *The
Doctrine of the Asse,* published in 1661, and *Rules of Life; Being
Good Wishes to the Clergy and Laity; For whose use the Asse's Complaint Was Written,* published in 1663. Following in the footsteps
of other distinguished schoolmasters who provided text-books
for their scholars John Twells, who was master of Newark
Grammar School from 1674 until 1713–14, published in 1683
the *Grammatica Reformata, Or A General Examination Of The Art of
Grammar,* ... *Designed for initiating the Lower Forms in the Free-
School at Newark upon Trent.* One of his predecessors at Newark
was Benjamin Willey who graduated B.A. in 1668 and M.A. in
1672 at Magdalene College, Cambridge, and held the mastership for a short time from 1670. Willey was the author of verses
On The Last Dutch War and is described as 'sometime Master of
the Free-School of Newark upon Trent' in the volume of
Poetical Recreations which appeared in 1688.[4]

As well as being a distinguished high master of Bury St.
Edmunds Grammar School Edward Leeds was the author of
books for use in school. His *Methodus Graecam Linguam Docendi*

was published in 1690 and was followed in 1693 by *Ad Prima Rudimenta Graecae Linguae Discenda Graeco – Latinum Compendium.*

William Crowe of Gonville and Caius College, Cambridge who was master of Whitgift Grammar School, Croydon from 9 December 1668 until 10 April 1675, provided in 1663 *An Exact Collection or Catalogue of our English Writers On the Old and New Testament* and in 1672 *Elenchus Scriptorum in Sacram Scripturam Tam Graicorum, quam Latinorum, &c.* John Oldham, who entered the school from St. Edmund Hall, Oxford about 1675 and remained as usher until 1678, achieved a reputation as a poet so that 'he was honoured with a visit by the Earls of Rochester and Dorset, Sir Charles Sedley and other persons of distinction'. The Reverend D. W. Garrow relates that 'Mr. Shepherd, the head-master, was not a little surprized at this visit, and would have taken the honour of it to himself, but was soon convinced that he had neither wit nor learning enough to make a party in such company'.[1]

William Johns, who left the university before he had taken his degree to become schoolmaster at Prince Henry's Grammar School, Evesham in Worcestershire in 1663, wrote a play which earned for him a place in Anthony Wood's list of 'writers' from All Souls College, Oxford. The play, which was published in 1678, was called *The Traytor to himself; or Man's Heart his greatest Enemy, a moral Interlude in Heroic Verse, representing the careless, hardned, returning, despairing, and renewed Heart, with inter-marks of Interpretation at the close of each several Act* and performed by the Evesham schoolboys 'but simply' at their breaking up.[2] Of Henry Munday, a postmaster of Merton College and graduate of Corpus Christi College, Oxford, who came as master to Henley Grammar School in 1656, Wood wrote that the school 'being well endowed and replenish'd with Scholars, was very beneficial to him'. The master unfortunately allowed his propensity to 'Physic' and authorship to consume so much of his time and energy at the expense of the school that he was about to be dismissed when he died in 1682.[3]

Another distinguished schoolmaster and author was Dr. Francis Gregory who entered Trinity Hall, Cambridge from Westminster School. He began his schoolmastering career at his old school as usher to Dr. Busby and moved in 1654 to become master first at Woodstock[1] and then at the newly established school at Witney in Oxfordshire where he stayed until his death in 1707. At the Restoration Gregory's devotion to the royalist cause was recognized by an invitation, which he accepted, to preach the sermon at the service of thanksgiving in St. Mary's Church, Oxford and by his appointment to a royal chaplaincy. His published works include an anthology, partly composed by his pupils at Woodstock, to commemorate the King's return, printed in 1660 and entitled *Votivum Carolo, or A Welcome to his Sacred Majesty Charles the II.* In the introduction to this volume the schoolmaster wrote, 'Children are the Hopes of Gods Kingdome, and his Majesty's too; my work is, to teach them Religion, Loyalty, and Learning; Religion towards their God; Loyalty towards their King; and Learning to fit them for the service of both. Besides, I cannot better evidence my own Allegiance, then by Teaching young Gentlemen Theirs.'

Gregory's interest in ecclesiastical matters was exemplified by the publication in 1674 of *The Triall of Religions; With Cautions To the Members of the Reformed Church Against Defection to the Roman* and his diligence as a schoolmaster by a Greek-Latin lexicon[2] and an English, Latin, Greek vocabulary[3] and *Instructions concerning the art of Oratory for the use of Schools.*[4] The first usher to be appointed to Witney Grammar School and to serve under Gregory was Edward Hinton of Merton College and St. Alban Hall, Oxford who published a translation from Greek of *The Apophthegms or Remarkable Sayings of Kings and Great Commanders.*[5]

In 1695 Andrew Tooke was appointed to the ushership at Charterhouse where he had received his education before entering Clare College, Cambridge. Thirty-three years later he succeeded Dr. Thomas Walker as master and continued in that office until his death in 1732. In November, 1704 Tooke was made a fellow of the Royal Society and earlier in the same year became Professor of Geometry at Gresham's College, a post which he resigned in 1729. He was the author of many learned books including *The Pantheon, Representing the Fabulous Histories of the Heathen Gods and Most Illustrious Heroes* which was first published in 1713 and which proved so popular that it reached its twenty-ninth edition in 1792.[6]

Two schoolmasters who engaged in literary work while performing their school duties followed one another at Felsted School in Essex. Simon Lydiatt, M.A., of Christ Church, Oxford who was appointed in 1690, compiled a book of Greek epigrams entitled *Stachyologia or Spicilegium* which was published in 1696 and used in the school as a text-book and which was somewhat extended in its fourth edition by the author whose desire to enlarge it further was restrained by the reluctance of his publishers. Lydiatt's successor, at Christmas, 1712, was Hugh Hutchin of Lincoln College, Oxford who came to Felsted from the mastership at Christ Church Cathedral School in Oxford and whose previously published works included an edition of Justin Marty's *Apology*, in 1700.[1]

Another interesting schoolmaster whose literary work belongs to the period after he had given up his teaching career was Richard Carr. Carr has already been mentioned as the probable author of the advertisement which appeared in *The London Gazette* of Monday–Thursday, 20–23 April 1674, and which gave notice that the schoolmaster at Saffron Walden taught Latin, Greek and French and that his assistant gave instruction in arithmetic, merchants' accounts and writing. But Carr's true interests lay elsewhere and in 1683 he resigned the mastership in order to enter Leyden University as a student of medicine. He took his M.D. degree at Cambridge, became a fellow of the Royal College of Physicians in 1687[2] and has left a book on medicine.[3]

4. Problems and Insufficiency

Schoolmasters were inevitably beset by problems and difficulties. Some of these were temporary and of no great significance. Others were more distressing in their nature and sometimes their effects were felt by the school for many years. A protracted contention began in 1651 between the authorities of Repton School and Gilbert Thacker who lived in a house which adjoined the school and whose family had sold land to the school at a time when it contained about fifty boys. In 1651 the number in the school had increased to about two hundred with a corresponding volume of noise under Thacker's windows and annoyance from boys trespassing on his ground. As a result of action for trespass brought against the master, William Ullock, and two ushers of the school it was agreed that the plaintiff might build a wall to prevent boys from encroaching on his property. He was not willing to do this and twelve years later a renewal of the quarrel was provoked apparently by the actions of the master and usher who took to putting their rubbish where it could be seen by passers-by and by Thacker from his windows. Thacker and his wife by turns erected a dam to stop the refuse being washed past their front door when it rained and to cause it to flow towards the schoolhouse, and the boys of the school broke it down. Finally the disputants came to blows. Thacker followed the master's wife into her house and struck her while Mrs. Thacker entered the master's study and complained to him about his wife. The scholars remained indoors for a week or stayed away from school for fear of arrest when Thacker issued writs against them. At length in 1664 the school authorities retaliated by obtaining a Bill of Chancery to restrain their violent neighbour whose actions, it was claimed, were likely to ruin the school which in its reputation for producing men distinguished in church and state was second to none in that part of the country. The quarrel was submitted to the arbitration of Philip, earl of Chesterfield in 1665 and again in 1666 without result but was eased by the death of William Ullock in 1667. It was finally settled in 1670 in favour of Thacker.[1]

Rugby School suffered a temporary set-back after 1682 in which year twenty boys including five boarders were admitted with a new headmaster, Leonard Jeacockes. In the next year the number of entries fell to two, to one in 1684 and then for two years there were no admissions. It has been conjectured that the cause of decline is to be traced to an epidemic in the town where the death-rate rose steeply in 1680 and 1681 and again in 1685 and the two following years. Since there was a good intake of boys in 1682 this explanation is not completely satisfying and it may be that some other reasons account for the lean years, perhaps unpopularity or failing health on the part of the master who died in 1687. It is noticeable that in 1688 twenty-five boys were admitted or readmitted and that outbreaks of smallpox in Rugby in 1710 and 1733 had no perceptible effect

on the number of boys in the school.[1] Felsted School was directly
affected by smallpox which continued from October 1711 to the
following April. The troubles of that unhappy period, which
brought much 'prejudice and loss' to the school, caused a break-
down in the health of the master, Simon Lydiatt, and no doubt
hastened his death in November 1712 after a long and distinguished rule of twenty-two years during which, according to
Daniel Defoe, he had raised the school 'to the Meridian of its
Reputation'.[2]

A not unusual complication in the life of the grammar schools
which engaged the attention of some masters arose from the
differences of opinion which might exist between the master and
his assistant. An unhappy example of strife between a master
and his usher is furnished by the career of Thomas Chaloner.
Driven from Shrewsbury School by the arrival of the parliamentarian forces on 22 February 1644–45 Chaloner taught in nine
different places during the following eighteen years and finally
settled at Newport in Shropshire as first master of the grammar
school established there in 1656. His mastership here as elsewhere was successful and it is unlikely that he would have left
Newport, as he did in 1662, to return to Shrewsbury School if it
had not been for the conduct of his 'under-master' which
Chaloner described as 'imperious and crafty'. The case of
Chaloner is made more pathetic by the fact that there is little
doubt that the under-master, of whose behaviour he complained, was his own son Thomas who had been invited in 1658
by the founder, William Adams, to assist his father in the school,
and who now in the interest of his own advancement rendered
the thought of further association with him unbearable to his
father.[3] It is likely that differences had arisen between the
schoolmaster, Edward Pearce, and usher, John Deane, of
Bristol Grammar School since additional orders made by the
corporation in 1704, shortly after the usher's resignation, allowed
his successor in that office to appeal to the mayor and aldermen
against the master's orders and directions if he found 'any
Mischief or Inconvenience' in them.[4] James Hume who became
master of Dulwich College in 1706 was without the assistance of
an usher until in 1709 John Beresford was appointed to the post.
Master and usher did not work together in harmony for long

since in the next year Hume complained of 'notorious and wilful failure in the discharge of his duties' by Beresford who retorted that a man like Hume could hardly be expected to speak the truth.[1]

The common causes of friction between masters and ushers may be gleaned from statutory regulations about their respective responsibilities and rights of appeal to the governors. It appears that some ushers disliked being supervised, refused to accept rulings about the method and order of work and objected to correction when the master found irregularities in their departments. Ushers, on the other hand, were sometimes given reason to complain that, in transferring scholars from the lower school, masters chose those who were likely to pay them best with the result that children were removed to the upper school before they had reached the requisite standard of attainment and to the prejudice of the ushers.[2]

A dispute between the master and his usher, though it was doubtless exasperating to the disputants and hardly conducive to the smooth running of the school, was not a matter of major importance. What was really damaging was the negligence of schoolmasters which caused parents to withdraw their children from the schools. An examination of the reasons for the neglect of their schools by schoolmasters must, of course, take account of the fact that they were often compelled to hold some other office which most likely and most conveniently was a cure of souls. Not every case of insufficiency is attributable to the demands made by the care of a parish or other ecclesiastical employment and it is questionable if pluralism provides a wholly acceptable explanation for any instances of negligence and inefficiency. A matter for surprise is the failure of governors in some cases to take steps to remedy an unsatisfactory situation and in others to do more than remonstrate with offending schoolmasters.

Berkhamsted School suffered shameful neglect by its teaching staff and this made it necessary for parents either to bring teachers into the town from outside or to send their children away from the town to be taught. In 1668 this scandalous situation roused the people of Berkhamsted to request the warden of All Souls, Dr. Thomas Jeames, to hold a visitation as he was empowered to do every three years by the Act of 1549. On 4 May the master, Thomas Fossan, and the usher, John Seare, presented themselves before Dr. Jeames when it was adduced against them that during the five years in which they had held their offices they had neglected their duties, had often been absent from the school, had not prepared any pupils for the universities, and had failed to attend regularly the parish church on Sundays and holy days and to keep up the custom of morning and evening prayers in school. During their five years' tenure of office the number of the schoolboys had fallen from seventy, at the time of their appointment, to between ten and twenty. Evidence as to the former prosperous and successful condition of the school under diligent masters and to its present sorry state was given by old boys, by the rector and doctor of Berkhamsted and by a woman who had lost her chief means of livelihood which was to take as boarders boys attending the school. The boys themselves and their complete lack of knowledge of grammar testified to the frequent absence of their teachers. The master had been known to refuse to teach the boys and was reported to have welcomed the drop in number which meant less work for him. The master and usher were dealt with leniently since they were allowed to continue on condition that they were in school for at least three hours in the morning and three hours in the afternoon and that they attended church with their scholars on Sundays. The rector and churchwardens were asked to inspect and to make a report on the school for consideration at a further meeting on 24 August. The school was well rid of the offending master and usher when on the day after this meeting they resigned. This example of neglect may be partly, if not wholly, explained and excused by the facts that the master was also rector of Little Gaddesden and the usher lived four or five miles away from the school at Ivinghoe where he was overseer to the poor.[1]

The master of Hanley Castle Grammar School in Worcestershire was also vicar of the parish[2] and, according to a petition of 30 July 1714, signed by thirty-seven parishioners and addressed to the school trustee, Anthony Lechmere, this combination of duties in the person of James Badger since 1691 had done serious harm to the school. The good reputation of the school as a

preparation for the universities had attracted the sons of gentlemen from many counties until the coming of Badger nearly
thirty years before. It was alleged that he had done little to earn
the salary of forty pounds a year, had allowed the school
buildings to fall into disrepair and had neglected his scholars so
that parents had withdrawn their children, and those pupils who
remained had forgotten what they had learned before they came
to him. The petitioners asked that the schoolmaster should be
replaced or at least that he should be compelled to employ a
competent usher. Their efforts were unavailing and the situation
remained unchanged until the death of Badger, at the age of
seventy-seven, eleven years later.[1]

Another master of palpable inefficiency was Edward Griffith
of Nottingham Grammar School who was not, however, prepared to relinquish his office without a struggle which he carried
on successfully against the governors for ten years. It was in
August 1697 that the master was first charged with want of
proper attention to his duties and with causing harm to the
school, and on this occasion he undertook not to accept any
ecclesiastical charge and not even to do any preaching. Griffith
invited his accusers to test the efficacy of his teaching method
and the proficiency of his pupils. The examiners were evidently
dissatisfied with what they found. Four months later Griffith
was dismissed from his mastership on the same grounds of
negligence and of causing the people of Nottingham to send
their children to schools outside the town, and was given notice
to quit the schoolhouse by the following Lady Day when his
salary would be stopped. On 5 May the wardens of the school
were directed to renew the order of dismissal and, if Griffith did
not resign, to take steps to have him evicted. If, however, he
would give a written assurance that he would withdraw at once
the school wardens were authorized to continue to pay his
salary until Christmas. At Christmas Griffith was still schoolmaster at Nottingham and in January 1699–1700 the 'house'
capitulated and he was confirmed in the mastership until
further notice. It was another seven years before the wardens
got rid of Griffith who carried away with him eighty-five pounds
as compensation for his dismissal.[2]

The master and usher of King's School, Peterborough were

embarrassed by a multiplicity of duties. David Standish who took over a flourishing school in 1707 combined with the mastership the rectory of Woodstone and a minor canonry. The unsatisfactory consequence is shown by one of the rules made by the dean and chapter three years later which required that the master and usher should come to an understanding about their attendance so that there should always be at least one of them present during school hours. At a meeting in 1714 the chapter remonstrated with and accepted the resignation of the usher whose duties as a minor canon had caused him to appoint a substitute to perform his school duties. On the same occasion the dean administered a warning to the master, but in 1720 the chapter was still dismayed at the falling number of scholars and neglect of the school buildings which they attributed to the fact that their rule of 19 June 1710 about attendance at school had not been duly kept.[1]

A fall in the number of boys at Shrewsbury School marked the long mastership of Richard Lloyd, an old Salopian and sizar and fellow of St. John's College, Cambridge, who came to the school in 1687 and was apparently at first successful. An important contributory cause of the decline was undoubtedly, as the historian of the school has pointed out, the fact that for some of the time Lloyd held canonries at Hereford and Brecon and was vicar of Sellack in Herefordshire. Lloyd was breaking the school regulation that masters should not hold any parochial or other cures and in 1717 this violation was made the ground of a suit in the Court of Chancery against the master and the second master, Rowland Tench, who was also curate of Astley, when it was alleged that the master's neglect had caused parents to withdraw their sons from the school and to send them elsewhere so that the number of boys in the highest school was now only eight. As a result of this petition Lord Chancellor Macclesfield allowed the master six months in which to decide between the school and the benefice and it seems likely that Lloyd chose the former since he continued in the school until June 1733.[2]

At a meeting at Goldsmiths' Hall, London on 7 March 1681–82 Samuel Holmes presented to the Worshipful Company of Goldsmiths a petition which was supported by the mayor and aldermen of Stockport in Cheshire and others charging Samuel Needham, the master of the grammar school, with negligence and stating that he had been instituted to a living at some considerable distance from the school. It was therefore requested that the schoolmaster should be dismissed and Holmes appointed in his place. The petition no doubt came as a surprise to the company since the school had prospered under Needham who had been appointed to the mastership eight years before on 6 March 1673–74 with the recommendation of the mayor and aldermen and forty-two townspeople. The schoolmaster who was present at the meeting was able to show a certificate in his favour signed by some of the local clergy and others of high social standing and to satisfy the company that any negligence might justly be attributed to Holmes who had acted as his deputy in the school during his absence. Nevertheless the court decided that it was not possible to perform adequately the functions of schoolmaster in Stockport and parish priest elsewhere and out of consideration for Needham agreed to postpone the election of his successor until Lady Day 1683 provided that he discharged faithfully his duties to the school during the intervening period.[1]

Absenteeism was one of the complaints against Francis Brockett of Dulwich College made in 1679 to Dr. Gilbert Sheldon, archbishop of Canterbury, since the schoolmaster had a curacy in London which kept him away from school every week for two or three days. It was further alleged that he refused to teach without extra payment for himself although the inhabitants claimed that their 'children ought to be taught freely, paying only for entrance and two shillings a year'. Brockett was master at the time of the archbishop's visitation from 1664 to 1667 and his outbursts of fiery temper no doubt occasioned the admonition in the rules of 9 October 1667 to 'Forbear from all passion towards the Scholars, but especially from Blows'. Evidence of this unfortunate temper is afforded by the order for Brockett's arrest issued on 27 October 1677 because he had caused Thomas Bowdler of Camberwell 'to be violently assaulted and wounded by sewall of his schollers' and had 'threatened to teare the said Deponent in peeces'. In spite of complaints and contention with the governors Brockett maintained his position in the school until his death in September 1680.[1]

Bedford Grammar School provides an example of extraordinary absenteeism on the part of the masters in this period and of inexplicable failure on the part of a governing body to rectify matters. In 1665 the town council as the governing body of Bedford Grammar School requested the fellows of New College, Oxford to exercise their right of appointing the master and to name a successor to John Allanson who had died recently. The late master had apparently seen very little of his pupils for he had been absent from the school and serving as a naval chaplain, leaving his place to be supplied by a deputy, Daniel Langhorne, a condition of affairs which had been allowed to go uncorrected by the governors.[2] In 1672 John Longworth, B.C.L., fellow of New College, was elected to the mastership, holding this office in conjunction with the living of Oakley. Five years later he resigned his benefice and went to America. He did not, however, resign the mastership of the school and neither the town council nor New College made any move to replace him. There are no records until three years later when, in the continued absence of Longworth, William Willis was appointed as deputy master on 4 October 1681, to continue in that office until the following May. The deputy master was a Wykehamist who had been admitted to New College as a scholar in 1675 and removed from his fellowship there four years later on the ground of non-residence. The council's hopes of Willis 'that by his diligence he would have restored the School to its antient Glory & reputacon, the flourishing whereof would have indirectly advantaged the Inhabitants and Tradesmen of this Towne by Boarders & resort of friends' proved vain and in 1683 'the excesses which that unhappy man ran into ... were such as made it necessary for him to retire'. The council's letter of 30 July 1683 to New College does not throw light on Willis's misdemeanours which, as they wrote, 'we had rather you should heare of from others, than by our informacon'.[3] Meanwhile the usher of the school, John Rewse, had charge of all the scholars and on the following 9 November was paid fifty shillings over and above his salary for his additional labours. Longworth was still recognized as master and the next appointment to the mastership was again on a temporary basis to continue for a period of three years if, meanwhile, the absentee had not returned. The temporary master was Nicholas Aspinall who was elected by New College on 8 November 1683 at the recommendation of the town council and who remained in control of the school for the next thirty-five years.[1]

Other governing bodies showed a deeper interest in the welfare of their schools and a more vigilant supervision of the conduct of affairs which led in some cases to the expulsion of unsatisfactory masters. No reason is forthcoming for the dismissal of the master and usher of Ashbourne Grammar School in 1672. The master, Thomas Goodread, M.A. of Christ's College, Cambridge, who was elected on 17 December 1666, appears to have resigned his place without protest on 3 April 1672 in obedience to the order of the governors and to have received £11 15s. which was due to him. At the same time £6 7s. 8d. was paid to Francis Hallowes, the usher since 11 November 1662, who engaged to give up his place 'without disturbance' when it was required of him by the governors.[2] William Johns of Evesham Grammar School in Worcestershire was discharged in 1687 on the ground that he had been absent for 'weekes past'[3] and at Henley in Oxfordshire John Meddens or Meadows was charged with 'misgovernment' in 1691 and dismissed in 1700 after being away from the school for more than a month.[4]

The history of schools which suffered through the insufficiency of their masters at the end of the seventeenth century and throughout the eighteenth century makes distressing reading. According to Mr. A. F. Leach's analysis it was 'the pernicious practice of employing parsons as schoolmasters' which led to 'the degradation or ruin of many grammar schools in the eighteenth and early nineteenth centuries'. While allowing that the practice of combining the professions of schoolmaster and parish priest resulted in many cases from the fact that the school income by itself was inadequate to support a man of university standing Mr. Leach asserted that 'the remedy was worse than the disease' and accepted the decline of a school under its vicar-schoolmaster as 'the usual result' which followed this 'fatal conjunction' of offices.[5] This judgement deserves careful examination for, as has been hinted, it is a debatable question whether pluralism in itself caused priests-schoolmasters to neglect their schools. For the purpose of this investigation it seems permissible to take examples outside the limits of our period since Mr. Leach was concerned with pluralism as a cause of the general decline of grammar schools which became marked in the eighteenth century. But, as we have already seen, discussion of this problem is relevant to the history of grammar schools in the later Stuart period as well as in later times.

Mr. Leach used hard words which, nevertheless, seem to have some justification when they are applied to gross pluralism of the sort presented by the history of Felsted School during the mastership of John Wyatt from 1725 to 1750. Wyatt served the vicarage of Hatfield Peverel from 1731, the rectory of Woodham Mortimer from 1745, the rectory of Peldon from 1746 and also held the rectory of Little Waltham. In 1731 Hans De Veil was appointed usher and from 1732 combined the vicarage of Saling with the ushership and from 1740 held in addition the vicarage of Felsted. Mark Gretton who was the next usher was also vicar of Good Easter from 1746, rector of Margaret Roding from 1747 and perpetual curate of Little Dunmow from 1749. When Wyatt left there were nine boys at Felsted School.[1]

In the later Stuart period, as we have seen, it is not, at any rate, unusual to find that the deterioration of a school is associated with a master who also held a benefice. And there is ample evidence in the eighteenth and early nineteenth centuries of schools which declined under the rule of their vicars-school-masters.[2] Sometimes, indeed, the vicars were schoolmasters only in name who, while they received the salaries of two offices, were content to employ a deputy to do the teaching. Such was the situation at Winchcombe where the two grammar schools, the King's School and Lady Chandos' School, had in the eighteenth century been combined and met in the Chandos school building and where from 1793 to 1832 the vicar, John James Lates, was accustomed to pay a deputy who gave only elementary instruction.[3] Similarly at Fotheringay when Robert Linton, who had been appointed master in 1790, became vicar of the parish in 1814 he apparently performed his duties in the school through a deputy who was not a graduate and who taught only elementary subjects.[1]

That the negligence of priests-schoolmasters was a factor in the decline of the grammar schools in the seventeenth and eighteenth centuries is, of course, indisputable. It is not easy in every case, however, to estimate the measure of the master's responsibility for the degradation of a school when, as we have seen, other circumstances were also contributing to bring about the same result. In 1819 the Commissioners to inquire concerning Charities reported that when Dr. John Lempriere was master from 1792 to 1809 there were never more than two, usually one, and sometimes no scholars on the foundation at Abingdon School. In 1766 when John Bright was master, there were a hundred and three boys, including forty boarders, in the school and the decline in number which began soon after that year was apparently due in the first place to a contested municipal election in which the master and the corporation took opposing sides. In answer to their inquiries the commissioners found that the decadence of the school was ascribable to the facts that the inhabitants did not desire a classical education for their children, that four guineas a year were charged for instruction in writing and arithmetic, that the time for the beginning of morning school had been changed from six o'clock in the summer and seven o'clock in the winter to nine o'clock throughout the year, and that the master had been absent 'in the necessary attendance upon the duties of two cures, which the corporation permitted him to retain in contravention of the articles of the founder'.[2]

What must be questioned is Mr. Leach's assertion that to appoint to schoolmasterships men who also had pastoral and preaching responsibilities was to court disaster. It is essential to remember that, in the absence of provision for the training of teachers, often the man best qualified for the mastership of a grammar school was a clergyman and that in the nature of things some schools could not have survived as long as they did without the teaching given by the man who was also responsible for the spiritual welfare of a parish. In theory, as has been suggested, there seems to be no reason why a man should not run a school successfully and minister to the needs of a parish. In practice, whether he did so or not depended largely on his energy and ability.

The inhabitants of Camberwell were given no cause to complain that William Jephson from 1733 to 1761 neglected his duties as master of the grammar school although after 1741 he held the livings of St. Clement, Eastcheap and St. Martin, Orgar. In 1818 a former pupil who had been under Jephson from 1751 to 1759 stated that in addition to the twelve free scholars there were day boys paying fees and 'a great many boarders'. The fact that there were three ushers shows that the school was flourishing under its priest-schoolmaster.[1] Samuel Cole raised the fortunes of Guildford Grammar School while he performed the duties of rector of Merrow. In 1777 Cole was commended by the corporation and rewarded with a gift of a hundred pounds for his assiduous efforts, during the past eight years, in raising the number of pupils to over sixty and for providing at his own expense for the employment of assistant masters. The history of Guildford Grammar School illustrates the dependence of schools upon the diligence and competence of their masters for in 1765 the school under Cole's predecessor, John Pearsall, was reported to have had no pupils for almost a year, a condition which was ascribed to the master's negligence and misconduct and which doubtless had been aggravated by the fact that he was also vicar of Warehorne in Kent.[2]

These examples show what could be done by capable men who combined school and parochial duties. The conclusion is that, in an age when there was a crisis in confidence in the grammar schools, some men were able by their exertions and abilities to attract pupils and bring prosperity to their schools while others failed because they lacked the qualities of character and learning necessary in the exacting task of teaching. It is reasonable to suppose that many, if not all, who found in pluralism an excuse to be absent from their schools or to transfer their scholastic responsibilities to deputies would have proved, in any circumstances, unsatisfactory schoolmasters.

But the picture is incomplete and less than justice is done to schoolmasters unless consideration is given to the 'very great discouragements' which they had to overcome or bear with fortitude. Attention has already been drawn to long hours,

L

large classes and the problem of discipline. Add to these the prospect of a low basic salary and uncertain increments, and dependence upon or subserviency to school trustees and it occasions no surprise that many judged the calling of school-master 'too mean for a Scholar to undertake, or desire to stick too many yeares'. We shall examine these additional factors in succeeding chapters.[1]

VII

THE SALARIES OF
SCHOOLMASTERS

Among the Wase papers is a letter, dated 28 January 1673–74 and signed by the master, William Foster, and the usher, James Pemberton, which describes the grammar school at Heskin in Lancashire in idyllic terms:

> The school is a tall & stately structure of Hewn Stone. Within ye walls it is 19 yards one foot & 2 inches in length: 5 yards & an half in breadth. Ye groundroome is exactly well boarded & decently seated, above staires are 2 comendable fire rooms, a study for ye bookes, another roome for materialls toward ye repaire of ye schoole, besides a large staire case all uniforme & well boarded. The Situation thereof is very pleasant ye adjacent fields being very fruitfull. To ye North and Norwest it hath a delicate prospect over a vast compass of even lying lands, pleasant rivers, & stately woods, ye yard about it for ye boys recreation, & Masters benefitt containes 5 acres of land. About a stones cast west from ye schoole at ye foote of a Sandy bank issueth forth a pleasant spring (another Hippocrene) the water whereof is exceeding wholsome, whereat ye schollars drink, for indeed we have but few houses near us, the water falls downe from a stone trough about a yard to ye earth in so gentle a streame yt a man may drink it up as it comes. Mr. Radcliff ye afore*said* Master made it with his owne hands.

If indeed they were at all discontented with the conditions of their employment the master and usher betray no sign of it in this delightfully serene account of their school. And yet 'since yt dreadfull fire in London 1666' they had received only thirty pounds a year in salaries between them, instead of the normal fifty pounds, and did not know when they would again be paid in full.[1]

Foster and Pemberton were not the only schoolmasters whose salaries were affected by this disaster. In an undated letter Joseph Ashworth, the master of Merchant Taylors' School, Crosby in Lancashire, informed Wase that his salary of thirty pounds and his usher's salary of twenty pounds were 'Att present shortened . . . by reason of the sad fire in London they arising out of rents for Houses there'.[2] The endowment of Dorstone Grammar School in Herefordshire was twenty pounds a year, payable out of tenements in London, and the school-master's salary, which had 'bin intermitted for some time, long of ye late dreadfull fire there' was not restored to him until Michaelmas 1672.[3] The destruction of the hall and most of the houses belonging to the Company of Grocers affected the payment of the Oundle schoolmasters, William Taylor and his successor William Speed, for more than twenty years. In 1687 Speed reckoned that he was owed two hundred and eighty-five pounds; his resignation two years later, without warning of his intention, and his removal to a school at Hampstead were probably influenced by the continued difficulty of obtaining his money from the company.[4]

The condition of these schoolmasters was not unlike that of some men during the Civil War when salaries remained unpaid because of the difficulties which trustees met in collecting the rents.[5] Their circumstances were exceptional and may therefore appear to be inappropriate to the purpose of this chapter which is to assemble evidence in an attempt to reach some conclusions about the rates of pay of schoolmasters in the later Stuart period. But in fact their misfortunes serve to draw attention, even if somewhat dramatically, to the uncertainty which might exist in the amount of a schoolmaster's salary from one year to the next, and this matter is certainly relevant to our purpose.

A conservative estimate, made by Professor Charles Wilson, is that in 1688, out of a population of about five and a half millions, 'something over three million persons, in palace, castle, manor, farm or cottage were dependent on agriculture for their income'.[6] To this majority belonged the men in school-rooms and schoolhouses for they derived their basic wages from lands and rents though additional increments were forthcoming in the way of gratuities and fees from the parents of all or some of their pupils. The endowment of a grammar school usually consisted either of an annuity, the amount of which was specified at the time of the foundation and made chargeable in perpetuity upon the founder's estate, or of property, bequeathed by the founder or bought by trustees with money left by the founder. As a method of providing a salary for a schoolmaster, the endowment of the school with a fixed rent-charge had the advantage of cushioning its recipient against the effects of deflation. The obvious disadvantage of such a bequest was that a sum of money which represented a liberal allowance when the first master was appointed, might become less than sufficient in the changed circumstances and times of his successors. Where the endowment was in the form of so many fields or houses, the amount of the salary was subject to fluctuations, as the value of property changed, and dependent on the integrity and competence of the men who administered the school estate. The question then arises as to the hazards resulting from the nature of these sources of income, for schoolmasters, like men in other walks of life, were liable to suffer financial vicissitudes.

A man might be judged by results and, if found wanting, made to forfeit his stipend, as was Randall Nicoll in 1701 when the boys of Aldenham Grammar School failed to reach the standard of learning required of them.[1] Occasional expenditure for essential purposes which made additional demands on the school funds might cause the schoolmaster's pay to fluctuate. Thus in 1705 the churchwardens, as managers of Darlington Grammar School in the county of Durham, deducted eight pounds from the salaries of the master, Jonathan Sissons, and usher, John Hodson, in order to pay for school books and repairs to the school building,[2] and a fall in salary from twenty pounds a year to £12 10s., when in 1669 a Mr. Rees succeeded Tully Wells at Wellingborough Grammar School in Northamptonshire, is apparently explained by the same reasons.[3] Provision for a pension was not normally allowed and a newly appointed master might find himself called upon to support his predecessor, as did Richard Ashburne when in 1726 he succeeded James

Bateman who retired from the mastership of Bolton-Le-Moors Grammar School in Lancashire for reasons of health after serving the school for twenty-one years.[1] A rise in salary in keeping with the value of school property was sometimes obstructed by the refusal of the tenant to pay an increased rent as Simon Lydiatt of Felsted School in Essex found in 1690 when Sir John Fock demanded that his lease should be renewed on the same terms as before. Fortunately for Lydiatt his cause was championed by the school patron, Lord Keeper Nottingham, so that finally Fock was compelled to pay arrears of rent to the amount of three hundred and fifty pounds for which the master and usher had waited six years.[2]

An important factor in the uncertainty about salaries was the readiness of some school trustees to keep the wages of their schoolmasters at the lowest possible level. The fluctuation in the scale of pay, occasioned by this tendency to save money on the schoolmaster, is well illustrated in the history of Solihull Grammar School in Warwickshire. George Long, who was master from 1663 to 1668, was paid thirty-five pounds a year. The school authorities also allowed for an usher, Goodman Blunt, during Long's mastership. Mr. Brandley and Jonathan Coore followed in the space of two years and then George Ward was appointed at a salary of twenty-eight pounds a year or twenty pounds if he employed an usher. After one year at the school the master chose to dispense with the services of his usher. The chronicler of Solihull and its church suggests that a reduction in Ward's salary to thirteen pounds and ten shillings in 1685 resulted from a dispute between the master and feoffees. Perhaps there had also been a fall in the number of his scholars. Two years later the situation improved and the master's salary was raised to twenty pounds a year. Presumably it was the opportunity of a mastership at the age of twenty-one years which induced Josiah Foster, M.A., of Brasenose College, Oxford, to accept the post, made vacant by Ward's death in 1689, at a salary of thirteen pounds and ten shillings and with the added condition that he should 'cast whatever levies, accompts, or other writings' the parish officers required. The conditions of his appointment explain Foster's departure after eighteen months. The next master, William Hiron, who came in

1692, also agreed to combine the office of schoolmaster with that of 'general scribe, and accountant for the Parish' in return for which he received an annual stipend of twenty-five pounds out of which he had to pay his usher. In 1694 he was succeeded by John Hunter who remained for ten years at a salary of twenty-two pounds a year with an additional eight pounds for an usher.[1]

The constitution and conduct of governing bodies will be examined in the next chapter. But, in the present context, it is worth noting that the financial status of many schoolmasters would have been improved if they had been allowed to reap the full benefits from increases in the value of school property. The niggardly control of school revenues by trustees, and their stubborn resistance to pressure to raise the salaries of school-masters are evident in the correspondence which passed between the Bedford Corporation and the authorities of New College, Oxford.

John Allanson, formerly a scholar of Winchester College and a chaplain of New College, was appointed to the mastership at Bedford in 1663 at a salary of twenty pounds a year.[2] He was master only until Michaelmas, 1665[3] and was succeeded by John Butler, a scholar both of Winchester and of University College, Oxford.[4] In 1666 the rents and fines from the school property were realizing more than three times the amount paid to the master, and thirty years before this date the income of the school was already ninety-nine pounds a year.[5] Since the town council refused to pay the master a fair share of the school income Butler evidently sought to provide himself with an adequate salary by taking increased fees from his pupils with the result that a dispute arose between the master and the towns-people in 1668. The council voted that the children of the inhabitants should be taught grammar freely and that the only proper fees which the schoolmaster was entitled to receive were charges of twelve pence from every pupil at his entrance to the school and, subsequently, of twopence a quarter for instruc-tion. Butler's position would have been indefensible if he had been receiving an adequate portion of the school income. The warden, Dr. Michael Woodward, and fellows of New College supported Butler and on 9 November wrote on his behalf to the council. 'What man of parts', they asked, 'will come among you, when ye Teacher's stipend shall (as at this time) bee lessened at your pleasure & when, for every inhabitant's sonne, hee must thresh (as some call it) at 2d a Quarter?' Since the council were 'pleased to spare noe more', the letter continues, 'ye Schoole shall want an Able Teacher' and 'ye Colledge must lose a good preferment, which, (assure yourselves) it will not suffer'. The council were therefore requested 'to allow Mr. Schoolemaster what lately hath been allowed' and also to recall their 'Edict of Two pence'. If they refused to do so then the college authorities would have to take 'such Course as by our Counsell wee shall bee advised unto'.[1] Writing to the warden and fellows of New College on 21 February 1668–69, the mayor of Bedford, Thomas Underwood, declared that the corporation were free to offer what salary they pleased and that although, in fact, twenty pounds was the established stipend Butler had received an increase of six pounds a year in the previous December.[2] In reply to this letter the New College authorities refused to accept the explanation that twenty pounds was the customary salary since the corporation could not claim that this was the salary of the master at the time when the school income was only twelve pounds a year. They considered that the master should be paid forty pounds a year and the usher twenty pounds and warned the council that their policy could only react to their own disadvantage and to the ruin of the school.[3] More than two years later, on 11 July 1670, the master's salary was raised to thirty pounds and that of the usher to twenty pounds. Another attempt to move the council was made by the college authorities when they elected John Gascoyne as usher on 8 January 1671–72.[4] In the following August Butler resigned the mastership and suggested to New College that the vacancy in the school might prove a useful opportunity to negotiate improved conditions for his successor.[5] Nothing apparently came of this suggestion. The council continued their policy of refusing to use the school income for its proper purposes and on 27 January 1691–92 both the master, Nicholas Aspinall, and the usher, John Robinson, had to suffer decreases which brought their respective salaries down to £26 13s. 4d. and £13 16s. 8d.[6] In November 1706 Aspinall's offer to be responsible for repairs to the school for the next eleven years at a cost of ten pounds a year was accepted although it does not appear whether he was prompted by the possibility of adding something to his salary or exasperated by the council's complaint that the repairs were 'very burthensome & chargeable'.[1]

We have seen in a previous chapter that often a schoolmaster was able to increase his income by fees and gratuities. Often, too, he was provided with a house free of rent and this was worth four or five pounds a year to him.[2] He might, if the house was 'capable and convenyent' for the purpose, take pupils as boarders. Indeed in 1663 the Bedford Corporation argued, with some justification, that their schoolmaster was in a favourable position to augment his salary in this way since Thomas Butler, who was master from 1656 until he was turned out at the Restoration, had used the master's house to 'good profit; having many gentlemens children under his tutourage'.[3] Similarly the Witney schoolmaster was evidently expected to supplement his salary of thirty-five pounds a year since the school statutes stipulated that children related to the founder were to be given the best room for their lodging.[4] The influx of boarders attracted by the good reputation of schools enabled some schoolmasters to live in comparative affluence and even, it appears, to acquire a considerable fortune.

In 1663 Edward Leeds entered upon the mastership at Bury St. Edmunds Grammar School at an annual salary of forty pounds which was augmented by fees from boarders. The number of boys in the school was limited by the original statutes of 1550 to a hundred but the demand for places induced the governors to set a limit of a hundred and twenty in the new statutes, confirmed by the bishop of Norwich on 2 September 1665, and to use their special power to extend that number to a hundred and sixty before the end of the month.[5] Anthony Wood's friend and former teacher at Thame Grammar School in Oxfordshire, David Thomas, moved first to Dorchester Grammar School as master 'where he continued till the time of his death in Aug. 1667, having before obtained a comfortable estate by the great paines he took in pedagogie, and by the many sojourners that he alwaies kept in his house'.[6] Robert Jennings who held the mastership of Abingdon School for twenty years until 1683 was able to pay five thousand and eight hundred pounds for the Plowden estate at Shiplake in Oxfordshire to which he retired.[1]

No doubt in many other cases the masters were expected to supplement their meagre salaries by having boarders in their houses. But this expedient, like fees and gratuities, could provide only an uncertain increment. 'Were the particular salaries of Masters throughout the Land, as in a Table set forth, it is not to be fear'd least their ample patrimony should excite the Covetousness or Envy of the Reader', wrote Christopher Wase. Indeed his opinion is that 'nothing rather might seem a more effectual motive to the well dispos'd to enlarge their beneficence, then the weighing the assiduous labors of Teachers against their incompetent maintenance'.[2] Wase did not provide for his readers such a table of salaries, nor did he support and strengthen his plea for augmentations of the schoolmasters' wages by quoting testimony which he had received during the five years which preceded the publication of his book. A salary scale, compiled from his papers, is given as an appendix to this chapter and the necessary task of interpreting the material is facilitated by the comments of Wase's correspondents. We are thus conveniently presented with a sample of schools in twenty-five counties during the 1670s. And although the statistical evidence is far from complete, yet it affords a base from which to further our inquiries into the financial situation of schoolmasters during the later Stuart period and, in some cases, down to the end of the eighteenth century and beyond.

Charles Hoole gave it as his opinion that the master of a grammar school should receive not less than a hundred pounds a year and that the salaries of ushers should be between thirty and eighty pounds a year.[3] A useful comparison for Hoole's suggested optimum salary in 1660 is found in the hope expressed by his contemporaries, to which Dr. Anne Whiteman has drawn attention, that all benefices might be raised to eighty or a hundred pounds a year. Dr. Whiteman has also shown that in the diocese of Salisbury, between the years 1660 and 1663, out of 372 livings, the value of which is known, 219 were worth less than a hundred pounds and 153 less than eighty pounds.[4] It must be remembered that Hoole was anxious for the recognition of the importance of the school-master's work and for a supply of able men who would be attracted to that profession by the prospect of high salaries. It is hardly surprising, therefore, that the salaries of Wase's school-masters fall short of Hoole's ideal figure. Writing on 27 April 1675 about schools in Warwickshire, Samuel Frankland noted Birmingham Grammar School as 'the best endowed schoole in these parts'. Next came Sutton Coldfield and Nuneaton, each with about eighty pounds a year, and Rugby School with fifty pounds. In all these schools the master was provided with a house and garden and was required to pay the stipend of an usher if he had one.[1] Frankland's information may be amplified from other sources. In March 1677–78 the income of Birming-ham Grammar School had risen to two hundred and fifty-two pounds and eighteen shillings, and by 1702 to three hundred and twenty-two pounds. The schoolmaster's salary which was fifty pounds in 1655 rose by two increments to eighty-eight pounds and fifteen shillings in 1702 and that of the usher during the same period from twenty pounds to forty-four pounds six shillings and eightpence. Unhappily, for reasons which do not appear, the increments of twenty pounds to the master and ten pounds to the usher, which were made by the governors in 1702 were withdrawn by them three years later.[2] At Nuneaton, according to the terms of the new charter of 18 April 1694, the schoolmaster's salary was settled at sixty pounds a year or fifty pounds if he employed an usher who was to receive twenty pounds.[3] Among the better paid men was the high master of Manchester Grammar School whose salary in 1685 was sixty pounds a year. This was a flourishing school which employed an usher at a salary of twenty-eight pounds and a master for the petties at twelve pounds a year.[4]

These schools offered some of the most lucrative posts and schoolmasters might count themselves fortunate if their salaries were a third of the sum at which Hoole aimed. The point is underlined by Frankland's concluding statement that the rest of the schools in Warwickshire, which numbered almost twenty, rarely offered more than twenty pounds a year for the master.[5]

In 1659 a salary of forty pounds a year for the masters and

twenty pounds for the ushers was suggested by the anonymous author of *Chaos: Or, A Discourse, Wherein Is presented to the view of the Magistrate . . . . a Frame of Government by way of a Republique* in his scheme for the erection of a grammar school in every town. These were the amounts which, as has been shown, the warden and fellows of New College considered suitable for the master and usher of Bedford School in 1669. Forty pounds was allowed for the master of Charlbury Grammar School in 1675[1] and for the master of Palmer's School at Grays Thurrock in Essex in 1710.[2] In offering this salary to Henry Pitts in 1657 the Nottingham town council felt justified in insisting that the master of the grammar school should not preach without their permission or undertake any pastoral charge while he continued in that office.[3]

According to Gregory King's 'scheme of the Income, and Expence, of the several Families of England, calculated for the year 1688' a schoolmaster with a basic salary of forty pounds made the same sort of livelihood as the lower paid clergy, shopkeepers, tradesmen and artisans. Below these categories, in King's analysis, came only common seamen at twenty pounds a year, labourers at fifteen pounds a year, common soldiers at fourteen pounds a year, and cottagers and paupers with a yearly income of six pounds and ten shillings.[4] It is probably true to say that with all his ups and downs, though he may have been kept in order, even subservience, by his governors, the schoolmaster was respected in the community. Indeed, as a university graduate his status was that of a gentleman and his place in the social scale similar to that of a lawyer, doctor of medicine, merchant and officer in the army or navy.[5] It is, therefore, not unreasonable to suggest that forty pounds a year should be regarded as a minimum salary for a schoolmaster in the latter half of the seventeenth century. But, as Frankland's return for Warwickshire indicates, most of the schools in that county offered no more than twenty pounds to their schoolmasters, and founders after the Restoration evidently considered that this amount was an adequate endowment for the schools at Heptonstall in Yorkshire, Cradley in Herefordshire, Chirbury in Shropshire,[6] Midhurst in Sussex[7] and South Leverton in Nottinghamshire.[8] The master at Eye Grammar School in

Suffolk only attained the salary of twenty pounds in 1692 when he was allowed to add the usher's salary to his own because there were not enough boys in the school to engage the attention of two men.[1]

As for the condition of schools with endowments and schoolmasters with salaries less than twenty pounds a year, some of Wase's correspondents may be allowed to speak for themselves and for their fellows. On 18 October 1673 John Paris, the master of Wye Grammar School, wrote that his school was 'endowed but with sixteen pounds per annum, without any house, library, or exhibitions, having nothing to commend it, but the privacye and antiquitye which have made it the nurserye of most of the Gentry in these parts of Kent'.[2] Robert Powell's account of Gainsborough Grammar School in Lincolnshire was written on 22 November 1673. The schoolmaster was then paid twelve pounds a year and since no schoolhouse had been built he had to obtain permission 'to teach Schoole in a quire, divided from the Chancel; All this considered, I need certifie you no more, concerning the queries in your letter, when the condition of the schoole is so low . . . and if benefactors would give but some land for a stipend, it would flourish.'[3]

Ormskirk Grammar School in Lancashire was 'endowed very poorly' with twelve pounds a year. 'Some augmentacons have bin left by other persons', wrote Ellis Rycroft on 17 November 1673, 'but I Dare *say* they are left very desperate'.[4] The surname of the master of Stokesay Grammar School in Shropshire in 1673 was Bromley. 'His Xtian Name I have not as yet', wrote William Fosbrooke, the curate of Diddlebury, on 16 August '& for ought I understand by my friend, he is loath to reveale it, he being a younger Cantab: & withall fearing lest ye menconing of his Name with so small an Income might prove a Degradation, For he is suddenly to Remove.' The school was endowed with ten pounds a year out of which a shilling a week was deducted for the poor.[5] At Bungay in Suffolk the master of the grammar school was paid five pounds a year. Wase's correspondent considered that a 'general account' would be sufficient since 'through ye smallness of ye Masters stipend' the school was 'so inconsiderable'.[6] The endowment of Chipping Norton Grammar School in Oxfordshire was eight pounds a year and this fact sufficiently explains the anxiety of the schoolmaster, Charles Dance, in 1675 to enlist Wase's aid in obtaining information about a small legacy, worth six pounds and thirteen shillings a year, which, so he understood, had been left to the school out of an estate at Steeple Aston. 'If there be any life in that which is due to ye schoole out of Martins estate', wrote Dance in a post-script, 'you will doe me a great Kindnesse if you will be pleas'd to Vouchsafe me a line with your convenience'.[1] Unfortunately there is no comment on the situation of the schoolmaster at Bitterly in Shropshire who was entirely dependent for his income on the fees paid by his pupils.[2] The same condition of employment applied to the schoolmaster at Chard Grammar School in Somerset which was founded in 1671.[3]

The range of salaries of ushers was as wide as that of masters. At the beginning of the eighteenth century the post of usher at Birmingham carried a salary of £44 6s. 8d.[4] while at Burneston in Yorkshire the mastership and ushership were respectively worth sixteen pounds and five pounds and eight shillings a year,[5] and at Darlington in the county of Durham £29 12s. 11d. and six pounds.[6] These are extreme cases and, although salaries of twenty pounds a year for ushers were not unknown,[7] normally they were between ten and sixteen pounds. In the 1670s the usher at Whitchurch in Shropshire earned ten pounds a year,[8] at Blackburn in Lancashire £14 6s. 8d.,[9] at Ashbourne in Derbyshire £14 15s.[10] and at Aldenham in Hertfordshire £16 13s. 4d.[11] It is apparent that while an usher was paid much less than the master of his school he might be better off than other men who were in charge of smaller and poorer schools. Like the masters, the ushers received a share of any fees and gratuities and eked out their meagre salaries by some other employment when and where this was possible. Though some men remained ushers all their working days the position was obviously suited to young unmarried men who could regard it as temporary while they waited for something better. It is, therefore, no matter for surprise that at Durham School between 1678 and 1687 there was a quick succession of ushers who were paid ten pounds a year, Thomas Thomson from 1678 to 1680 and then Thomas Hutchinson who was followed by William Salkeld in 1682 and William Singleton in 1683, Barnabas

Hutchinson in 1684, Leonard Deane in 1686 and John Pakin or Parkin in 1687.[1] Abraham Gregory combined the ushership at the King's School, Gloucester, with the vicarage of Sandhurst until in 1671, at the age of twenty-seven years, he received preferment as a canon of Gloucester and rector of Cowley.[2] For others, like David Thomas and Francis Gregory, an ushership provided an apprenticeship in their chosen profession.[3]

The tragedy of many schools, and of their schoolmasters, was in the nature of the endowments which, since they were in the form of specified sums of money, allowed of no improvement in spite of inflation. Charles Dance's salary at Chipping Norton, for example, consisted of a crown stipend of six pounds a year and a further benefaction fixed at two pounds a year. The endowments at Kinnersley, Newbury and Brailes were likewise payable out of crown revenues so that with the rising cost of living, and in the absence of further benefactions, they grew steadily less capable of supporting schoolmasters. And here, once again, the theme of the decline of the grammar schools has re-asserted itself.[4]

In Yorkshire examples of fixed endowments combined with eventual decline in status are furnished by the histories of Burneston Grammar School and Syddall's School at Catterick. In 1820 the master of Burneston School was receiving a salary of sixteen pounds a year for instructing seventeen boys and girls in writing and arithmetic. The original foundation in 1688 was that of a free grammar school with a master at an annual salary of sixteen pounds and an usher at a salary of five pounds and eight shillings a year.[5] The school at Catterick was founded in 1658 when the former vicar of Catterick, Michael Syddall, made provision by his will to build a school, a hospital and a chapel and to pay twenty pounds a year to a university man who, apart from taking a fee of five shillings from each pupil on admission to the school, was to teach Latin and Greek without charge to children of the parish. In 1688 Syddall's trustees built the school, hospital and chapel. In 1796 the school ceased to be a grammar school. In 1821 the charity amounted to forty-five pounds of which the schoolmaster received the original salary of twenty pounds in return for teaching reading, writing, arithmetic and the church catechism to sixteen children.[6] In the course of time many schools lost their status as grammar schools or ceased to exist, a situation from which they might, perhaps, have been saved to flourish if the founders had bequeathed lands instead of fixed rents.[1] Founders and benefactors little deserved to have their well-intentioned efforts ridiculed by eventual failure.

Two other matters concerned with the remuneration of schoolmasters are relevant to the decline of schools. The first, to which attention has already been called, was the lack of proper provision for men who, because of old age or infirmity, had to relinquish their posts. It is true that some founders ordered their feoffees to 'take some regard of the necessity of' such men, 'as charity shall require', and there is evidence that this duty and responsibility were sometimes recognized and accepted.[2] William Hanby was evidently unable to perform the duties of usher at Durham School after 1678 and continued to receive the full amount of his salary, ten pounds a year, in the form of a pension down to 1690.[3] In finding Rowland Tucker incapable of performing the functions of usher, on account of his age and infirmities, and ordering his dismissal on the following Midsummer Day, the Bristol Corporation, on 31 May 1681, decreed that he should be paid a pension of ten pounds a year, the amount to be deducted from the salary of his successor. In the outcome the pension was raised to twenty pounds a year and the new usher, Thomas Stump, was not in fact required to contribute to the support of his predecessor.[4]

But, since school endowments did not normally allow for additional charges, it followed that some men, through no fault of their own, were compelled to continue in office long after they had passed the peak of their powers, and in old age and infirmity to witness the deterioration of schools which had flourished under their earlier energetic and capable leadership. This surely explains why the number of pupils at Bristol Grammar School was diminished towards the end of Charles Lee's long tenure. Lee who began his mastership in 1764 remained in office until he died in 1811 since the Bristol Corporation refused to grant him a pension.[5] The lack of any provision for retirement on a pension doubtless kept George Innes at Warwick School too long. He inherited only one or two boys and no boarders from John Roberts whose unsuccessful mastership extended from 1763 to 1791. Innes immediately raised the number of day boys to nine and during his early years 'had a flourishing seminary of private boarders'. After 1812 ill-health forced him to give up his boarders and he seems to have confined his teaching to two or three day boys until his death in 1842 at the age of eighty-three years.[1]

The second consideration was pointedly expressed by Christopher Wase: 'Nothing is of its own nature more expensive then want'. He was concerned with the unseemliness of the situation, the lack of incentive to labour and the distraction from duty which resulted when men in positions of authority were subjected to 'the manifold indecencies of indigence'.[2] He might have added that, when grievance about conditions of employment was added to the already heavy burden of schoolmastering, men were liable to show less than the desirable restraint in dealing with their charges and that poor rates of pay made for low quality in teachers. Marchamont Nedham summed up the whole matter when he wrote ''Tis the Salary which makes Schools and Learning flourish'.

In this survey of schoolmasters' salaries we have found evidence throughout the later Stuart period to support the judgement passed by Nedham in 1663:

> Ministers themselves, who instruct us to expect future rewards, yet without a fair present maintenance would fall into the contempt of the vulgar, and their labours prove ineffectual. And this is the case of Schools: no imployment more publickly useful, none more toylsome and painful; yet no one more sleighted even to reproach; no one less rewarded or regarded. 'Tis a great scandal to the Nation, and certainly as great a grievance (if rightly considered) that no one sort of men are greater sufferers in this kind, then Schoolmasters.[3]

Whether or not this is a just appraisal of the situation as a whole it is difficult to say since there is a lack of evidence for figures of salaries in professions comparable with that of schoolmasters in endowed schools. We know that in 1729 William Stukeley was dissatisfied with his practice as a doctor in Grantham in

M

Lincolnshire which was bringing in fifty pounds a year.[1] This income certainly seems meagre when it is compared with that of a successful writing master. In 1712 William Massey became 'Latin-usher' to Richard Scoryer, a writing master 'who had a flourishing boarding school at Half-farthing-house' in Wandsworth, Surrey. Scoryer was succeeded in 1714 by Edward Powell under whom Massey continued for a year and of whom he had a high opinion 'not only as a dexterous penman, but also as a scholar, very well versed in classical learning'. Massey records that, when he lived with him and for some time afterwards, Powell earned nearly a thousand pounds a year from his school.[2] Evidently, for a man whose ability was esteemed and whose school prospered, the profession of a writing master could prove a highly lucrative one. Teaching in private classical schools also offered the prospect of higher incomes than could be won from established schools. Attention has already been drawn to the information supplied to Christopher Wase by John Rowland that in the small town of Eltham in Kent, three schoolmasters who were running their own schools were each earning two hundred or two hundred and fifty pounds a year.[3] In comparison with such men the schoolmasters in endowed schools seem to have occupied an unenviable position. And yet it was not unknown for men to give up their own schools in order to accept posts in endowed schools. Thus Stephen Clarke moved from his private school in Cottingham in Yorkshire to the grammar school at Thornton in 1676.[4] Samuel Ogden became master at Wirksworth Grammar School in 1695 after keeping a private school in Derby,[5] and in 1707 Richard Johnson left a private school in Kensington to take up the mastership of Nottingham Grammar School.[6] The decisive factor in bringing about these moves was no doubt the measure of security which was offered by endowed schools and which some men eventually found more attractive than independence and the possibility of greater financial rewards in private enterprise.

Probably, then, schoolmasters with a modest basic wage, free tenancy of a house and emoluments, were not so badly off. Some, especially if they took boarders, made a good living. Indeed the most impressive feature of this investigation is the disparity of incomes between schoolmasters at the top and those at the lower end of the salary scale. A similar inequality existed among the clergy at the beginning of the eighteenth century. Information supplied to the governors of Queen Anne's Bounty and published in 1711 revealed that out of 9,180 benefices, 5,082 were worth less than eighty pounds, 3,826 less than fifty pounds and 1,216 less than twenty pounds a year.[1] Commenting on the situation of the poorest clergymen Dr. G. F. A. Best wrote that a man 'whose clothes, family, place and manner of living, pronounced him poor – might labour under grievous disadvantages. His poverty would cripple his pastorate in many obvious ways. He would lack books and the society of educated persons.'[2] Many schoolmasters must surely have laboured under similar disadvantages. In such unfavourable conditions the system of pluralities was unavoidable and, as we have seen, often the solution which brought relief was the combination in one man of the offices of schoolmaster and parish priest.

Appendix

Salaries of schoolmasters in the 1670s, compiled from the Wase manuscripts, C.C.C. Oxon 390/1–3, in the Bodleian Library.

The schools are arranged in descending order of salaries. When the date of foundation is not given in the manuscript it is here supplied from authorities, the *Report of the Schools Inquiry Commission,* 1868, Volume I, Appendix IV (R.), N. Carlisle's *A Concise Description of the Endowed Grammar Schools in England and Wales* (C.), and the *Victoria County Histories* (V.). Where dates of foundation conflict I have given them all, followed in each case by the initial of the authority. Such additions are marked with an asterisk. In some instances the dates of foundation given by authorities differ from those in the manuscript and attention is drawn to these differences in the Notes (p. 262).

School	County	Date of Foundation	Salary £ s. d.	Source
Nuneaton	Warwickshire	1552 or 1553*	80 0 0	390/2, f.211
Sutton Coldfield	Warwickshire	1541(R.). Before 1544(C.). 1540(V.)*	80 0 0	390/2, f.211
St. Albans	Hertfordshire	About 1569(R.). 1548(C.).*	52 0 0	390/1, f.213
Rugby	Warwickshire	1567*	50 0 0	390/2, f.211
Cambridge, Perse School	Cambridgeshire	1615	40 0 0	390/1, f.46
Faversham	Kent	About 1576	36 0 0	390/1, f.259
Hipperholme	Yorkshire	1661¹	31 0 0	390/2, f.243
Beachampton	Buckinghamshire	1669²	30 0 0	390/1, f.31
Colwall	Herefordshire	1612*	30 0 0	390/1, f.197
Chudleigh	Devonshire	About 1667	30 0 0	390/1, f.91
Lewisham	Kent	1652³	30 0 0	390/1, f.256
Mere	Wiltshire	About 1667	30 0 0	390/2, f.231
Oxford, Nixon's Free Grammar School	Oxfordshire	1658	30 0 0	390/2, f.117
Usk	Monmouthshire	1621*	30 0 0	390/3, f.28
Whitchurch	Shropshire	1550	30 0 0	390/2, f.156
Ashbourne	Derbyshire	1585	28 0 0	390/1, f.71
Southampton	Hampshire	1553(R. and C.). 1550(V.)*	25 10 0	390/1, f.174
Blackburn	Lancashire	1509 or 1510(R.). 1514 (V.)*	25 0 0	390/2, f.1
Deptford	Kent	1672	24 0 0	390/1, f.258
Cradley	Herefordshire	1668	20 0 0	390/1, f.198
Chirbury	Shropshire	1676	20 0 0	390/2, f.135
Dorstone	Herefordshire	1643	20 0 0	390/1, f.199
Heptonstall	Yorkshire	1642*	20 0 0	390/2, f.243
Kingsbridge	Devonshire	About 1671	20 0 0	390/1, f.94

School	County	Date of Foundation	Salary			Source
Houghton Conquest	Bedfordshire	1632*	16	0	0	390/1, f.5
Wye	Kent	1447(R.). 1545 (C.)*	16	0	0	390/1, f.268
Bakewell	Derbyshire	1636*	15	0	0	390/1, f.73
Gainsborough	Lincolnshire	1589	12	0	0	390/2, f.38
Houghton Regis	Bedfordshire	1654	12	0	0	390/1, f.3
Newbury	Berkshire	Reign of King John[1]	12	0	0	390/1, f.20
Ormskirk	Lancashire	1614[2]	12	0	0	390/2, f.22
Stokenchurch	Oxfordshire	1675	12	0	0	390/2, f.123
Bishop Auckland	Durham	1604 or 1605*	10	0	0	390/1, f.112
Buckingham	Buckinghamshire	Reign of Edward VI (R. and C.), 1540 (V.)*	10	0	0	390/1, f.33
Ewerby	Lincolnshire	1667	10	0	0	390/2, f.37
Honiton	Devonshire	1640*	10	0	0	390/1, f.93
Houghton Le Spring	Durham	1574	10	0	0	390/1, f.114
Kelverdon	Essex	1636[3]	10	0	0	390/1, f.124
Martock	Somerset	1661	10	0	0	390/2, f.169
Wrexham	Denbighshire	1603*	10	0	0	390/3, f.12
Wilden	Bedfordshire	1624	9	0	0	390/1, f.8
Brailes	Warwickshire	1534	8	1	8	390/2, f.203
Abthorpe	Northamptonshire	1642[4]	8	0	0	390/2, f.72
Chipping Norton	Oxfordshire	Before 1547 (R.) Reign of Edward VI(C.). 1540(V.)*	8	0	0	390/2, f.115
Towcester	Northamptonshire	Reign of Edward VI[5]	7	14	2	390/2, f.100
Stokesay	Shropshire	1616	7	8	0	390/2, f.153
Newdigate	Surrey	1641	6	13	4	390/2, f.197
Kinnersley	Herefordshire	Before 1674	6	2	0	390/1, f.202
Bungay	Suffolk	Before 1563*	5	0	0	390/3, f.167
Bitterly	Shropshire	Before 1678	No stipend			390/2, f.137

VIII

SCHOOL GOVERNORS

When Stephen Newcomen was helping Wase with his inquiries he was able to give him 'a sight of such orders, and directions' as the governors had drawn up for the better administration of Boxford Grammar School in Suffolk. Since there were thirty-seven governors, some of whom lived in places remote from the school, it was considered convenient that one of them, who was to be styled the warden and who lived near but not in the town of Boxford, should be empowered to summon meetings of the governing body at which not less than fifteen members must be present. The procedure to be followed 'upon the death, cessation, or deprivation' of a governor or schoolmaster was prescribed:

> So soon as the Sumons are gone forth (according to the primary Institution, and Patent) for a congregation, and assembly and the Governours mett everyone is to take knowledge that he is there mett not to doe or performe something for his owne proffit or gaine, but setting aside all private Respects and sinister ends is only to aime at the glory of God the love of his Country, the good Instruction, and education of youth, upon *which* dependeth the benefit, & prosperity of the Commonwealth.

Governors were to be above the age of twenty-one years,

> or rather more Auncient; Religious of wise knowledge, and experience fit to manage, and improve the Lands, Tenements, Goods, Stocks, and Chattels of the said Schoole to best advantage.

Provision was made for an annual service and sermon in the parish church after which the warden and governors were to go to the school to see how the master and boys were progressing and to receive from every scholar 'some Speech, Prose, or

Matter, as commendable proofes of their proffiting'. Part of their duty on this occasion was to make a survey of the school-house and lands in order to ensure that payments to the teaching staff were satisfied.

As Newcomen pointed out, these directions, if rightly observed, 'would not a little conduce to the well ordering and flourishing of the said Schoole'.[1] Certainly they imply that the governors had a proper appreciation of their duties and responsibilities and a sincere and selfless desire to further the best interests of their school. Even so it is unlikely that they met with Wase's unqualified approval since they failed to mention one aspect of school management which seemed to him to be of the first importance.

In general Wase's opinion was that the composition of governing bodies needed to be reviewed in the light of experience of their working. While disclaiming any desire to make changes unduly in established constitutions, he suggested that in present and future deliberations 'variety of Paterns compar'd' might 'be serviceable towards determining the choice with more success'. In particular Wase was concerned about the relation of the schoolmaster to his governors. It seemed to him that absolute dependence upon trustees for his stipend and security could not 'but retard the endeavours' and might 'endanger to shake the stedfastness of the best resolv'd Teacher'. Moreover it was unreasonable that a master of arts, who was considered fit to have charge of boys, should himself be reduced to the status of a pupil in the matter of the school income, 'the onely man in the Parish judg'd proper from whom the value of his estate be conceal'd'. The remedy was, of course, obvious and had already been applied at Shrewsbury where the master joined with the mayor in letting the school lands. Such a partnership in authority and responsibility satisfied Wase's plea for 'a right esteem' of the schoolmaster who was, after all, 'a fellow-Laborer with their Minister'. It had the further advantages, as he pointed out, of relieving the townsmen from any temptation to misapply, and of preventing the master from impairing, the school funds.[2]

What Wase was here content to suggest Marchamont Nedham in 1663 had already made bold to express in his forthright

way. After stating that the original endowments of schools
had been 'very fair and honourable' and that in times past
provision for schoolmasters had been 'very competent', he asked,
'but what do we add to our forefathers stock?' His answer was:

> The Trustees and Governours in the several Corporations
> share the Improvements amongst themselves, take all above
> the Salary for lawful prize, and leave the Master to the bare
> old allowance, notwithstanding the vast increase of the old
> Rents. So that by this means Schools are become Im-
> propriations, and lay men (ignorant fellows) run away with
> the incouragements of Learning, & receive the rewards of
> the Masters industry.[1]

The constitution of governing bodies, to which Wase directed
attention, and their conduct of school affairs, which earned
Nedham's condemnation, are, then, the themes of this chapter.
It will be useful to our purpose to follow the example of the
Schools Inquiry Commissioners, reporting in 1868, and to
divide governing bodies into three main groups.

The governance of a school might be entrusted to one or two
men who were the heirs of the founder or who owned certain
houses or lands. When Charles Darby, the master of Martock
Grammar School in Somerset, was corresponding with Wase in
1674 the sole governor of his school was the founder's son,
William Strode. In 1675 the presentation to the schoolmastership at Llanegryn in Merioneth was in the hands of Lewis Owen,
the founder's nephew, and was to be continued in his heirs. At
Ashford in Kent, so Wase was informed, the patron of the school
was Sir Norton Knatchbull, the founder's nephew and owner of
Morsham Hatch, and the owner of this manor was always to
have the right of presenting to the schoolmastership.[2] Out of
seven hundred and eighty-two endowed schools, which were
investigated by the commissioners between 1865 and 1867 and
which at some time in their history had purported to give instruction above the rudiments, about one hundred were controlled by one or two persons by virtue of inheritance or ownership of property.[3]

The particular weakness of this method of governance lay
in the possibility that an heir, who did not share his ancestor's

enthusiasm for education or inclination to philanthropy, might discontinue the payment of the charity. The point is well illustrated in the history of Needham Market Grammar School in Suffolk. A bequest for the building of a school and an annual grant of twenty pounds for its upkeep were given grudgingly by Sir Francis Theobald, by his will of 20 January 1631–32, because he was not allowed to forget or evade the obligation to realize the promise and intention of Sir Francis Needham, whose heir he was. The payment of the annuity was not maintained by his son and grandson so that in 1674 the school was deserted. When an inquisition was held by the Commissioners of Charitable Uses in 1688 the schoolmaster was William Richardson who, contrary to the school ordinances, was a nongraduate but seemingly gave satisfactory service. His salary of four pounds and ten shillings was paid by the parents of his scholars and he taught no children free of charge since no money was provided for that purpose. It was therefore ordered that the founder's grandson, Robert Theobald, should settle the annuity upon trustees in order to ensure its regular payment in the future.[1]

The form of governance eventually determined for the school at Needham Market was, in fact, the one most frequently chosen by founders. They nominated, as trustees, individuals who were counted worthy to have charge of their charities and who were judged not to stand in need of any recompense for their services. The second group of governing bodies consisted, therefore, of societies specifically created for the administration of schools. They held their meetings once or twice a year at the school and normally were responsible for electing new members when vacancies occurred.[2] In 1868 about three quarters of the existing grammar schools were controlled by individual trustees who were responsible for administering the endowments and appointing the masters.[3]

Such associations varied in the number and social status of their members. The choice of the schoolmaster at Little Thurlow in Suffolk was entrusted to the incumbents of Great and Little Thurlow who were accustomed to consult the chief inhabitants before making an election.[4] At Botesdale in Suffolk, in accordance with Sir Nicholas Bacon's ordinance of 10 October 1566, his heir elected the schoolmaster and there were two governors, one for Botesdale and the other for Redgrave, who served for one year only and nominated their successors.[1] The governance of the school at Houghton Regis in Bedfordshire was committed to six, and at Ashbourne in Derbyshire to fifteen 'of the most substantiall inhabitants'.[2] The governors of Newland Grammar School in Gloucestershire were 'parishioners, in number about twelve'.[3] Of the feoffees of the grammar school at Whitchurch in Shropshire 'some few' were 'Gentlemen, the rest persons of pretty good estates', all of them parishioners or having estates in the parish.[4] The minister and churchwardens were the school governors at Cradley in Herefordshire.[5]

It is evident that the success of such schemes for the governance of schools was very much a matter of chance since it depended on the characters of the men appointed and on their response to the trust placed in them. They could indeed be ignorant of, indifferent or even hostile to the claims of education. To some the responsibility of school government might become wearisome and any actions which might involve disputes or legal proceedings, though these were for the good of the school, might seem best avoided. When their experience of education was limited to their own school they were likely to be unconscious of its failings and of possibilities of development and improvement. Where the position of trustee was tenable for life the harmful effects of an unfortunate selection could continue to be felt by the school over a long period of time. All these possible weaknesses in the scheme of school management by individual trustees are easily discernible. A review of some of the evidence will show that misgivings about the operation of the system are fully justified.

Some of Wase's correspondents witnessed to the negligence and incompetence of school trustees. Reports from Stow-on-the-Wold in Gloucestershire and Tenterden in Kent suggest that the trustees were unwilling or unable to rouse themselves in the defence of their schools. In an undated letter, written by Benjamin Callon, Wase was advised that he would find Stow-on-the-Wold 'a very sad example of iniury'. It appears that 'about 50, or 60 yeares since there was a very hot contention about misimployed lands' and that from that time there had 'beene but little done' to redress the situation. 'Every corrupt knave has used us at his pleasure,' Callon concluded, 'and no man could, or at least would defend our right.'[1] At Tenterden, according to the schoolmaster, Stephen Hassenden, who wrote on 12 January 1673–74, there was 'a combination of envious persons at this Time endeavouring to subvert the very Foundation of the schoole' and for the past two years they had withheld the annuity.[2] Wase's information from Richard Grimbaldston, the master of Huyton Grammar School in Lancashire, was that the school endowment, which had formerly been sixteen pounds a year, had been reduced 'through carelesness' on the part of the trustees so that in July 1675 the stipend was the annual interest on £192 10s.[3]

The shortcomings of trustees were not confined to indifference and inefficiency. The affairs of schools were sometimes committed to men who used their offices to further their own interests. An example of the unscrupulous use of trusteeship is furnished by the history of Wotton-under-Edge Grammar School in Gloucestershire. In 1647 after the two patrons John Smith and Lord Berkeley had appointed to the mastership Thomas Burton, an old boy of the school and M.A. of Lincoln College, Oxford, Smith obtained for himself a new lease of the school lands at Nibley and made the master enter into a written agreement to resign his office, whenever his resignation was demanded, or pay a fine of five hundred pounds. Smith was in a strong position since the refusal of the master to renew the lease would certainly lead to his dismissal and any future appointment would be made on the same terms. In April 1706 George Smith's exercise of the patronage was in accord with the wishes of some of the leading inhabitants when he appointed Samuel Bennett, another old boy of the school and a graduate of University College, Oxford. Once again the master was bound by a written agreement of resignation and Smith obtained a new lease to the property at Nibley without paying a fine at renewal and at a rent of thirty-two pounds and ten shillings which was a tenth of its actual value.[4] But George Smith had met his match in Samuel Bennett who in 1710, with support from the people of Wotton-under-Edge, began legal proceedings to annul Smith's possession of the lease of school lands. The outcome, if not a complete victory for the schoolmaster, at least rescued the school from strangulation at the hands of its trustee. On 16 December 1718 the Master of the Rolls ordered Margaret, the widow of George Smith who had died in 1712, to surrender the lease and the deed of resignation, which her husband had obtained from the master, and to pay full value for all school lands except the property known as Warren's Court, to which the Smith family claim for a lease at one-third of its actual value was allowed. The buoyant effect of this release from deprivation was evidenced by the measures for improvement and reform which followed within two years of the confirmation of the decree in 1723, when costs of over four thousand two hundred and twenty-five pounds were allowed against the defendants. In accordance with a scheme approved, on 1 March 1724–25, there were increases in the Smiths' rent, which went up to sixty pounds a year and in the master's salary, which was raised to forty pounds a year. A new board of seven managers, of which the mayor and the vicar of the parish were always members, was made responsible for the administration of the school property and the investment in land of any overplus of the rents. In 1726 four hundred and fifty pounds were allotted for building a new schoolhouse.[1]

One further example of the misconduct of individual trustees deserves notice because the misappropriation of school funds by the six 'honest and substantial Inhabitants' who formed the governing body was eventually ended by the intervention of the school visitor. The story was reported by Thomas Leigh who, writing from London on 5 October 1675, told Wase that he had received it from Henry Rix who had recently been appointed to the mastership at Newport in Essex. The schoolmaster's information was that the school at Newport was founded in 1588 by Mrs. Joyce Franckland, daughter of Robert Trapps, a goldsmith of London, her son William Saxey being co-founder. In the founder's will the endowment of impropriated tithes of Bansted in Surrey, two houses in Distaffe Lane in London and two houses in Hoddesdon in Hertfordshire, was valued at twenty-three pounds and ten shillings, of which twenty pounds was assigned to the master, two pounds to the visitor, and thirty shillings to repairs of the school building. The master's salary 'was but little improved notwithstanding ye great improvement of ye aforesaid rents' until, about 1663, Dr. Robert Brady, master of Gonville and Caius College, as 'Visitor overthrew certain concurrent Leases, which ye feoffees had made contrary to law, & assured ye improved rents to ye Master'. As a result of his action in 're-deeming' the revenues 'out of ye clutches of ye rapacious Feoffees, & improving ye rent' the whole annual salary amounted in 1675 to eighty-three pounds; and since the visitor received forty shillings for every advance of twenty pounds in the income he was now paid eight pounds.[1]

Some founders entrusted the administration of their charities to the college in the university, or to the city company with which they were associated, or to the corporation of the town or borough in which the school was situated. These societies, together with cathedral chapters, form the third group of governing bodies, associations already in existence for other purposes when the schools were founded. According to the returns of the commissioners, published in 1868, ninety-three grammar schools were wholly or partly administered by such societies. Oxford and Cambridge colleges were the trustees of seventeen schools and had powers of visitation and appointment to the masterships in eleven other schools, twenty-seven schools were governed by thirteen city companies, seven of which were each responsible for one school, in twenty towns the grammar schools were mainly controlled by the municipal corporations, and eighteen schools were connected with cathedrals.[2] The act of connecting his school with a university college, city company or municipal corporation satisfied the founder's sense of loyalty and affection, promised permanence and security for the new foundation, and assured continuity in the school managers. It certainly did not rule out the possibility that school funds might be misappropriated and misapplied.

The history of East Retford Grammar School in Nottinghamshire provides an interesting example of mismanagement by the corporation which continued even after it had been exposed by an inquisition. A Commission of Charitable Uses in 1699 found that for the past twenty-nine years the bailiffs and burgesses had misapplied the rents and profits of the school property and were then allowing for the master and usher only twenty-nine pounds a year out of a revenue of £145 5s. 8d. By the decree of 17 June the corporation were ordered to pay within one month arrears to the amount of £3,372 4s. 4d. for the support of the school, schoolmaster and usher, and a further sixty pounds as a recompense to the master, Henry Boawre, for the injury they had done to him, by retaining the rents, during the twenty-nine years of his mastership. The corporation were forbidden to take fines when leases were renewed and ordered to charge rents equal to the full value of the lands, to pay all rents and profits to the school and to give account of their stewardship annually to the representative of the archbishop or of the dean and chapter of York. Objection to this judgement was made by the bailiffs and burgesses and on 3 October 1700 it was claimed in their defence that some of the estates named in the commissioners' decree were not and never had been part of the school property, that no evidence had been adduced to prove that they belonged to the school and that it was impossible to distinguish between school and corporation lands. It was further alleged that the commissioners had no power to make a decree about property which was given for charitable uses before the first year of the reign of Queen Elizabeth. Evidently the suit was not actively prosecuted for there is no record of any further proceedings. It may be that, as the Commissioners to inquire concerning Charities surmised in 1820 and as the corporation defence maintained in 1700, the decree of 17 June 1699 could not be upheld in the case of a Crown grant made in the time of Edward the Sixth and that the Statute of Charitable Uses was reckoned to apply only to bequests from the Crown since the first year of Queen Elizabeth. Mr. A. F. Leach doubted this assumption since this was not the law as it was interpreted and followed in other cases. He suggested that possibly an amicable arrangement was reached and that the schoolmaster was sufficiently satisfied. But, as the commissioners reported in 1820, 'the bailiffs and burgesses have ever since the decree, received and applied the rents and profits of the school in the same manner as before'. In 1801 the master's salary was twenty-nine pounds a year and that of the usher twenty-one pounds.[1]

More effective was the intervention in 1698 by the bishop of London, Dr. Henry Compton, as visitor of Colchester Grammar School in Essex, in response to a formal protest made against the municipal authorities in the administration of the school affairs.

By a decree in Chancery the trusteeship was taken from the bailiffs and eventually, although not until September 1707, conferred on Sir William Luckin of Messing, Sir Isaac Rebow and five others.[1]

A situation very similar to that at East Retford was revealed in 1735 at Bath by the Commissioners of Charitable Uses. This case is worthy of remark since here, too, the decree of the commissioners, dated 10 June 1735, was never carried into effect. It did, however, bring about a change of attitude on the part of the governors towards their school. The commissioners found that the corporation of Bath had 'notoriously mismanaged, neglected, misconverted and misapplied the revenues of the lands' given by Edward the Sixth for the maintenance of the grammar school and ten poor persons. They had paid between ten and thirty pounds to the schoolmaster, which was very much less than the annual income, and nothing at all to any poor person. 'In manifest violation of the said trust' the corporation had 'constantly applied the same to their own or private uses', had kept no account of income and expenditure, had 'mixt and blended the said lands and premises with other lands' and had transferred ownership to other persons so that most of the school property was no longer distinguishable from that of the corporation. The commissioners decreed that the corporation 'should be for evermore absolutely removed and displaced from the said trust' which was to be managed by a new body of trustees including Henry duke of Beaufort, Charles earl of Orrery, Thomas lord Weymouth, John lord bishop of Bath and Wells and John lord Berkeley. The corporation were further ordered to pay five hundred pounds 'in satisfaction of the great damage thus done to the charity' and to give an exact account of school property within three months under a penalty of five thousand pounds. It seems likely that the duke of Beaufort and the others refused to accept the responsibility placed on them. In any event, the corporation of Bath continued to administer the school and school property. Between 1752 and 1755 they paid £3,933 13s. 9d. for a new school and schoolhouse.[2]

These illustrations show the misfortunes which might befall a school when a municipal corporation had control of the school revenue. Lands or money donated for a school sometimes became indistinguishable from the property and funds of the corporation through carelessness and failure to keep a separate account of the school trust fund. Where fixed sums of money were specified in the original terms of foundation as salaries and exhibitions the corporation might consider that any increased revenue resulting from changes in the value of money and property could legitimately be appropriated to their own purposes. It is evident that corporations, no less than individual trustees, were disinclined to raise the salaries of schoolmasters and were liable to succumb to the temptations presented by the management of educational endowments.

This is not to claim that unworthy motives must be attributed to every corporation which sought to regain or retain control of the local school. The corporation of Oswestry in Shropshire, it is true, had a bad record of school government since in 1635, as the result of an inquisition by a Commission of Charitable Uses, they were discharged from any responsibility for the grammar school and school property and replaced by the bishop of St. Asaph. Forty years later the corporation wished to reverse this decree though, according to the schoolmaster, John Evans, they would have been satisfied to obtain the right of presenting to the mastership.[1] If the case was prosecuted the corporation were unsuccessful since at the beginning of the nineteenth century the master was still chosen by the bishop of St. Asaph.[2] In 1688 the corporation of Langport Eastover in Somerset recorded that they had lately spent a large sum of money on restoring the buildings of their 'Ancient Schole'. They were understandably jealous of their right to appoint the schoolmaster and manage the school which was challenged by Robert Hunt the executor of Thomas Gillett who, by his will of 6 December 1675, gave the school its endowment. When in 1686 the corporation instituted legal proceedings it was found that Robert Hunt and, after him, his son and heir, John, had failed to fulfil Gillett's charitable intentions, so that on 25 July 1698 the defendant owed £728 2s. 11d. to the school. On 12 March 1704–05 the Court of Chancery ordered that this money should be used to purchase land and that the school should be administered by Gillett's trustees together with five representatives of the corporation.[3]

Some municipal corporations were restless when the local

school was controlled wholly or partly by a city company or university college. In 1647 the corporation of Stockport in Cheshire earned a severe rebuke from the Company of Goldsmiths of London because they chose Thomas Peirson as master of the grammar school. The corporation more than once evinced an inclination to appoint the master while the company showed themselves determined to allow no encroachment on the right of presentation and dismissal which had been vested in them by Sir Edmond Shaa in his will dated 20 March 1487–88. On this occasion the mayor and aldermen drew attention to the inadequacy of the basic salary of ten pounds and tried to justify their assumption of the presentation on the ground that from before Good Friday to Christmas Day in the preceding year the school had been without a teacher so that parents had been compelled to send their children to other schools at some distance from Stockport. The company insisted on their absolute right to nominate the master and having received the humble apology of the corporation were ready to accept their recommendation of Peirson as a suitable candidate and to prefer him, although he was not a graduate, to another applicant, William Duncan, M.A., of Cambridge. In 1668 the corporation refused to accept the company's choice of Daniel Leech as master and ejected him from the school. At their meeting on 6 September the company heard a petition sent by a hundred townspeople for the reinstatement of Leech, and also representatives of the mayoral faction who alleged that the new master was unsatisfactory since he was not a graduate and that he had signed a note of resignation. The dispute dragged on until Leech, having failed to satisfy a board of examiners in London that he had the ability necessary to prepare pupils for entrance to the university, was paid a gratuity of ten pounds on 1 September 1669 and dismissed. His successor, Joseph Whittle, B.A., of Brasenose College, Oxford, was appointed on 29 September after he had satisfied the board of examiners of his sufficiency.[1]

One objection to companies and colleges, justifiable in most cases, was that they were non-resident trustees. This was presumably a cause of complaint by the corporation of Stockport in 1647. Moreover, the delegation or sharing of duties might lead to jealousy between the company or college on the one hand and

N

the managers in the school locality on the other. Records of the bitter rivalry which could arise between a municipal corporation and a university college, when both bodies had responsibility for the same school, are preserved in the histories of Shrewsbury School and Bedford School.

The legal right of the master and seniors of St. John's College, Cambridge to elect the masters of Shrewsbury School was secured by the ordinances of 11 February 1577–78 which allowed the bailiffs of Shrewsbury to reject for sufficient and just cause a college nominee and to ask for another nomination. And yet in 1635, 1646, 1672 and 1688 the Shrewsbury Corporation asserted their claim to appoint a master. In 1672 the occasion of this illegal insistence was a vacancy in the room of the second master. The corporation, ignoring the college nomination, elected Oswald Smith of Christ Church, Oxford, who had recently graduated B.A. During at least seven years of litigation which ensued the corporation refused to retreat from their position in spite of the opinion of their own counsel that they had no case. An account of this dispute was sent to Wase by David Morton, a fellow of St. John's College, in a letter of 15 November 1675.

I am not to dissemble with you, that of late there hath been some dispute between ye Town of Salop & our College, about putting in a second master into that School: They recommending one to our choyse whom though we did not disapprove, (being satisfied as to his worth) yet we thought ourselves obliged to lay aside for one more statuteably qualified according to ye Ordinances of ye School: this notwithstanding, ye Town of themselves chose ye other into Possession of ye School, upon pretence of the First Foundation by K. Edw. 6. Hereupon ye College brought ye Case to ye Counsell board, whence it was referred to ye Lord Keeper, as his Majesties Visitor; & by Him heard in Easter Term latly who gave sufficient intimations of his Opinion, yt ye Right was in Us; yet suspended his definitive sentence, till there might be (if possibly) some friendly accommodation between Us, as to ye Present Case, & then He declared He would settle it beyond Controversy for ye future. And in this Posture we now stand; and therefore I presume to return you here Mr Andrewes as present 2d Master, so, in Right, though Mr Smith be yet in Actuall possession of ye place.[1]

The counsel for St. John's College showed that the sole concern of the master and seniors was to fulfil the trust which was placed in them. The case was still undecided in 1679, but in the outcome the corporation seem to have been successful on this occasion since Oswald Smith continued in the second mastership until his death in 1715. The possibility is that the college nominee, Richard Andrews, M.A., of Shrewsbury School and St. John's College, Cambridge, was offered and accepted a benefice. When the third mastership became vacant in 1688 the college named Henry Johnson. Once again the corporation, perhaps encouraged by Oswald Smith's successful retention of the second mastership, proposed and installed their own candidate, Robert Matthews. The master and seniors of St. John's College resigned themselves to the situation and expressed their readiness to elect Matthews if Johnson would withdraw, no doubt flinching from the possibility of another expensive lawsuit and finding sufficient consolation and justification in the facts that both candidates were natives of Shrewsbury and members of their own college. Johnson refused to surrender but there is no evidence that he instituted legal action to support his claim to the third mastership before his death in 1690.

A dispute over the right of nominating the schoolmaster at Bedford began when, in January 1717–18, the master and fellows of New College, Oxford appointed Matthew Priaulx, a fellow of the college, to the post. On 16 January the usher, Benjamin Rogers wrote to the new master to inform him that the corporation had already elected their own candidate and had locked the doors of the school.[2] No attempt was made by the corporation to evict or harm Priaulx when he arrived in Bedford and was admitted to the school, through the back door, by the usher who delivered to him the keys. But the corporation tried to stay the granting of a licence to teach by the ecclesiastical court and it was made clear to Priaulx that they were determined to prosecute the case and were confident that if the decision of the Court of Chancery went against them they could rely on the

influence of Whig supporters in Parliament to bring their cause
to a successful issue. The suggestion, made by the Member of
Parliament for Bedford, that Priaulx should be imprisoned until
the corporation's candidate could be secured in his possession
of the school was rejected in favour of an election by freemen of
the town.[1] Accordingly Benjamin Holloway was elected as
schoolmaster on 9 April 1718 and set up a rival establishment in
the Town Hall.[2] The usher, Benjamin Rogers, departed from
the school in January 1720–21 and the three ushers, William
Hodgson, Thomas Beedley and John Collin,[3] who followed him
in quick succession were paid by Priaulx out of his own pocket
while he begged the college authorities to pay him the arrears
of his salary.[4] The case dragged on in the local assizes and then
in the Court of Chancery until a judgement was given in July
1725. The right of the master and fellows of New College to
appoint the master and usher was ratified and costs were allowed
to both sides out of the charity. It was ordered that arrears should
be paid in full and that the masters' salaries should be one-third
of the rents yielded by the charitable bequest which then
amounted to one hundred and fifty pounds a year.[5]

The corporations of Shrewsbury and Bedford claimed, in the
face of clear evidence to the contrary, that they had the right to
appoint the schoolmasters in their towns, and the Shrewsbury
burgesses stated that they were better fitted than the college
to discharge this function. The two corporations may have been
guilty of nothing more than perversity, obstinacy or local pride,
but in the circumstances they were not above suspicion of deceit
and the desire to control the elections for their own selfish
advantage. In the case of Bedford, politics, if they did not origin-
ate, at any rate aggravated the situation since the Whig sym-
pathies of the corporation were in conflict with the Tory leanings
of the college. Perhaps the members of the Bedford Corporation
were irritated by an attempt on the part of the college to obtain
for the schoolmaster an increase in salary which the corporation
could well have afforded if they had used the school resources to
their limit.[6] As the historian of Shrewsbury School has pointed
out, the master's authority and influence as a trustee would be
nullified by the fact that the bailiffs, who were his fellow trustees,
had elected him to his office, while the right of appointment to

masterships enabled members of the corporation to offer remunerative posts to friends and relatives who had been educated at a university. Both corporations were prepared to squander school funds on prolonged litigation and to disregard the harmful effects upon the school of such proceedings. Indeed the number of scholars at Bedford School fell to sixteen or seventeen before the dispute ended.[1]

It is impossible to know how widespread were inertia, inefficiency and corruption among those who had the governance of grammar schools in the later Stuart period. Of course there were trustees who performed their duties honourably and to the best of their abilities. Not all corporate bodies were corrupt and some were not always so. In a letter of 22 February 1675–76 John Oddie, the schoolmaster of Blackburn Grammar School, described his governors as 'Faithfull' and attributed his own salary of twenty-five pounds a year and his usher's salary of £14 6s. 8d. to their careful improvement of the school income.[2] In 1676, as we have seen, the governors of the grammar school of Edward the Sixth at Birmingham raised the salary of the schoolmaster to sixty-eight pounds and fifteen shillings and that of the usher to £34 6s. 8d. and their new statutes of that year contained the sensible provisions 'that no person being Tenant of any of messuages and lands belonging to the Schole' should ever hold office as governor and that valuation of school property was always to be 'with the privity of the Cheife Schoole Master'. In the eighteenth century the situation at Birmingham deteriorated and on 23 January 1710–11 the schoolmaster, James Parkinson, was upheld in an action which he had brought before the Attorney General alleging that the governors 'had lavished away great and unnecessary sums in rebuilding' and that they arrogated to themselves the exclusive right to dispense the school revenue. In 1723 the Commissioners of Charitable Uses found that for the past twenty years no scholar had been elected to exhibitions and fellowships in the universities and that this was 'a manifest breach of Trust in the persons, who acted as Governors'.[3] In 1699 a change for the better in the attitude of the corporation of Bristol towards their grammar school was shown by the allocation of a hundred pounds from fines to repairs of the school buildings, and in 1700 by the gift of a hundred pounds to

Balliol College, Oxford, towards the building of chambers for exhibitioners sent from the school. On 12 December 1711 the corporation granted the request of William Goldwin, who had been master since 1709, for an increase in salary and raised it from sixty to eighty pounds a year.[1]

Nevertheless there is ample evidence to support Wase's plea for careful consideration and comparison before deciding on the composition of governing bodies. As things were the management of schools might be in the hands of men who were inexperienced and unacademic. No wonder, then, that Wase advocated the alliance of country schools with some hall or college in the university.

> The fruit of Country Schools in good measure depends upon an opinion of the Master, to the Electors of whom more then truth and honesty is requir'd: therefore prudent Founders have been circumspect as to that point; and where certain Towns-men upon the place have been allow'd most proper Governors as to the management of the Revenue, and Execution of the Statutes, yet Colleges in one of the Universities have been judg'd sometimes more competent Patrons, and rather with the Diocesan consulted in the compiling those Ordinances of Government.

Wase expressly confined this recommendation to country schools since

> all Corporations stand not in the same terms for skill, or choice of candidates as do Collegiat Churches and Ecclesiastical Patrons or Noblemen, or the greater Companies of London.[2]

He shows no awareness of the jealousy and rivalry which, as we have seen, might be occasioned by the working of such a scheme. Educational endowments might be controlled by careless or unscrupulous men who had little or no regard for the welfare of schools. Though we may wish to avoid being as doctrinaire as Marchamont Nedham in his sweeping condemnation of trustees yet we must acknowledge that there were good grounds for complaint about the misapplication of school funds.

It is probable that the development of annual audits investigated by chartered accountants has done more than anything else to stem the kind of negligent or dishonest behaviour which has been exposed in this chapter. Obviously the controls which Common Law provided in this period were too weak to check it. In any event someone had to instigate a case in order to get any help. Instances of bribery and corruption as well as of inertia in the management of schools may be multiplied throughout the eighteenth century. Some examples will serve to show that in governance, as in discipline and curriculum, the story of the grammar schools in the later Stuart period reveals the pattern of things still to come. At Botesdale Grammar School there had been no trustees for fifty years when in 1738 the rector of the parish, Mr. Gibbs, called attention to this disregard of the founder's intention.[1] The earl of Chesterfield as hereditary governor confessed in 1782 to a complete ignorance of the charities and funds which supported Repton School.[2] In 1792 the duke of Devonshire was the sole trustee of Buxton Grammar School in Derbyshire and there had been no master for some years.[3] John Goodall, master of Lincoln Grammar School, withdrew his application for the mastership of Stamford Grammar School, left vacant by the death of William Hannes in December 1730, when the corporation refused to accept his condition that they should relinquish the fines on rents and renewal of leases which rightly belonged to the school.[4] In January 1722–23 the vicar of Earls Colne in Essex, Thomas Bernard, paid a hundred pounds to the Towle family for the mastership of the grammar school, and in 1756 Robert Young obtained the post at a fixed salary of twenty-five pounds a year with a pound for each boy, up to the number of fifteen boys, on condition that he collected the rents and gave the residue to the school patrons.[5] At Brentwood when at long last Thomas Tower of Weald Hall rebuilt the schoolmaster's house between 1773 and 1775 he directed a large part of the school income, which he had lately enjoyed, to raise the value of the chaplaincy of Brentwood Chapel.[6] Carlisle received no answer to his letter of inquiry about Cheltenham Grammar School, but his information in 1818 was 'that the Parishioners of this Place are much dissatisfied with the management of their School' by the fellows of Corpus Christi College, Oxford.[7]

At best, we must conclude, in general and in a worsening situation school governors did little or nothing to prevent or delay the decline of grammar schools. It is not unreasonable to surmise that apathy and discouragement among schoolmasters were attributable to or aggravated by indifference and irresponsibility on the part of their governors. At worst, the ultimate and distressing situation, as described by Nicholas Carlisle at the beginning of the nineteenth century, was

> that many of our numerous and ample Endowments have fallen to decay, by the negligence or cupidity of ignorant or unprincipled Trustees; who have silently, or by connivance, suffered the furtive alienation of the very Lands which they were called upon so solemnly to defend, and which were in a great measure ordained for the Education of their own Children.[1]

IX

THE GRAMMAR SCHOOLS AND
PRIVATE ENTERPRISE

1. Introductory

More than fifty years ago Miss Irene Parker wrote:

> The change from the flourishing, energetic grammar schools
> of the 14th, 15th, and 16th centuries to the decaying lifeless
> ones of the 17th and 18th is so remarkable that it has been
> considered as the chief feature of the period, and the schools
> which make those years really interesting and noteworthy
> have been overlooked.

Miss Parker's signal contribution to a more complete account of
educational facilities and opportunities was to draw attention
to the dissenting academies which sprang up after the Restoration and were the direct outcome of the government's policy to
suppress all that was Puritan in education. These institutions,
which offered a training in preparation for the Ministry, Law
and Medicine, belong properly to the realm of higher education
and students when they entered were normally expected to have
had the equivalent of a grammar school education.[1] The purpose
of this present study has been deliberately and expressly to con-
centrate on the grammar schools, and more particularly in the
later Stuart period. But in the same period there were private
schools and institutions offering instruction at the secondary
level. These, too, are worthy of note and, as actual or potential
rivals of the grammar schools, they certainly cannot be overlooked.

While acknowledging that the dissenting academies were
'progressive institutions', Dr. Hans has challenged Miss Parker's
contention that without them the history of education from
1660 to 1800 'would indeed be a dull and barren record'.[2] The
purpose of Dr. Hans's research was to show that the eighteenth

century was 'a period of as brilliant schemes and philosophic
works as the seventeenth century' and 'also a period of actual
realisation of modern education'. In the course of his study he
points to 'schools and institutions which were free from religious
control and which formed the main current of modern education
in the eighteenth century'.

As a practicable means of obtaining statistical evidence Dr.
Hans chose to investigate the secondary and higher education of
3,500 men, born between 1685 and 1785, who won for themselves
a place in the *Dictionary of National Biography*. This method which,
as he says, focuses attention on 'the intellectual élite' and 'accen-
tuates the position of the privileged groups' was adopted since
'to undertake a statistical investigation of the educational conditions of the whole population of England is a tremendous task
which is hardly possible for one man to achieve' and since 'the
data are insufficient, especially in the field of secondary education'. Dr. Hans's classification of 3,000 of his selected men
according to their national and social origins produces an
English and Welsh group of 2,313 men including 713 sons of the
nobility and gentry, 750 sons of professional men, 361 sons of
merchants and traders and 308 sons of farmers, craftsmen and
workers.

Of the sons of noblemen and gentlemen, 239 were educated
at home by private tutors. Sixty-two sons of merchants were also
among those who enjoyed the privilege of private tuition in their
own homes. For 191 sons of professional men, including 133 sons
of clergymen, home education meant, in the majority of cases,
that they were taught by their fathers. At the lower end of the
social scale 87 sons of farmers, craftsmen and workers, who
achieved eminence without the advantage of formal school
education, were 'almost invariably . . . men of outstanding
natural ability who educated themselves, sometimes in the most
adverse circumstances'. The large group of 597 men, who did
not attend schools of secondary level, is completed by fourteen
sons of military and naval officers and civil servants, and four
men of unknown origin.

According to Dr. Hans, 'the more discerning parents of the
titled aristocracy and of the gentry' chose to have their boys
educated by private tutors. Other families in this social group,

for the most part, sent their sons to Eton and Westminster. These two schools, together with Winchester, St. Paul's, Shrewsbury, Merchant Taylors', Rugby, Harrow and Charterhouse, were patronized by the aristocracy and the wealthy in the eighteenth century.[1] It is not surprising, therefore, that the largest group, 697 selected men, came from these nine schools. The other grammar schools 'could hardly be called nurseries of the élite' for 170 of these schools are represented in the survey by only 530 old boys. Private schools contributed 283, and dissenting academies 206 of the selected men.

This part of Dr. Hans's thesis is largely concerned with a segment of the population for which higher education at a university, dissenting academy or catholic college was 'the high road to eminence'.[2] It shows that home and private tutors and private schools played an important part in the education of 'the intellectual élite'. But, as we shall presently see, private tutors in the homes of the nobility and gentry, private classical schools, private teachers for mathematics and modern languages, vocational schools were all familiar, even essential parts of the educational system in the seventeenth century. The distinctive feature in secondary education in the eighteenth century was the so-called academies which, although they might include the classics in their schemes of education, paid particular attention to modern subjects and provided vocational training for those who wanted it. The general course of study in these institutions included English, arithmetic, geography, history, French and drawing, to which pupils might sometimes add painting, music, riding and fencing. The academies prepared students for the universities, for the Army, Navy or Mercantile Marine, for commerce and for professions which called for technical ability. Their origin may be traced to the fashionable establishments which were set up in the seventeenth century to meet the vocational needs of young noblemen and gentlemen. The element of newness in the eighteenth century academies was, therefore, not the broad curriculum but the social standing of the pupils for, as Dr. Hans wrote, most of them 'catered for the lower middle class (teachers, artists, merchants, farmers) and craftsmen. The fees were moderate and poor students with proved ability were trained gratis'.

The pattern which emerges from Dr. Hans's investigation of selected men shows that the educational tendencies of the seventeenth century continued in the eighteenth century. Valuable as this evidence is, it is not, and does not purport to be 'a true picture of the general distribution of educated men in the eighteenth century'.[1] Since the grammar schools were losing their hold and educating a decreasing percentage of boys, what, in fact, were parents doing with their sons? What other possibilities were there for the training of boys whose parents chose not to send their sons to the endowed schools? Was there a perceptible or measurable increase in the number of private teachers and private schools in the eighteenth century? And, if so, does this justify the generalization that the proportion of boys receiving secondary education surpassed or, at any rate, did not fall below the level for the seventeenth century? These are the questions which need to be asked of the eighteenth century since they are obviously and closely linked with the effect of private enterprise upon the grammar schools and the extent to which parents, who did not favour the grammar schools, made use of private teachers and establishments. To these problems we must address ourselves even if, in the outcome, we are unable to resolve them. Dr. Hans was not directly concerned with the questions which have been posed. Nevertheless to attempt to answer them means inevitably to draw upon the facts and figures which he was at pains to supply by searching out and enumerating private teachers and institutions. But first we must turn to survey the field of private teaching in the later Stuart period in order to ascertain what were the opportunities for secondary education outside the grammar schools.

2. Private Education

Not all those who were qualified by rank and wealth to provide private tutors for their children subscribed to the view that this method of education was necessarily the best. Robert Boyle (1627–1691) wrote of himself that when he was eight years of age he was sent to Eton by his father, Richard Boyle, the first earl of Cork, 'ambitious to improve his early studiousness, and considering that great men's children breeding up at home tempts them to nicety, to pride, and idleness, and contributes much more to give them a good opinion of themselves, than to make them deserve it'.

The earl had intrusted his son's earlier education to a Frenchman and to a chaplain who had taught the boy 'to write a fair hand, and to speak French and Latin'.[1] The danger of allowing children to associate with inferiors was a matter of concern to Lady Harley and a strong reason for sending them away to school. In a letter of 19 January 1670–71 she wrote to Sir Edward Harley, 'My judgment is not for the boys being kept at home, for it is not possible to keep them from associating with servants and getting a strange clownish speech and behaviour, which our boys have already, and the longer they live at home the worse it will be.'[2]

The great Dr. Richard Busby who reigned over Westminster School from 1638 to 1695 sought, with a large measure of success, to persuade noble families to send their sons to him. To Busby came the children of families like the Howards, Digbys, Sackvilles and Cavendishes who were accustomed to entertain private tutors in their households for the education of their children. In 1660 William Russell, earl of Bedford, sent to Westminster his two younger sons when they were eight and nine years old. This was in the nature of an experiment since their two elder brothers had been prepared for the university by the earl's chaplain, the Reverend John Thornton.[3]

Nevertheless, although many aristocratic families patronized Eton, Winchester and Westminster, the majority considered that the training offered by these schools was unsuitable and unnecessary for their sons, and more especially for the eldest son who would inherit the title and estates. Private tuition at home followed by a period of residence at one of the universities and Inns of Court and completed by travel abroad was an educational programme favoured by the aristocracy and squirearchy at the end of the seventeenth century. John Locke, who tested every subject by its practical value in later life, was of the opinion that a gentleman might dispense with a large part of school learning 'without any great disparagement to himself, or prejudice to his affairs' and that gentlemen who sent their sons to school were hazarding their 'Innocence and Virtue for a little Greek and Latin'. Accordingly he advocated private tuition in the confidence that 'he who is able to be at the Charge of a Tutor at

Home, may there give his Son a more genteel Carriage, more manly Thoughts, and a Sense of what is worthy and becoming, with a greater Proficiency in Learning into the Bargain, and ripen him up sooner into a Man, than any at School can do'. It is hardly likely, however, that families were able to find and employ the paragon of breeding and learning who was Locke's ideal tutor or, indeed, that they were prepared to follow his advice to 'spare no Care nor Cost to get such an one'.[1]

The post of tutor was obviously one of importance and, as Miss G. Scott Thomson wrote, 'there must have been many tutors whose influence counted infinitely more in moulding the character of their pupils than did that of the father and mother'.[2] William Higford in 1660 mentioned three estimable men who had been tutors in his family.

> Sir John Higford, who was an eminent man in his country, had for his tutor the famous Bishop Jewel; my father, Dr. Cole, an excellent governor; myself, Dr. Sebastian Benefield, native of Presbury, a very learned man: all three of Corpus Christi College, Oxon.[3]

Ideally the tutor and parents worked harmoniously together to train the children, as in the household of William Russell, the fifth earl and later the first duke of Bedford, at Woburn Abbey in Bedfordshire. For his family of six boys and three girls, William Russell engaged as tutor the Reverend John Thornton, already mentioned, soon after that gentleman had taken his degree at Trinity College, Cambridge in 1646. Thornton who 'lived and died a Nonconformist' was paid thirty pounds a year for acting as tutor to the children and chaplain to the earl. He also took upon himself the offices of librarian, secretary, almoner and medical adviser.[4] The interest and care which some parents took in the education of their children is apparent in the account which Mrs. Lucy Hutchinson gives of her husband, Colonel John Hutchinson, during the time of the Commonwealth:

> As he had great delight, so he had great judgment, in music, and advanced his children's practice more than their tutors: he also was a great supervisor of their learning, and indeed himself a tutor to them all, besides all those tutors which he

liberally entertained in his house for them. He spared not any cost for the education of both his sons and daughters in languages, sciences, music, dancing, and all other qualities befitting their father's house.[1]

Happy were the men who found employment in such pleasing circumstances and whose qualifications and endeavours were recognized and appreciated by their patrons. All too often tutors must have found themselves exasperated and frustrated by the interference of fussy parents and accused 'one time of too much severity, another of neglect, and another time for giving too hard tasks'.[2] Moreover their treatment and remuneration were not such as to invite properly qualified men to accept tutorships. Indeed in many households the position of the tutor had in no way improved since in 1619 Thomas Morrice had called attention to their low status, which was that of 'an inferior subject', and to their incompetent allowance.[3] One chaplain described himself as 'the highest servant in the house, either out of respect to my cloth, or because I lie in the uppermost garret'. He, and others like him, was allowed to dine at his master's table but expected to retire before the sweet course was served.[4] In the *Guardian* of 29 June 1713 Richard Steele drew attention to the position and pay of many of these men. 'As the case now stands,' he wrote, 'those of the first quality pay their tutors but little above half so much as they do their footmen.' The scant respect for education was shown, said Steele by the 'monstrous' situation in which 'men of the best estates and families, are more solicitous about the tutelage of a favourite dog or horse, than of their heirs male'.[5] It was a cause of wonderment to Bishop Burnet that parents who were to bequeath vast estates to their children and who spent lavishly on other things were 'so frugal and narrow' in the matter of their children's education.[6]

In the circumstances it is not surprising that tutors were often men of poor quality and that the advantages of individual attention were not apparent in every case. In 1634 Henry Peacham criticized the inefficiency of the majority of tutors. 'For one discreet and able Teacher,' he wrote, 'you shall find twenty ignorant and careless; who . . . where they make one Scholler, marre ten.'[7] Nearly a century later Daniel Defoe referred to them as 'those murtherers of a child's moralls, call'd tutors' and indicated that they were lacking in more than learning. 'That taking tutors to teach young gentlemen is not onely the ruine of their heads, but of their moralls also.'[1] Sir John Reresby (1634–1689) received his instruction up to the age of fifteen years from a tutor who lived in the house. Then Sir John's mother moved to London and both he and his brother Edmond were sent to school in Whitefriars, 'where', wrote Sir John, 'I soon found the disadvantage of learning at home, many boys much younger than myself being much better scholars'.[2]

In the category of educational establishments for the privileged minority must be placed the academies of the sixteenth and seventeenth centuries. The projects for academies in England after the style of those which already existed in France were an effort to furnish at home for young nobles and gentlemen that training which they usually sought abroad 'where it proved costly to their souls many times as much as to their bodies'.[3] An early attempt to erect an academy was the proposal of Sir Humphrey Gilbert about 1570. In this suggested institution, which was to be called Queen Elizabeth's Academy and which was intended for the Queen's Wards and other young nobles and gentlemen, provision was to be made for instruction in Latin, Greek, Hebrew, logic, rhetoric, moral philosophy, natural philosophy, physic, civil and common law, divinity, French, Italian, Spanish and High Dutch, methods of defence, dancing, vaulting, music, heraldry and riding. In the seventeenth century a scheme for an academy, drawn up by Edmund Boulton in 1620, was sponsored by George Villiers, first duke of Buckingham, who proposed in the House of Lords that 'some fit and good Course might be taken for Erection and Maintenance of an Academy, for the breeding and bringing up of the Nobility and Gentry of this Kingdom, in their young and tender Age, and for a free and voluntary Contribution, from Persons of Honour and Quality, for that Purpose'.[4]

This proposal was cut short by the death in 1625 of the king, James I, and by the unsettled conditions at the beginning of the new reign. However, in 1635, Sir Francis Kynaston obtained a licence to set up an academy under the name of the Museum Minervae in his house in Bedford Square, Covent Garden.

Professors were appointed for philosophy and physic, music, astronomy, geometry, and languages, and they were empowered to elect also professors for horsemanship, dancing, painting, engraving, etc. This scheme probably did not survive its author who died in 1642. Another attempt was made in 1648 by Sir Balthazar Gerbier but this academy, which was apparently on the same lines as that of Kynaston's Museum Minervae, was shortlived. Of Sir Balthazar Gerbier, a painter, architect, courtier and 'a man of projects', Professor Foster Watson wrote that

> the interest of his proposed Bethnal Green Academy lies in the fact, that to him as a financial speculator, an educational institution on a large scale for the sons of nobles and gentlemen seemed a promising commercial undertaking. It is a good indication of the strong desire for the courtly subjects of education and the difficulty of adequate supply for the demand.[1]

These schemes had been transitory, and in England of the Restoration period the supply of fashionable academies was not sufficient to meet the demand of the nobility and gentry. Some academies indeed there were like that of Monsieur Henry de Foubert in London which seems to have met with a large measure of success and where instruction was given chiefly in the courtly exercises. This establishment was chosen by Sir Edward Harley for the further education of his son Robert when he left Mr. Birch's school at Shilton in 1680. On 6 July Sir Edward Harley broached the subject in a letter to Lady Harley.[2] He wrote that

> Monsieur Foubert, who for his religion was driven out of France, has set up an Academy near the Haymarket for riding, fencing, dancing, handling arms, and mathematics. He is greatly commended and has divers persons of quality. I was with him and like him very well so that if you dislike not I would have Robin spend some time there.

The success with which Monsieur Foubert met may be gauged from a letter which he wrote to Robert Harley on 29 November 1681 when he asked him to inform them if he intended to return to the academy since they were so full that there were no rooms

o

to spare.[1] Foubert's effort 'to lessen the vast expense the nation is yearely at, by sending their Children into France, to be taught these militarie Exercises' was supported by the encouragement and recommendation of the fellows of the Royal Society.[2]

Other academies offered a wider curriculum which included modern languages and the usual exercises. One such academy flourished about 1670 at Tottenham High Cross in Middlesex and seems to have belonged to Mr. A. Bret. In his prospectus Bret says that

> so many of these things shall be performed as can be expected from a School newly Erected for this purpose. Namely, First, The Grammar for the English, Latine, Greek and Hebrew, shall be taught: Secondly, There shall be at present, an apartment for French, and hereafter for Italian and Spanish: Thirdly, Provision is made of Maps and Globs, with Instruments and Books for Astronomy, Geography and Geometry: Fourthly, There is a Master for Writing and Arithmetick: Fifthly, Masters are also provided for teaching Musick, Dancing, Singing, Painting, Fencing and Military Discipline: Sixthly, Repositories for Visibles shall be immediately provided, out of which may be produced, Herbs, Drugs, Seeds, Mineral Juices, Metals, precious Stones, Birds, Beasts, and Fishes, that cannot be produced in Specie, shall be shewed in their Pictures: Seventhly, Comenius his Interludes, shall be Acted at least four times a Year: – Riding the Managed Horse, is a business of that Charge, that it cannot be Attempted till there be such a number of Gentlemen upon the Place as will bear the charge of it. Ordinary Persons shall be entertained at 20l. per annum, or under, to learn what they please; Gentlemen at 25l. per annum; and persons of greater Quality at 30l.

To this school Arthur, earl of Anglesey, then Lord Privy Seal, sent his grandsons, Lord Dacey and Sir James Pore. Another academy of the same sort was that of a certain Mr. Banister in Chancery Lane near the Pump. The subjects of study included Latin and Greek grammar, rhetoric, astronomy, geography, geometry, arithmetic, writing, painting, French, singing, music, dancing, wrestling, fencing, riding the managed horse. According to the information given in the advertisement at the end of Mr. Bret's pamphlet,

> any Person that desire it, may be Accommodated in Mr. Banister's House with Diet and Lodging at reasonable Rates, and may learn all, or as many of these things as they please; or they may come thither at set times and be Instructed in the things before mentioned.[1]

An academy which evidently had an excellent reputation was run by Mr. Meure from about 1690 until about 1705. On 18 December 1704 Robert Pitt wrote to his father, Thomas Pitt, governor of Madras:

> My two brothers are at Mr. Meure's Academy, near Soho Square, esteemed the best in England. They learn Latin, French, and accounts, fencing, dancing, and drawing. I think of settling them in Holland for their better education next summer; and, should my wife's father-in-law, Lieutenant-General Stewart, accompany the Duke of Marlborough, of placing them under his care, to see a campaign.[2]

According to John Locke gentlemen sent only 'their younger Sons, intended for Trades' to the grammar schools. Even this measure of support surprised him since these schools seldom if ever prepared their scholars for 'Trade and Commerce, and the Business of the World'.[3] In fact there had arisen a class of specialist teachers to meet the demand of those who had to earn their living in commercial employments. These were the so-called writing masters, who taught arithmetic, merchants' accounts and penmanship. To one of these men Sir Dudley North was sent from Bury St. Edmunds Grammar School when his parents' intention to place him as a merchant was encouraged by his 'backwardness at school and a sorry account that the master gave of his scholarship'. Sir Dudley's own inclinations were towards the life of a merchant for 'the young man himself had a strange bent to traffic and, while he was at school, drove a subtle trade among the boys by buying and selling'. And so since 'it was considered that he had learning enough for a merchant but not phlegm enough for any sedentary profession', he was removed from the grammar school and, according to the scheme for making a merchant of him, 'the next step was the being placed in London at a writing-school, to learn good hands and accounts'. Here it was necessary for him to learn also self-discipline for 'the writing-school was a place of entire liberty: he might come and go as he would: he might learn if he pleased; and as freely let it alone'. Fortunately, however, Sir Dudley 'minded his business at times well enough, and acquired amply what he came there for, which was fair writing and accounts'.[1] A private teacher whose main subject was writing but who also taught arithmetic was James Hodder whose school was in Lothbury Garden.[2] In 1661 Hodder published his book entitled *Hodder's Arithmetick: Or That necessary Art made most easie. Being explained in a way familiar to the capacity of any that desire to learn it in a little time.* In his preface to the reader the author says that he had 'for sundry years kept a Writing-School in this City, and thereby gained some experience in that commendable Art'. 'And now,' Hodder writes, 'for the better compleating Youth as to Clerk-ship, and Trades, I am induced to publish this small Treatise of Arithmetic.' In 1671 was published *Hodder's Decimal Arithmetick: Or, A plain and more Methodical way of Teaching the said Art, Then hath hitherto been publish'd. By James Hodder, late Writing-Master in Lothbury, London, now Keeper of a Boarding-School in Bromely by Bow.* Another book which its author described as 'peculiarly fitted for merchants and tradesmen, made useful for all men, familiar to the meanest capacity; and for the public good laid down in a school method' was the work of Noah Bridges. His book was published in 1653 with the title *Vulgar Arithmetique.* Its publication had been helped by the Council of State which, on 18 June 1653, granted 'the petition of Noah Bridges for license to print, bind, publish, and dispose of a treatise by him set forth concerning arithmetic, provided the book be of his own making'.[3] Bridges was a teacher of arithmetic during the Commonwealth period and kept a school in his house at Putney. From his advertisement it is clear that Bridges's school cannot be adequately described as a writing school since there was taught 'the Greek and Latin Tongues; also Arts and Sciences Mathematicall, viz. Arithmetique, fair Writing, Merchants' Accounts, Geometry, Trigonometrie, Algebra, etc.'[4]

In addition to book-keeping, accounting and writing the

qualifications necessary to the youth who aspired to be a successful merchant included some knowledge of foreign languages and
of foreign weights and measures. The need was supplied by the
teachers of foreign languages, the number of whom had been
steadily increasing from about the middle of the sixteenth century.
A French traveller in England at the end of the seventeenth
century remarked on the large number of schools which had been
established by Huguenots who had fled from persecution especially after the revocation of the Edict of Nantes in 1685.[1] Miss
Kathleen Lambley has drawn attention to a successful French
School in Nottingham after the Restoration which was kept by
Jacob Villiers, an Englishman who had learned the language
when he travelled and taught in France.[2] In 1680 he published
in London *Vocabularium Analogicum, or the English-Man speaking
French, and the French-Man speaking English: Plainly shewing the
Nearness or Affinity betwixt the English, French and Latin.* The book
was written, said Villiers in his address to the reader, 'to gratify
my Friends, as also to oblige those Gentlemen and young Ladies,
who are my Scholars, and to encourage all such who shall have
a mind so to be'. The greatest demand was for instruction in
French, but text-books and teachers were available for those who
wished to acquire some proficiency in Italian, Spanish and
German.[3]

Another group of specialists was formed by the teachers of
mathematics who had sprung up in response to the steadily
increasing demand for instruction which would furnish the
technical skill to deal with problems of surveying, horology,
navigation, gunnery and fortification. In 1655 Sir Ralph Verney
considered sending his son to Mr. John Kersey of Charles Street,
Covent Garden. In reply to Sir Ralph's letter of inquiry Kersey
wished to make clear that the training which he gave was not
meant to be a preparation for commerce and that if Jack was
intended for a merchant or some other trade then the best course
would be 'to place him at Board with such as make that businesse
only their profession'. On the other hand, said Kersey, 'if his
designe is only to learne some thing in the Mathematiques, I
shall doe him what service I am able, if he can be conveniently
lodged and dyeted neere my house'. The fee for this instruction in
mathematics was twelve shillings a week.[4]

Not all teachers of mathematics would have claimed, as Kersey did, that their work had no reference to trade and commerce. The instruments which some of them made and the techniques of navigation which some of them taught were obviously of importance to the merchants as well as to their shipmasters. It was not necessary for one man to be expert in every aspect of the merchant's profession. But he would need to be sufficiently informed to protect himself against grievous errors and fraudulent practices. Though he might not require skill in navigation yet he might wish to be abreast of modern developments in aids to navigation and to be able to assure himself of the efficiency of the men who had command of his ships. Such knowledge belonged to the realm of mathematics which, as Dr. John Newton noted with regret in 1677, was entered neither by the writing master nor by the grammar schoolmaster. Of these mathematicians and their teaching Professor E. G. R. Taylor wrote:

> While a few of them were men with a university background, the majority were not. They were almanack-makers, astrologers, retired seamen, surveyors, gunners, gaugers – in fact they were themselves mathematical practitioners who simply handed on their art. But, as might be expected, they all worked in close association with the instrument-makers, and as the handling of instruments was the very badge of this new profession, it was quite usual for a teacher to design a novel one of his own, and to impart its 'description and use' only to those who would come to him for instruction. Textbooks (and many published their own) were compiled from teaching notes, or from material lifted bodily from earlier works, and it is perhaps little wonder that with such meagre help progress was so slow.[1]

The little information on this subject in the Wase correspondence indicates that the competition which vexed and embarrassed the grammar schoolmasters came from the private classical schools. William Walker, the master of Grantham Grammar School, who wrote on 11 November 1673, found difficulty in obtaining information about free schools in Lincolnshire.

Something I hear from Lincoln, but the Master there being angrie with the Bishop for setting up a private School in the Town, and with me for speaking some good words of the Bishop (as he supposes) for that, he gave me rather an Invective than a Narrative.[1]

On 27 April 1675 Samuel Frankland of Coventry reported that in the county of Warwickshire all the free schools were 'as to the number of scholars lower then formerly' because many school-masters had begun 'to teach private Schooles to ye great detri-ment' of the public schools. 'Unlesse Authority take some effectuall course for relieveing us from these encroachments,' he wrote, 'we shall still be brought lower, though we lay out our time & strength wholly in this publique work.'[2]

A private school which was attractive to the local gentry flourished at Bicester in Oxfordshire for almost a century after it was opened in 1669 by Samuel Blackwell who became vicar of the parish in 1670. Edmund Verney of East Claydon chose to send his two sons to Bicester rather than to Eton, Winchester or Westminster although the serious illness of the schoolmaster in March 1679 caused him to withdraw the boys for a short time and to reconsider his decision about their education. The situa-tion was aggravated by the fact that there was no usher and Verney therefore brought his sons home. On 3 April the two boys returned to school at Bicester. A new usher had arrived but con-ditions were far from satisfactory. 'Mr. Blackwell mends but very slowly, and the Usher Talks of going away very suddenly,' wrote Edmund Verney on 10 April.

The Truth of it is Mrs. Blackwell is so Greedy and Covetous, That she will not allow any Usher Reasonable Hyre, neither are my Children so carefully ordered as at first; therefore I Take that Schoole to Be growne worse, and Have thoughts to Remove them ere it Be Long to Eaton, Winchester or Westminster. Winchester I know, and Like very well, but only it is a Place at a greate Distance from mee: I do Intend so soone as fine weather comes in, to Go to Eaton my selfe, that I may satisfy myselfe in ye Place.

Evidently the good reputation of Bicester School was quickly restored since the Verney boys remained there until 1681.[1] The school was fortunate to have as its usher White Kennet who after his ordination in 1684 probably also acted as Blackwell's curate. Kennet, who left in 1685 to become vicar of Ambrosden and in 1718 bishop of Peterborough, showed his continuing interest in the school by his friendship for the schoolmaster and gifts of books to the library.[2] Blackwell left in 1691 on his appointment to the living of Brampton in Northamptonshire and the school continued under the next vicar, Thomas Shewry, who compiled the catalogue of the school library which contained one hundred and fifty books presented for the most part by supporters in the neighbourhood and fellows of Oxford colleges. Evidently the school curriculum extended beyond the study of the ancient languages for the library included not only a majority of Latin authors with works in Greek and three volumes of Hebrew but also editions of English books mostly of history and geography.[3]

An interesting school which prospered in the period following the Restoration was kept by Samuel Birch at Shilton, near Burford, in Oxfordshire. This private school 'was remarkable for producing, at the same Time, a Lord High Treasurer, a Lord High Chancellor, a Lord Chief Justice of the Common Pleas; and ten Members of the House of Commons, who were all Cotemporaries, as well at School, as in Parliament'.[4] The future Lord High Treasurer was Robert Harley, afterwards earl of Oxford, who was a pupil at Mr. Birch's school from 1671 to 1680. He had as his schoolfellows the future Lord High Chancellor, Simon Harcourt, afterwards first Viscount Harcourt, and the future Lord Chief Justice, Thomas Trevor, afterwards Lord Trevor. The earl of Clare was informed in 1679 that Mr. Birch's school was 'very full' and that 'no chamber was to be had without three beds in a room'.[5]

Apart from his success as the master of a private school Samuel Birch is noteworthy as an unlicensed nonconformist schoolmaster, a former chaplain of Corpus Christi College, Oxford, who began his schoolmastering in 1664 at a house in Shilton which he rented after he was ejected from the living of Bampton in Oxfordshire. His career as a schoolmaster almost ended soon after it began, for in 1665 the Bishop's Court ordered his dismissal because of his failure to receive communion at church and because he did not have a teacher's licence. The local gentry were not prepared to lose the services of such an excellent schoolmaster, refused to allow him to follow his own inclination to return to a small estate which he owned near Manchester, and set him up in a large house where he could pursue the calling for which he was so admirably suited. When on one occasion he was imprisoned his supporters gave bail for him and obtained his release 'the very next day'. It was not, however, until the last years of his life that he was allowed to work in peace and without continual interference from the civil and ecclesiastical authorities.[1]

Another successful private schoolmaster was Samuel Ogden who had been ejected from the living of Mackworth in Derbyshire in 1662 because of his nonconformity. Four of his pupils were admitted from his school in Derby to St. John's College, Cambridge, the first on 18 May 1681 and the last on 14 November 1686.[2] Among Ogden's pupils was Thomas Parker who proceeded to Trinity College, Cambridge in October 1685 and became Chief Justice, Lord Chancellor and earl of Macclesfield.[3] This private school was too successful for the liking of Thomas Cantrell, the master of Derby Grammar School, who in 1695 brought an action which was heard in the Court of Arches. Ogden's schoolmastership was declared to be contrary to the canons of the Church and detrimental to the welfare of the free school and he was compelled to close his school. His teaching career was not yet ended, however, for Sir John Gell, as patron of the free school at Wirksworth, offered him the mastership which he accepted and held until his death in 1697.[4]

It has been shown that some grammar schoolmasters who were forced to resign their posts at the Restoration because of their religious or political allegiance opened their own schools.[5] The dissenting schoolmasters were joined by those dissenting ministers who solved the problem of making a living by offering their services as teachers in return for voluntary subscriptions from their supporters and sympathisers. If Birch and Ogden were typical of these men the Restoration reaction may be said to have benefited the cause of education by driving them into the ranks

of the schoolmasters. The numerical strength of the dissenting
teachers is implied, as Professor Foster Watson has reminded us,
by the fact that ten years after the Act of Uniformity in 1662,
Archbishop Sheldon directed his suffragans to take all possible
measures to restrain those who were teaching without licences
within their jurisdiction.[1]

In these circumstances it is not surprising that some of the
replies to Wase's questions about free schools express resentment
at the encroachment of private schoolmasters and anxiety about
the damaging effect that private schools were having upon the
public grammar schools. Richard Grimbaldston of Huyton
Grammar School in Lancashire evidently felt deeply about 'one
Thomas Hickcock a Quaker' who 'with his deluding tongue' had
drawn away many of his scholars. In July 1675 Grimbaldston
wrote:

> I could wish he were dealt with according to the Lawe; And
> that the parents of those children, who send them to him
> may be debarred their Freedom; so that when they send
> them to the Free school again, they may pay 2s the quarter;
> for I hear he will only teach 10 boyes; & have 5s per
> Quarter; I hope if his Lordship the Reverend father In God,
> our Bishop of the Diocese, be acquainted herewith he will
> see that Course be speedily taken herein.[2]

Admittedly private schoolmasters were a cause of embarrassment to the masters of grammar schools. The effect of private
enterprise upon the endowed schools should not, however, be
exaggerated.

3. The Extent and Effect of Competition

It is generally agreed that the first sixty years of the seventeenth
century was a period when the endowed grammar schools
flourished. It has been pointed out elsewhere that boys went
up to four Cambridge colleges, St. John's, Gonville and Caius,
Christ's and Peterhouse, from eight hundred and fifty-seven
grammar schools.[3] The statistical evidence for private education,
as accurately as this can be ascertained from the same registers,
is that three hundred and one private schools and sixty-three
private tutors sent boys to the four colleges between 1600 and

1660.* The implication of this evidence is, therefore, not that the public grammar schools suffered from the competition of private teachers, but that private enterprise played an indispensable part in the expansion of secondary education in the first half of the seventeenth century.

It is evident that qualitatively as well as quantitatively private schoolmasters made their presence felt in the early Stuart period. In his book, published in 1660, Charles Hoole testified to the progressive spirit of some of these men who showed by their example that it was 'a matter very feaseable to raise many of our Grammar-Schooles to a far higher pitch of learning, then is ordinarily yet attained to in England'.[1]

Among schoolmasters sending boys to the university in the first half of the seventeenth century were Hezekiah Woodward (1590–1675), a man 'esteemed eminent in his profession', who had opened a private school in London at Aldermanbury about 1617.[2] Another was Thomas Farnaby (1575?–1649), described by Anthony Wood as 'the most noted school-master' and 'the chief grammarian, rhetorician, poet, Latinist, and Grecian of his time', who taught in the grammar school at Martock in Somerset and then moved to London where he set up a private school in Goldsmith's Rents, behind Redcross Street, Cripplegate, and taught 'young noblemen and other generous youths, who at one time made up the number of 300 or more'. From London Farnaby went to Sevenoaks in Kent about 1636 'and his school was so much frequented, that more churchmen and statesmen issued thence, than from any school taught by one man in England'.[3] Mr. Lawrence Stone has drawn attention to the facts that the admission registers of St. John's College, Cambridge, Gonville and Caius College, and Christ's College, for the years between 1626 and 1637, contain the names of thirty-eight boys who came from the private school kept by

---

* The information in the registers for the period 1600 to 1800 about boys who were educated privately is not complete. Moreover, it is not always easy to distinguish private schools from private tutors or to know if boys, who are simply stated to have been educated at home, were prepared for the university by their fathers or by private tutors. The figures from the registers, here and elsewhere in this chapter, are only of schools and tutors sending boys directly to the university, and take no account of schooling and tuition before the final stage of secondary education.

Matthew Stoneham at Norwich while only eleven boys came from the local grammar school.[1]

During the Commonwealth period the number of private schools increased, set up by clergy and fellows driven from their livings and colleges because they did not seek to disguise their allegiance to the king. Among the sequestrated clergy was Charles Hoole (1615–1667), 'a master of his art, acknowledged by his contemporaries and rivals',[2] who taught in a private school between Goldsmith's Alley in Redcross Street and Maidenhead Court in Aldersgate Street, before moving about 1651 to another private school in Tokenhouse Gardens in Lothbury.[3] Another clergyman who turned to teaching was Richard Lloyd (1595–1659) who had a private school in Oxford in the parish of St. Peter-le-Bailey.[4] He was the author of *The Schoole-Masters Auxiliaries to remove the Barbarians Siege from Athens, advanced under two guides*, which was published in London in 1653–54 and which has been described as 'probably the best theory of teaching reading and spelling in the period'.[5]

At the Restoration a new factor in the situation was the intrusion of unlicensed nonconformists into schoolmastering. Of course the grammar schools suffered as a result of the loss of boys whose parents were offended by the anglican monopoly of the schools and who were not afraid to risk loss of reputation and even persecution by their support of the dissenting schoolmasters. This is evident, as has been shown, in the complaints made against the dissenters by the recognized schoolmasters and in the legislation of 1662 and 1665 to restrain them.[6] But while it is one thing to recognize the fact of their invasion, it is quite another to measure the extent of their encroachment upon the preserve of the privileged and protected grammar schoolmasters. Mr. A. G. Matthews has calculated that at some time after their ejection a hundred and one dissenting ministers turned to teaching as a means of livelihood and that nine of these kept academies which offered training in preparation for the Ministry.[7] To this number must be added the dissenting schoolmasters who were dismissed by the grammar school authorities and who continued to teach privately. Perhaps, then, the total number of unlicensed nonconformist teachers was about a hundred and fifty.[8]

It must be remembered, however, that most of the dissenting

schools were small and that there must have been many non-conformists who were unwilling to be associated with unlicensed schoolmasters and who preferred to send their sons to the recognized grammar schools. As we have seen, dissenting schoolmasters who found supporters were always liable to interference by the authorities and might at any moment be compelled to break up their schools and to move to another area. Ralph Button, who was Professor of Geometry at Gresham College from 1643 to 1648 and who in the latter year became Proctor of the University of Oxford, Canon of Christ Church and University Orator, was removed from his offices at the Restoration and subsequently suffered imprisonment for six months because he taught the sons of two knights in his house at Brainford in Essex.[1] At Evesham in Worcestershire an unlicensed teacher was forbidden by the borough council to open a private school. In a resolution of 15 September 1669 it was ordered that William Westmacott should not be allowed to reside in the borough since he did not hold the doctrines of the church, his views would spread beyond his private schoolroom and cause discord, and his school would be harmful to the interests of the grammar school.[2]

Turning again to the admission registers of the four Cambridge colleges we find that during the sixty years following the Restoration the number of grammar schools sending boys to them fell, by a hundred and nineteen, to seven hundred and thirty-eight. The number of private schools sending boys to these colleges during the same period fell, by ninety-one, to two hundred and ten. Proportionately the fall in number was greater in the case of private schools than in that of the public grammar schools. Another calculation, based on the admission registers of St. John's College, Cambridge, Gonville and Caius College and Christ's College, is that 'By 1700 the public grammar schools were providing 70% of the education of College entrants from Norfolk, whereas sixty years before the proportion was less than half.'[3]

The decline in the number of boys entering the four Cambridge colleges is in unison with the decline in the number of entrants at the two English universities in the latter half of the seventeenth century. Mr. J. A. Venn's figures show that in the 1630s about a thousand and fifty-five boys went up to Oxford and Cambridge each year and that by the 1690s the number had fallen to about four hundred and ninety-nine.[1] Mr. Lawrence Stone has estimated that in the 1630s, with those who were educated at the Inns of Court, privately at home or at a foreign university, the number of young men receiving higher education was about a thousand two hundred and forty a year and that in the last decade of the seventeenth century the number had fallen to about eight hundred and twenty a year. The latter total includes about a hundred and fifty students who at the end of the century were entering the dissenting academies and between ten and twenty children of wealthy Catholic families who were sent abroad.[2] Anthony Wood's explanation of the decline in the number of entrants at the University of Oxford after the Restoration is that

> Presbyterians and Independents and other fanaticall people did forbeare to send them for feare of orthodox principles. Another party thought an University too low a breeding; entertain'd one at home, who infused principles of Atheisme. Others sent them beyond the seas and they return home factious and propagat faction. Another party (the papists), they send also beyond sea.[3]

The facts and figures which have been quoted show not only a change at the universities of Oxford and Cambridge but also a movement away from higher education as a whole. The decreased number of entrants at the two universities is, to some extent, explained, but is certainly not compensated by the increased number of students receiving private education at home and university education abroad and attending the dissenting academies. It is to be expected that secondary schools preparing boys for entry to the universities were involved in the educational depression. Attention has been drawn in an earlier chapter to signs, after the Restoration, of disinclination for a classical education.[4] The sum of the evidence is, therefore, that a decline from education of the sort leading to the universities rather than the competition of private classical schools was bringing about a deterioration in the public grammar schools.

It is in the eighteenth century, as has been shown, that the downward trend in the number of pupils attending the grammar schools becomes unmistakably clear. The effect of the flight from the grammar schools is clearly shown in the admission registers of the four Cambridge colleges. But so also is the decreased number of private schools contributing boys. During the years from 1720 to 1780 four hundred and six grammar schools and a hundred and thirty private schools sent boys to the four colleges. A comparison of these figures with those for the first sixty years of the seventeenth century shows that the numbers, not only of the grammar schools but also of the private classical schools, fell by more than a half.

Of the men who kept private classical schools in the eighteenth century two hundred and sixty-three have been enumerated by Dr. Hans. His calculation is that during the century there were more than a thousand and that at any one time there were not less than two hundred. But he also remarks the decline in the number of these private schoolmasters in the county of Norfolk from twenty-four in the first quarter to four in the last quarter of the century. The marked reduction in the number of private schools in this county may be attributable, as he suggests, to the movement of population away from an agricultural area. But it is also in line with a general decline in the number of private classical schools. Moreover, it must be asked how true it is to say that there was a movement away from the countryside. Recent research suggests that the enclosure of common land in the eighteenth century resulted in improved methods of farming and increased employment. And, according to Arthur Young, these improvements were particularly impressive in the county of Norfolk.[1] Dr. Hans estimated that the number of private classical schools rose to about three hundred in the middle of the century and dwindled to about a hundred at the end of the century.[2] All in all the evidence supports Mr. Lawrence Stone's contention that in the eighteenth century 'the multitude of little village schools run by the private enterprise of the parson, curate or free-lance schoolmaster slowly died away'.[3]

Resident tutors can hardly be regarded as rivals of the grammar schools at any time. They were the preserve of the nobility and gentry who, if they patronized the grammar schools, tended to choose a few which were socially acceptable. The evidence drawn by Mr. Lawrence Stone from the admission registers of St.

John's College, Cambridge, Gonville and Caius College and Christ's College, to refute the notion that the endowment of grammar schools between 1480 and 1660 brought secondary education within reach of the very poor, shows also that these schools did not normally receive the sons of peers and baronets, and that the custom of educating the sons of noblemen and of the squirearchy at home or at fashionable schools like Westminster and Eton was well established in the 1630s.[1]

To what extent the specialist teachers, the writing masters and the teachers of mathematics and modern languages, drew boys away from the grammar schools it is difficult to say. Mr. Ambrose Heal mentions seventy writing masters in London during the latter half of the seventeenth century.[2] There must have been many more scattered up and down the country. In their establishments boys might be helped 'to keep their English, by reading of a chapter (at least) once a day', taught writing and arithmetic and such preparative 'Arts, as may make them compleately fit to undergoe any ordinary calling'. They were, as Charles Hoole acknowledged, suitable for boys whose parents were prejudiced against Latin or who were unlikely to profit from the instruction given in a grammar school.[3] There is no suggestion in his writing that he looked upon them as the rivals of the grammar schools. Indeed some grammar school authorities, as we have seen, made use of the services of writing masters by inviting them to teach in their schools for a certain period each year or by sending boys to them.[4] It can hardly be doubted, however, that writing masters were beginning to benefit from the falling demand for a classical education which has been noted in the period after the Restoration.

For the eighteenth century Dr. Hans has enumerated twenty-four writing masters in London and sixteen outside London. The list may be supplemented from Heal's biographical notes of English penmen by one hundred and thirty-five writing masters in London and seventy-six in provincial districts. But, as Dr. Hans has stated, the establishments of many of them hardly merited the name of schools for 'the number of boarders was seldom more than five or six boys of various ages, who had to be taught individually' and the masters added to their incomes by giving lessons in the homes of wealthy parents.[5] Among writing masters in the eighteenth century teaching outside London were Moses Gratwick at Dunstable in Bedfordshire, Solomon Cook at Minchinhampton in Gloucestershire, James Heacock at Headley near Epsom in Surrey, John Langton at Stamford in Lincolnshire and Edward Lloyd at Abingdon in Berkshire.[1]

As for the other specialists, the teachers of modern languages and the teachers of mathematics, what they offered in the seventeenth century was clearly regarded as an addition, not an alternative, to the normal curriculum of the grammar schools. The point is illustrated by the failure of Reeve Williams in 1684 to obtain the mastership of the mathematical school in Christ's Hospital because he was not a classical scholar as well as a mathematician,[2] and because the boys on the mathematical side were expected to maintain their proficiency in grammar.[3] For young men at the universities there was no lack of private teachers to remedy deficiencies, if such they were reckoned, in their secondary education. At Oxford in 1700, as Dr. John Wallis observed, it was possible to obtain private instruction in chemistry, physics, anatomy, botany, mathematics, French, Spanish and Italian, as well as in music, dancing, riding and other physical exercises. He wrote: 'I do not know any part of usefull knowledge proper for scholars to learn; but that if any number of persons (gentlemen or others) desire therein to be informed, they may find those in the university who will be ready to instruct them: so that if there be any defect therein, it is for want of learners not of teachers.'[4]

Professor Taylor's long list of mathematical practitioners in Tudor and Stuart times contains the names of forty-five men in London and twenty-six in the provinces who were teaching mathematics between 1660 and 1714. Among teachers of mathematics outside London were John Taylor and Thomas Golding at Norwich, John Kendal at Colchester and John Buchanan at Steeple Bumpstead in Essex, Edward Hatton at Stourbridge and John Dougharty at Burdley in Worcestershire, Abraham Sharp at Liverpool and then for a short time at Plymouth, John Brampton at Sutton St. Mary's in Lincolnshire, John White at Tiverton in Devon, William Leybourne at Southall in Essex and Philip Cole at Chertsey in Surrey. Gilbert Clerke, ejected from his tutorship at Sidney Sussex College, Cambridge in 1655

P

because of his allegiance to the royalist party, taught mathematics at his home near Luffenham in Northamptonshire, and Adam Martindale, ejected from the living of Rostherne in Cheshire, in Cheshire and Lancashire. Some men taught in their own schools and also gave private lessons in the homes of their pupils as did John Wing of Pickworth in Rutland, and John Tipper of Bablake who was ready to visit pupils who lived within ten miles of Coventry.[1]

For the eighteenth century Dr. Hans has recovered the names of fifty-eight men who at one time or another gave private lessons in mathematics. This number includes twenty men who taught outside London and thirteen who began their careers by teaching privately and later took up posts as mathematics masters in private academies. Most of them were self-taught and acquired the knowledge which they imparted from text-books and periodicals. Among private teachers of other subjects in the eighteenth century those who taught modern languages were 'especially numerous', the 'regular supply of French teachers' being considerably increased by the influx of refugees at the time of the French Revolution. Dr. Hans found a few private teachers of geography but no teachers of history. There were also 'many private teachers of music, dancing, drawing and stenography'.

Finally, there were the private academies, which, as we have seen, made a distinctive contribution to secondary education in the eighteenth century by offering a general education as well as specialized training to those whose parents could afford moderate fees. Impressive, too, is the evidence of the rapid increase in the number of these establishments after 1750. For the first half of the century Dr. Hans found information about only eleven academies. Their heyday came in the latter half of the century and especially in the last two decades when there were about two hundred in existence, two-thirds of them in and around London. And yet they disappeared in the early years of the nineteenth century, presumably because they lacked support.

At the conclusion of his study Dr. Hans notes how, in the changed economic conditions at the end of the eighteenth century, opportunities for educational and social advancement were barred to boys of lower social status, the sons of farmers, craftsmen and labourers. The effect of the industrial revolution is evident towards the end of the century, he says, in the dwindling number of students entering the universities and in the sudden halt in the rise of scientists from these groups. Moreover, the migration of population into industrial regions inevitably caused a remarkable fall in the number of country schools run by clergy-men. Such was the sequel to a period during which thousands of boys of humble origin were enabled to enter the universities, the Ministry and the professions, and to climb the social ladder.[1]

Some of this reasoning seems suspect. As we have already seen the grammar schools showed a decline at least fifty years before the Industrial Revolution could have gained enough momentum to bring about such a change and, in any event, this movement never affected anything like the whole country. Moreover, any facile assumptions about how population moved and the character of society changed have been shown to be dangerous, and a comprehensive analysis of the social background of boys entering the universities during the eighteenth century has yet to be undertaken.

It has been shown how, after the Restoration, financial stringency resulted in the increase of fees and restriction in the number of free places at some grammar schools. But there were some who held that, whether it was necessary or not, it was desirable that the schools should close their doors to humble folk who could not pay fees. Such action, they said, would relieve the country of a superfluity of educated youths for whom there were not enough places in the Ministry, the Law and Medicine. We have seen that Christopher Wase ridiculed the suggestion that there were too many scholars for the professions.[2] He pointed out, too, that not all boys brought up in free schools entered the professions and that the lives of tradesmen were immeasurably enriched by their former studies. Nevertheless, he could not escape the fact that it was a cause for complaint that the grammar schools were helping to produce too many learned youths for too few openings.[3]

Moreover, the intellectual atmosphere of the eighteenth century does not seem to have been conducive to learning or to an interest in learning. In the realm of historical scholarship Professor David Douglas has noted the decline in and even distaste for learning after the notable endeavours and achievements of scholars in the seventy years following the Restoration. 'Philosophic generalization begat a contempt for erudition, and the men who had given their lives to the service of exact scholarship were despised as at best the drudges who had collected material for the lofty speculations of men of sensibility.'[1]

Professor Stuart Piggot found 'a parallel decline in antiquarian pursuits' exemplified in the life of William Stukeley (1683–1766).

> With regard to the unfortunate episodes of his later days – the Richard Cirencester forgery, the Oriuna fatuity, the wild guesses about Carausius and the British Kings – we can at least say that he was no worse than his contemporaries. Nothing comes out more strongly from a study of Stukeley's life and work than the changed intellectual temper in England after about 1730 . . . He is all too significantly a child of his age, and his own intellectual history but lives out the melancholy story of that of British learning at large.[2]

Such evidence discourages a ready assumption that the withdrawal of boys from the grammar schools indicates that enlightened parents were eager that their sons should avail themselves of new trends in education. Perhaps part of the explanation of the decline in the grammar schools is that parents, disillusioned by the value of a classical education, were content to allow their sons, once they had attained a basic literacy, to gain the rest of their learning in the school of life.

In sum, this survey of the field of private education has revealed a variety of schools and institutions which existed side by side with the endowed grammar schools and offered opportunities for post-primary learning. To what extent parents made use of these facilities it is impossible to say. Evidence of intellectual torpor in the eighteenth century hardly leads to an expectation that the movement away from public secondary schooling was compensated by a movement towards one or other of the forms of secondary education presented by private enterprise. Furthermore, it does not appear that, with the exception of the remarkable expansion of the private academies for a time after 1750, there was any advance either in the quantity or quality of private education during the eighteenth century. Favoured youths were given the advantage of some preliminary training before entering upon their chosen careers. But private education did nothing to alleviate the lot of boys barred from the grammar schools because their parents could not meet the cost of keeping them there. At the last, the decline in the grammar schools still appears as the significant factor in secondary education after the Restoration. The information obtained from the Cambridge admission registers underlines the notable deterioration in these schools. Evidence from the same source gives no reason to suppose that in the seventeenth century they were unduly inconvenienced by competition from the private classical schools or that in the eighteenth century the function of preparing boys for the universities was largely taken over by private schoolmasters. At the end of the eighteenth century, wrote Dr. Hans, 'the ground for the educational setback of the nineteenth century was prepared'.[1] An important factor in this regression was undoubtedly 'the crystallization of that all too familiar English association of educational opportunity with social status'. But, as Christopher Wase made clear, this restrictive tendency in education was already evident in the post-Restoration period. All in all, then, there does not seem to be anything excessive in writing, as Mr. Lawrence Stone did, of a 'prolonged educational depression which began in the second half of the seventeenth century and lasted for over one hundred years'.[2]

X

POVERTY

It is a fond conceit of many, that have either not attained, or by their own negligence have utterly lost the use of the Latine Tongue, to think it altogether unnecessary for such children to learn it, as are intended for Trades, or to be kept as drudges at home, or employed about husbandry.

So wrote Charles Hoole in his book published in 1660 and entitled *A New Discovery of the old Art of Teaching Schoole, In four small Treatises*, and proceeded to give his reasons why all children, as soon as they could read English well, should be sent to a grammar school. There were few children, Hoole maintained, who would not find even a smattering of Latin of singular use to them in reading English authors 'which abound now a dayes with borrowed words', and in conversing with the sort of men who delighted 'to flant it in Latine'. Moreover, he had 'heard it spoken to the great commendation of some Countries, where care is had for the well education of children, that every Peasant (almost) is able to discourse with a stranger in the Latine tongue'. The same praise might be obtained 'here in England . . . if we did but as they, continue our children at the Latine Schoole, till they be well acquainted with that language, and thereby better fitted for any calling'. Hoole was further concerned with the mischief which resulted from 'the non-improvement of childrens time after they can read English any whit well', which

> throweth open a gap to all loose kinde of behaviour; for being then (as it is too commonly to be seen, especially with the poorer sort) taken from the Schoole, and permitted to run wildeing up and down without any control, they adventure to commit all manner of lewdnesse, and so become a shame and dishonour to their Friends and Countrey.

If these reasons did not prevail or persuade those who were

prejudiced against Latin, then Hoole would have the children
sent to a writing school.

Evidently one of the most enlightened schoolmasters of the
seventeenth century was unimpressed by the contemporary
movement for modernization of curricula. Hoole parts company,
therefore, with men like Samuel Hartlib, Hezekiah Woodward,
John Dury and Sir William Petty who were in favour of saving
time spent in teaching Latin and Greek and introducing science,
modern history and geography and the languages of commerce
into the course of study in schools. But he is in line with writers
during the Commonwealth period in his advocacy of schooling
which continued beyond the rudiments until the pupils were
invited by 'some honest calling' or proceeded to the universities.[1]

In 1641 the greatest educational theorist of the day, the
Moravian, John Amos Comenius, had been in England and
expecting to take part in a reconstruction of the educational
system which would ensure that 'all young people should be
instructed, none neglected'.[2] The moment was unpropitious for
events were moving rapidly towards civil war. Disillusioned,
Comenius left England after a stay of only six months. But the
need and desire for educational reform had been kept very much
alive and had found expression in a remarkable outburst of
writing. Propositions of reform canvassed during the period of
the Long Parliament and Protectorate were concerned with
free and compulsory education for all children, modernization
of curricula, schooling suited to the aspirations and aptitudes of
the pupils and the supply and qualifications of teachers. If the
practical achievements in education had been disappointingly
meagre this was not because statesmen had lacked interest in
the subject but because their attention had been diverted from
it by more immediately pressing business. Hoole's proposal to
extend the benefit of education in and beyond the rudiments to
boys of every social group appears modest indeed, coming as it
did after the educational ferment of the previous twenty years.

At the Restoration schemes of educational reform and expansion were discarded. New schools which had been established
in Wales disappeared with the Puritan authorities who had called
them into being.[3] Even the old-established grammar schools,
which through the distracted times had shown their vitality and

maintained their prestige undiminished, were now suspect in some quarters as breeding grounds of sedition. Far from inculcating obedience and loyalty to established order in Church and State the grammar schools had produced those who rebelled against it, men like Oliver Cromwell who was trained at Huntingdon Grammar School, John Milton from St. Paul's, John Hampden from Thame Grammar School and John Selden from the Prebendal School, Chichester. What clearer proof was needed of the danger to society of too much education than the interest and enthusiasm evinced by rebels and regicides for the extension of educational opportunities?

Eighteen years after the Restoration, as we have seen, such views were still serious enough to rouse Christopher Wase's apprehension about the future of the grammar schools. Even if the schools escaped diminution or suppression, he said, criticism levelled against them, and therefore against the judgement of their founders, was bound to discourage would-be benefactors. How widely extremist and alarmist views about the influence of a classical education were disseminated or how effective they were in reducing the flow of charitable giving to grammar schools it is difficult to say. What is certain is that, though money was still forthcoming for new foundations and additional benefactions to some established schools in the later Stuart period, the era of lavish spending for the endowment of grammar schools was over. Our examination of the effects of inadequate endowments upon schoolmasters and upon the quality of their work, upon fees and free places in the schools, upon the curriculum and clientele, lends strong support to the contention that the weakness of many grammar schools was financial and that lack of money was the root of subsequent troubles. Wase was right to stress the need for new benefactions and augmentations of the masters' wages for already 'what was really plentiful in our forefathers days' had 'become really less then sufficient'.[1]

It may well be that poverty was the most important factor contributing to the decadence of many grammar schools in the eighteenth century. The suggestion has also been made that whereas the great expansion of the schools in Tudor and early Stuart times largely resulted from 'Protestant, and indeed Puritan, piety', the dwindling flow in endowments for new foundations coincided with 'the cooling off of religious enthusiasm'.[1] And yet there is no indication that in the late seventeenth and eighteenth centuries there was any lack of benefactors for all sorts of charitable causes. Professor C. Wilson has pointed out that of the charities still existing in London, Bristol and Norwich, about a third were set up during the fifty years after the Restoration.[2] What is more, the most striking philanthropic venture of the late seventeenth and eighteenth centuries was in the field of learning and actuated by the impulse of religion. It was Puritanism, revealed not in adherence to any theological dogma but as an attitude of mind, which made possible and maintained the movement whereby thousands of schools brought elementary education to tens of thousands of poor children to whom it would otherwise have been denied.[3]

At the beginning of this thesis attention was directed to the lavish outpouring of wealth which made the expansion of grammar schools the great educational achievement of the sixteenth and early seventeenth centuries. By way of conclusion, it is worth while to reflect on the organized movement for education of children of the poor which resulted from the philanthropic effort of the late seventeenth and eighteenth centuries. The charity schools were not intended to be preparatory to any form of higher education. Yet they were not unrelated to the grammar schools and a review of the charity school movement points the destitution of the older foundations.

The charity schools made a religious approach to the problem of pauperism by providing catechetical instruction for boys and girls between the ages of about seven and eleven years. Most of the time was taken up by reading and repetition of the Bible, the Catechism and the Book of Common Prayer. When they could read competently the children might go on to writing, and finally, and more rarely, to arithmetic. Such teaching promised the benefit, recognized and approved by anglicans and nonconformists, of raising up a firm resistance to the religious propaganda of Rome. It was regarded as a remedy for ignorance and vice and a safeguard against sedition and disloyalty. Industry and sobriety, obedience and gratitude, were qualities looked for in charity children when they left the schools.[4]

Though the system appears to be heartlessly utilitarian it is certain that many who supported it were moved by kindliness and compassion for the children of the poor. Moreover, they were convinced that the evil of neglected childhood was a dishonour to God. Christian duty demanded that they should respond to the challenge of irreligion and immorality which resulted from allowing children to pass what should have been their schooldays in idleness. In an age when social groups were clearly, and evidently divinely, defined their altruism and vision extended no further. As the historian of the charity schools wrote, 'It was beyond the range of their mentality to conceive that the poor were poor because Society was an ill-regulated machine, or that the body politic was, as a whole, responsible for the disease which attacked it.'[1]

Authorities have pointed out that the charity school movement owed its early success largely to the practice whereby charitable giving was organized by voluntary societies.[2] The new method in philanthropy, probably modelled on joint-stock enterprise in commerce, drew persons of modest means into the ranks of the philanthropists and released a source of revenue for charitable purposes hitherto untapped. The initial impulse for a charity school usually came from a small group of local people who pledged themselves to give subscriptions and set out to enlist the support of other people in the neighbourhood. Proposals for such schools elicited a ready response from the public with the result that schools maintained by local collections and subscriptions sprang up side by side with those which were endowed in the traditional way by wealthy individuals. Trustees of the subscription schools were elected in turn from the list of subscribers. During the first quarter of the eighteenth century the movement as a whole was invigorated by the energy and drive of the Society for the Propagation of Christian Knowledge which from 1699 onwards acted as a coordinating agency, promulgating the principles of subscription schools and combating inertia and opposition.[3] Statistical evidence about the numbers of schools and of children educated in them is far from complete. 'Nevertheless,' wrote Miss Gwladys Jones, 'it is possible to establish a steadily maintained interest in the education of the poor throughout the century.' In 1714 the number of the schools in the diocese of Lincoln was two hundred and by 1723 it had risen to two hundred and sixty-eight. In London in 1704 there were fifty-four schools which were educating over two thousand children. Twenty-five years later the number of schools had increased to a hundred and thirty-two and the number of pupils to five thousand two hundred and twenty-five.[1] The charity schools flourished because people were concerned that they should flourish or because groups of supporters had been built up who wanted them to survive. Such endeavour and enthusiasm are in striking contrast to the torpor and lack of driving power which characterized the authorities of many grammar schools in the eighteenth century.

There was a precedent for the provision of learning for poor children in the practice of the free grammar schools. The purpose of the older foundations, expressed in school statutes, was to place education higher than the rudiments within reach of children of all social groups. Reference to the poor is frequently made though 'rather in a way that indicates the desire to keep the door wide open for their reception, than the expectation that they would form the majority of scholars'.[2] The population of the grammar schools was highly heterogeneous, but it cannot be maintained that it normally ranged down as far as the sons of the labouring classes.[3] Notwithstanding the good intentions of founders, the grammar schools were closed to children whose families could hardly wait for the time when they would bring additional financial assistance by their labours or relief by their departure into apprenticeships. We have seen that freedom of the school did not necessarily preclude the demands for a sufficient academic standard and for fees at entry and occasional expenses during the course of schooling. Further, in the years following the Restoration, some free schools were able to maintain their status and even their existence only by minimizing the founders' intentions. The expansion of endowed English schools at the end of the seventeenth century still made no provision for children whose parents could not afford fees for their instruction. Indeed, as Miss Jones pointed out, the desire that these children should 'share in the advancement of learning . . . was a contributory factor to the movement for charity school education in the eighteenth century with which it is seldom credited'.[4]

The charity school system was complete in itself, an elementary training which offered little or no prospect for bright boys to climb the rungs of the educational ladder. Thus it came about that trends in education after the Restoration not only widened the gulf between anglicans and nonconformists but also drew attention to economic inequality and the difference in status between rich and poor. 'The essence of the contrast' between the old established grammar schools and the charity schools is to be found not in any difference of curriculum but, as Mr. A. E. Dobbs wrote, in 'a prodigious change in tone, associations, and social outlook. While mention of the poor in connection with the older foundations might refer generally to those who were not rich enough to obtain advantages elsewhere, the "poor" of the Charity Schools are a distinct social class'.

Indeed, so far as the curricula are concerned, a line of continuity is marked by the emphasis placed in both grammar schools and charity schools on religious instruction. Doubtless, as Miss Jones affirmed, teaching in the rudiments in charity schools was superior to that given in the schools of dames and parish priests.[1] But a most revealing comment, which is relevant to our consideration of the straitened circumstances of many grammar schools in the eighteenth century, was made by Mr. A. E. Dobbs when he wrote that 'there might be little difference between the subjects taught in a decayed Grammar School and the curriculum of a Charity School'.[2] The further study of the grammar schools in this book serves to confirm the truth of his statement.

The pattern of education which emerged in the eighteenth century was created by tradition and enterprise, charity and the conflict of principles. It was a far cry from Charles Hoole's uncomplicated design of learning in the petty school and then in the grammar or writing school, and from the plans for universal schooling, equality of opportunity and discrimination according to aptitude and ability which engaged the attention of reformers during the Commonwealth period. The Stuart Restoration swept away such fantasies and the provision of schools and schooling was once more left to voluntary effort. There was a variety of schools and institutions, good and bad, public and private, anglican and dissenting, elementary schools, grammar schools, commercial and vocational schools. In such a competitive and non-compulsory system the hazards of schools and schoolmasters were obviously considerable. Supported by the

Church, associated with the universities and shackled by restrictions placed upon them by the objectives of their venerable founders, the old established schools continued in the traditional way and, for the most part, offered to eighteenth-century society the material and method of study which had already been called in question in the seventeenth century. Those schools which were founded on ample endowments were assured of survival and largely independent of changing conditions and demands. The poverty of the grammar schools was revealed when in 1868 the report of the Endowed Schools Commission was published. Sir Joshua Fitch, who took part in the investigation of these schools, summarized the findings of the commissioners.

> The buildings and school furniture were, in a majority of cases, most unsatisfactory; the number of scholars who were obtaining the sort of education in Latin and Greek contemplated by the founders was very small, and was constantly diminishing; the general instruction in other subjects was found to be very worthless, the very existence of statutes prescribing the ancient learning often serving as a reason for the absence of all teaching of modern subjects; and, with a few honourable exceptions, the endowed schools were found, in 1865–7, to be characterized by inefficient supervision on the part of the governing bodies and by languor and feebleness on the part of teachers and taught.

The report marked the end of a 'melancholy chapter in English history', a chapter which began in the later Stuart period. For, while at the end of the seventeenth century the endowed schools largely maintained their privileged position as the recognized seminaries of secondary education, the causes of their subsequent decay were already present, and to some extent apparent, in their constitution and practice.[1]

ABBREVIATIONS USED
IN THE NOTES

Carlisle   Carlisle, N. *A Concise Description of the Endowed Grammar Schools in England and Wales.* Two volumes. London, 1818.

C.C.R.   *Reports of the Commissioners for Inquiring Concerning Charities.* Thirty-two volumes. London, 1819–40.

C.S.P.D.   *Calendar of State Papers, Domestic Series.*

D.N.B.   *Dictionary of National Biography.*

P.R.O.   Public Record Office.

V.C.H.   *Victoria History of the Counties of England.*

NOTES

PAGE 5
1. G. Davies, *The Early Stuarts 1603–1660* (Oxford, 1937), p. 349.
2. The ten counties chosen as representative for the purpose of his study are Bristol, Buckinghamshire, Hampshire, Kent, Lancashire, Middlesex (London), Norfolk, Somerset, Worcestershire and Yorkshire.

PAGE 6
1. W. K. Jordan, *Philanthropy in England 1480–1660* (London, 1959), pp. 22, 26, 282, 283, 288, 289.
2. W. K. Jordan, *The Charities of London 1480–1660* (London, 1960), p. 206.
3. K. Charlton, *Education in Renaissance England* (London and Toronto, 1965), p. 130.

PAGE 7
1. W. A. L. Vincent, *The State and School Education 1640–1660 in England and Wales* (London, 1950), appendix A, pp. 120–35.
2. See p. 208 below.
3. P. J. Wallis, 'The Wase School Collection', *The Bodleian Library Record*, iv, 2 (August 1952), 84, 86–104. This article was written to 'serve as an introduction to the collection, thus drawing attention to it, and at the same time to provide an index to the schools mentioned'.
4. P. J. Wallis, 'Histories of Old Schools: A Preliminary List for England and Wales', *British Journal of Educational Studies*, xiv, 1 (Nov. 1965), 49 footnote.
5. *The Works of Thomas Hearne, vol. iii, Containing the First Volume of Peter Langtoft's Chronicle* (Oxford, 1725), The Publisher's Appendix to his Preface, p. cxlv.
6. *Repton School Register 1557–1905*, ed. G. S. Messiter (Repton, 1905), p. 21; A. Macdonald, *A Short History of Repton* (London, 1929), p. 100.

PAGE 8
1. G. W. Fisher, *Annals of Shrewsbury School*, revised by J. Spencer Hill (London, 1899), pp. 160–71.
2. R. Nelson, *The Life of Dr. George Bull* (second edition, London, 1714), p. 10.
3. W. H. D. Rouse, *A History of Rugby School* (London, 1898), p. 86.
4. *V.C.H. Northants.*, ii, 254.
5. *V.C.H. Herts.*, ii, 66.
6. W. L. Sargant, *The Book of Oakham School with Register* (Oakham, 1907), p. 11.
7. J. E. B. Mayor, *Admissions to the College of St. John the Evangelist*, Part II (Cambridge, 1893), pp. 19, 27, 47, 49, 63, 66, 81, 89, 108, 110, Part III (Cambridge, 1903), p. 13.

PAGE 9
1. P. C. Sands and C. M. Haworth, *A History of Pocklington School* (London and Hull, 1951), pp. 50–52.
2. G. F. Russell Barker, *Memoir of Richard Busby* (London, 1895), pp. 121–2.
3. *V.C.H. Essex*, ii, 534.
4. L. Cust, *A History of Eton College* (London, 1899), p. 88; *D.N.B.*, xii, 1210.
5. Jordan, *Philanthropy*, pp. 283–4, 288–9.
6. R. F. Young, *Comenius in England* (Oxford, 1932), pp. 39–40 and footnotes.
7. *Comenius in England*, p. 10; *The Great Didactic of John Amos Comenius*, translated and edited by M. W. Keatinge (London, 1910), p. 98.
8. *Comenius in England*, p. 71.

PAGE 10
1. Ibid., pp. 25–51, 70.
2. For an appreciation of these men in the context of education see H. R. Trevor-Roper, 'Three Foreigners and the Philosophy of the English Revolution', *Encounter* (Feb. 1960), xiv, No. 2, 3–20.
3. *Commons' Journals*, ii, 121, 176.
4. *Comenius in England*, p. 65.
5. Fisher, pp. 138, 153, 174–6.
6. A. Raine, *History of St. Peter's School: York* (London, 1926), p. 97.
7. M. L. Banks, *Blundell's Worthies* (London and Exeter, 1904), pp. 27–29.

PAGE 11
1. *V.C.H. Derby*, ii, 237–8.
2. P. M. H. Bryant, *Harrow* (London and Glasgow, 1936), p. 18.
3. M. F. J. McDonnell, *A History of St. Paul's School* (London, 1909), p. 202.
4. J. M. Gray, *A History of the Perse School, Cambridge* (Cambridge, 1921), pp. 47–48.
5. Rouse, pp. 65–68.

PAGE 13
1. *V.C.H. Glos.*, ii, 327.
2. *Acts and Ordinances of the Interregnum, 1642–1660,* collected and edited by C. H. Firth and R. S. Rait (London, 1911), i, 879; F. Watson, 'The State and Education during the Commonwealth', *The English Historical Review* (1900), p. 71.
3. *Commons' Journals*, ii, 808, 827, 830–1.
4. Firth and Rait, i, 110, 302–3.
5. Ibid., i, 758, 830–5; *Commons' Journals*, iv, 662, 666; H. C. Maxwell Lyte, *A History of Eton College* (London, 1877), p. 243.
6. Firth and Rait, i, 883, ii, 84–85.

PAGE 14
1. Ibid., i, 984, 1077, ii, 57, 318, 490, 687.
2. Ibid., ii, 144–6.
3. T. Richards, *A History of the Puritan Movement in Wales* (London, 1920), pp. 226–31.
4. Vincent, p. 135.
5. *Commons' Journals*, vi, 369–70, 374, 396; Firth and Rait, ii, 342–8.

6. A. F. Leach, *Educational Charters and Documents 598 to 1909* (Cambridge, 1911), p. 538; *V.C.H. Durham,* i, 365.

PAGE 15

1. T. Richards, *Religious Developments in Wales 1654–1662* (London, 1923), pp. 54–57, 59, 60.
2. Firth and Rait, ii, 1095, 1401.
3. Ibid., ii, 1004.
4. *C.S.P.D.* (1655–56), pp. 372, 387–8.
5. *V.C.H. Essex,* ii, 512.
6. *The Old Order Book of Hartlebury Grammar School, 1556–1752,* ed. D. Robertson (Oxford, 1904), pp. 61, 75–76.
7. *Rugby, The School and Neighbourhood,* collected and arranged from the writings of the late M. H. Bloxham by W. H. Payne Smith (London and Rugby, 1889), pp. 26–28, 37.

PAGE 16

1. *Schools Inquiry Commission* (London, 1868), i, appendix iv, 37–90.
2. This estimate is based on the lists in the *Schools Inquiry Report,* vol. i, and in Howard Staunton's *The Great Schools of England* (London, 1877) with the removal of ten schools which are known to have been founded before 1660 and five schools which were founded and continued as elementary schools in the later Stuart period.

PAGE 17

1. R. S. Stanier, *Magdalen School* (Oxford, 1940), p. 136.
2. *C.C.R.* (1819), p. 201; J. S. Burn, *A History of Henley-on-Thames* (London, 1861), p. 99.
3. Carlisle, ii, 293–9, 304, 310, 318, 322.

PAGE 18

1. Carlisle, ii, 212–13; *V.C.H. Northants,* ii, 239.
2. *V.C.H. Notts.,* ii, 196; G. M. Livett, *Southwell Minster* (Southwell, 1883), p. 141.
3. Carlisle, ii, 433.
4. C. F. Russell, *A History of King Edward VI School Southampton* (Cambridge, 1940), pp. 256, 295; Carlisle, ii, 448.
5. R. Surtees, *The History and Antiquities of the County Palatine of Durham* (London, 1816), i, 160–1.

PAGE 19

1. Carlisle, i, 405.
2. *V.C.H. Yorks.,* i, 430; J. Lawson, *The Endowed Grammar Schools of East Yorkshire* (East Yorkshire Local History Society, 1962), p. 24.
3. Carlisle, ii, 607; E. F. Row, *A History of Midhurst Grammar School* (Brighton, 1913), pp. 67, 77, 78, 79; See also *C.C.R.* (1819), pp. 175–6.
4. *Clarendon Commission,* 1864.
5. Carlisle, i, 440.
6. *V.C.H. Warwicks.,* ii, 337.

PAGE 20

1. R. L. Archer, *Secondary Education in the Nineteenth Century* (Cambridge, 1921), p. 13.
2. W. O. Lester Smith, *To Whom do Schools Belong?* (Oxford, 1943), p. 65.
3. N. Hans, *New Trends in Education in the Eighteenth Century* (London, 1951), pp. 28–29.
4. Quoted in J. E. G. De Montmorency, *State Intervention in English Education* (Cambridge, 1902), p. 180.
5. *V.C.H. Herts.*, ii, 77; Carlisle, i, 536.
6. W. G. Walker, *A History of the Oundle Schools* (London, 1956), pp. 228, 231, 233, 234, 237.
7. *C.C.R.* (1828), xviii, 149; *V.C.H. Derbys.*, ii, 225.

PAGE 21

1. A. E. Gibbs, *The Corporation Records of St. Albans* (St. Albans, 1890), p. 133.
2. Carlisle, i, 525.
3. A. Macdonald, *A History of the King's School Worcester* (London, 1936), p. 167.
4. N. J. Frangopulo, *The History of Queen Elizabeth's Grammar School Ashbourne, Derbyshire, 1585–1935* (Ashbourne, 1939), pp. 121–2.
5. *C.C.R.* (1819), p. 181.
6. *The Gentleman's Magazine: and Historical Chronicle. For the Year 1804.* Part the Second, lxxiv, 806.
7. R. Simpson, *A Collection of Fragments illustrative of the History and Antiquities of Derby* (Derby, 1826), i, 478; Carlisle, i, 219; *C.C.R.* (1826–7), xvii, 5–6.
8. Carlisle, i, 426, 458; *V.C.H. Glos.*, ii, 437.
9. Carlisle, ii, 519, 577.

PAGE 22

1. T. Fowler, *The History of Corpus Christi College* (Oxford, 1893), footnotes to pp. 401–2.

PAGE 23

1. *Hobbes' Leviathan Reprinted from the edition of 1651.* With an Essay by the late W. G. Pogson Smith (Oxford, 1909), p. 166.
2. For recent support of argument which Wase was trying to counter, see Mark H. Curtis, 'The Alienated Intellectuals of Early Stuart England', *Past and Present*, No. 23 (Nov. 1962), pp. 25–43.

PAGE 24

1. C. Wase, *Considerations concerning Free Schools, as settled in England* (Oxford, 1678), pp. 1–2, 10–11, 51–52.
2. F. Madan, *Oxford Books* (Oxford, 1931), iii, 366.
3. 'By the care of King Charles I and archbishop Laud there was an archi-typographer setled in the University and for his encouragment he was to have the superior bedell's place of Law annexed to it'. (*The Life and Times of Anthony Wood*, ed. A. Clark, Oxford, 1892, ii, 231–2.)
4. Wase MSS., MS. C.C.C. Oxon 390/1, fols. 97, 99.

PAGE 25

1. *Electra of Sophocles: Presented To Her Highnesse The Lady Elizabeth; With an*

Epilogue, Shewing the Parallell in Two Poems, The Return, and The Restauration. by C.W. (The Hague, for Sam. Brown, 1649).
2. S. Rivington, *The History of Tonbridge School* (London, 1910), pp. 133–4; *D.N.B.*
3. *The Diary of John Evelyn,* ed. E. S. De Beer (Oxford, 1955), iii, 55.
4. MS. C.C.C. Oxon 390/1, fol. 123.
5. MS. C.C.C. Oxon 391/1, fol. 149.
6. *The Diary of John Evelyn,* iii, 525, 526.

PAGE 26

1. J. Johnson and S. Gibson, *Print and Privilege at Oxford to the year 1700* (London, 1946), p. 50.
2. A. Wood, *Athenae Oxonienses,* ed P. Bliss (London, 1817), iii, 884. Wase received one hundred and thirty-nine votes and his opponent seventy. (*The Life and Times of Anthony Wood,* ed. A. Clark, Oxford, 1892, ii, 232; Johnson and Gibson, p. 50.) Anthony Wood, who clearly disapproved of the manner of Wase's election, has also recorded an incident in Wase's Oxford career which caused amusement and annoyance. When King James II visited the university in 1687, the vice-chancellor received him with a 'short Latine speech' and then there was a pause while the vice-chancellor and others got on horseback; 'but Ch. Wase, the sup. beadle of law, being a meer scholar, and troubled with shaking hands, could not get on horseback, but was helped up, and when he was, he could not hold his staff upright, but cross ways, because he would hold the bridle, which caused laughter in some, and anger in others'. (A. Wood, *Athenae Oxonienses,* ed. P. Bliss, London, 1813, i, cvii.)
3. MS. C.C.C. Oxon 390/3, fol. 27.
4. MS. C.C.C. Oxon 390/2, fol. 75.

PAGE 27

1. Bodleian Library, MS. Ashm. 1820 b (83); *The Life and Times of Anthony Wood.* ii, 268.
2. MS. C.C.C. Oxon 391/1, fol. 114.
3. MS. C.C.C. Oxon 391/1, fol. 194.

PAGE 28

1. MS. C.C.C. Oxon 390/1, fol. 66.
2. MS. C.C.C. Oxon 390/2, fol. 22.
3. MS. C.C.C. Oxon 390/3, fol. 34. Wase's list of questions is much shorter than that of Nicholas Carlisle who asked eighteen questions preparatory to the publication in 1818 of *A Concise Description of the Endowed Grammar Schools in England and Wales.* Carlisle, however, did not ask for information about libraries; and while Wase asked for the 'succession of Masters' Carlisle asked only for 'the Head master's name'. The result is that whereas Wase's evidence contains lists of schoolmasters and ushers Carlisle usually does not give lists of former schoolmasters. (MS. C.C.C. Oxon 391/1, fols. 100, 101.)
4. MS. C.C.C. Oxon 390/3, fol. 162.
5. MS. C.C.C. Oxon 390/1, fol. 242.

PAGE 29

1. MS. C.C.C. Oxon 390/2, fol. 109.

2. MS. C.C.C. Oxon 390/3, fol. 162.
3. MS. C.C.C. Oxon 391/1, fol. 183.

PAGE 30
1. MS. C.C.C. Oxon 391/1, fol. 189.
2. MS. C.C.C. Oxon 390/2, fol. 46.
3. MS. C.C.C. Oxon 390/1, fol. 26.
4. MS. C.C.C. Oxon 390/3, fol. 185.
5. MS. C.C.C. Oxon 290/2, fol. 51.

PAGE 31
1. MS. C.C.C. Oxon 391/1, fol. 122.
2. MS. C.C.C. Oxon 391/1, fol. 67.
3. MS. C.C.C. Oxon 391/1, fol. 123.
4. MS. C.C.C. Oxon 391/1, fol. 129.
5. MS. C.C.C. Oxon 391/1, fol. 127.
6. MS. C.C.C. Oxon 391/1, fol. 69.
7. MS. C.C.C. Oxon 391/1, fol. 112.

PAGE 32
1. MS. C.C.C. Oxon 391/1, fol. 105.
2. MS. C.C.C. Oxon 390/3, fol. 160.
3. MS. C.C.C. Oxon 391/1, fol. 107. In a postscript to this letter of 20 November 1676, Cooke added: 'Sir, when you write to me agine, pray reform a mistake in your subscription for I am not Principall, but President of Jesus Coll'.
4. MS. C.C.C. Oxon 391/1, fol. 109.
5. MS. C.C.C. Oxon 391/1, fol. 70.

PAGE 33
1. MS. C.C.C. Oxon 390/1, fol. 141.
2. MS. C.C.C. Oxon 390/2, fols. 89, 91.
3. MS. C.C.C. Oxon 390/2, fol. 98.
4. MS. C.C.C. Oxon 390/2, fol. 78.

PAGE 34
1. MS. C.C.C. Oxon 390/2, fol. 215.
2. MS. C.C.C. Oxon 390/2, fol. 167.
3. MS. C.C.C. Oxon 390/2, fol. 247.
4. MS. C.C.C. Oxon 390/3, fol. 201 v.
5. MS. C.C.C. Oxon 390/2, fol. 133.

PAGE 35
1. MS. C.C.C. Oxon 390/1, fol. 37.
2. MS. C.C.C. Oxon 390/1, fols. 127, 129.

PAGE 36
1. MS. C.C.C. Oxon 390/1, fol. 20.

2. MS. C.C.C. Oxon 390/1, fol. 214.
3. MS. C.C.C. Oxon 390/1, fols. 189, 191, 195.
4. MS. C.C.C. Oxon 390/1, fol. 72.

PAGE 37
1. MS. C.C.C. Oxon 390/2, fols. 39, 42.
2. MS. C.C.C. Oxon 390/2, fol. 86.
3. MS. C.C.C. Oxon 390/2, fol. 211.

PAGE 38
1. MS. C.C.C. Oxon 390/3, fols. 152, 154.
2. MS. C.C.C. Oxon 390/2, fol. 186.
3. MS. C.C.C. Oxon 390/3, fol. 148.
4. MS. C.C.C. Oxon 391/1, fol. 85.
5. MS. C.C.C. Oxon 390/3, fol. 152.
6. Bodleian Library, MS. Wood D11, fol. 173.
7. Following the additional notes in the Wase manuscripts Mr. P. J. Wallis has
   remarked that there is information in the collection about ninety-eight schools
   which do not appear in Carlisle's list of endowed schools and that information
   about one hundred and sixteen other schools is supplementary to Carlisle's
   accounts of them; he also shows that two hundred and twenty-five schools are
   only mentioned by name. (P. J. Wallis, 'The Wase School Collection', *The
   Bodleian Library Record,* iv, 2, 82–83, 86–104.)

PAGE 39
1. Madan, iii, 284.

PAGE 40
1. E. Baines, *The History of the County Palatine and Duchy of Lancaster* (London, 1870),
   ii, 682; Carlisle, i, 645–6.
2. Dr. S. J. Curtis has suggested that an explanation of the term may possibly be
   found in the licence which freed the founder from the operation of the Statute of
   Mortmain and his school from outside control. He points out that according to
   the Statute of Mortmain in 1279 lands granted to the Church were liable to be
   confiscated by the Crown and that this measure had been enacted in order to
   prevent tax evasion by landowners who continued to hold as tenants lands
   which they had given to the Church. Exemption from the working of the act
   might be granted to a founder who accepted the provision that his school should
   offer tuition without charge to some of the pupils and whose endowment might
   therefore be regarded as a charitable bequest. Such an agreement was acceptable to many founders who were willing to give an advantage to children of a
   particular locality. (S. J. Curtis, *History of Education in Great Britain,* fourth
   edition, London, 1957, pp. 43–48.)

PAGE 41
1. Carlisle, i, 657, 841. The schoolmaster at Kirkby Stephen in Westmorland was
   required by the statutes of 1566 to take an oath in the parish church in the
   presence of the governors, churchwardens and twelve men of the parish that he
   would 'freely without exacting any money, diligently instruct and teach' the

children of the parish, and all others who should resort to him, 'in Grammar and other humane doctrine, according to the statutes thereof made'. (Carlisle, ii, 715.)

2. W. R. Whatton, 'The History of Manchester School', Manchester, 1828, *The Foundations of Manchester* (Manchester, 1848), iii, 25; *V.C.H. Lancs.*, ii, 581.

PAGE 42

1. T. W. Horsfield, *The History and Antiquities of Lewes and its Vicinity* (Lewes, 1824), i, 309; *Sussex Archaeological Collections* (Lewes, 1903), xlvi, 134, 142.
2. *Notes & Queries for Somerset and Dorset,* ed. F. W. Eaver and C. H. Mayo (Sherborne, 1893), iii, 245.
3. *Transactions of the Historic Society of Lancashire and Cheshire, Session 1855–56* (London, 1856), viii, 58–59.
4. *The Old Order Book of Hartlebury Grammar School, 1556–1752,* p. 200.
5. A. A. Mumford, *The Manchester Grammar School 1515–1915* (London, 1919), p. 477.
6. Carlisle, i, 676.
7. Whatton, ii, 28; Mumford, p. 479; Carlisle, i, 679.
8. Carlisle, i, 792–3.

PAGE 43

1. R. W. Goulding, *Louth Old Corporation Records* (Louth, 1891), pp. 2–3; Carlisle, i, 822–3; *A Translation of the Charter of King Edward the Sixth, Whereby a Free Grammar School was Founded for the Benefit of the Town of Louth, In the County of Lincoln* (Louth, 1813), pp. 3–4.
2. *Notes & Queries for Somerset and Dorset,* iii, 245.
3. *Deed of Foundation of the Free School of Robert Holgate York,* The Archbishop Holgate Society, Record Series No. 1.

PAGE 44

1. B. Varley, *The History of Stockport Grammar School* (Manchester, 1957), pp. 19, 24.
2. D. Wilmot, *A Short History of the Grammar School, Macclesfield* (Macclesfield, 1910), p. 10, appendix, xlv; Carlisle, i, 117.
3. P.R.O., Petty Bag Inquisitions, Bundle 29, No. 15, 19 Charles II.
4. *V.C.H. Notts.,* ii, 181.
5. Carlisle, i, 340; F. J. Snell, *Blundell's A Short History of a Famous West Country School* (London), pp. 41, 43.
6. Miss Dorothea Hurst, *Horsham: Its History and Antiquities* (London, 1868), pp. 103–5; H. Dudley, *The History and Antiquities of Horsham* (London, 1836), pp. 31–33.

PAGE 45

1. *V.C.H. Hunts.,* ii, 113.
2. *V.C.H. Beds.,* ii, 179.
3. Row, pp. 18–19.
4. Brasenose College, Oxford, Charlbury 2, 5, A Copy of the Orders of Charlbury School.

PAGE 46
1. L. L. Duncan, *A History of Colfe's Grammar School, Lewisham* (Printed for the Governors The Worshipful Company of Leathersellers of the City of London, 1910), p. 57; Carlisle, i, 579, 581.
2. Staunton, pp. 472, 481, 497, 509, 538; *Schools Inquiry Commission,* i, appendix iv, 65, 74, 77.

PAGE 47
1. Mrs. Margaret M. Kay, *The History of Rivington and Blackrod Grammar School* (Manchester, 1966), pp. 72–73, 84, 85, 155; J. Whitaker, *The Statutes and Charter of Rivington School* (London, 1837), pp. 223–4.
2. *The Quarterly Review* (1878), cxlvi, 68.
3. J. W. Adamson, '*The Illiterate Anglo-Saxon*' *and other Essays* (Cambridge, 1946), pp. 59–61; Carlisle, ii, 323.
4. Carlisle, ii, 137.
5. *Schools Inquiry Commission,* i, appendix iv, 76; *V.C.H. Notts.,* ii, 181.

PAGE 48
1. *Schools Inquiry Commission,* i, 566–7.
2. Wase MSS., C.C.C. Oxon 390/1, fol. 197; Carlisle, i, 484, 485.
3. W. H. Blanch, *Ye Parish of Camerwell* (London, 1875), pp. 250–1; O. Manning and W. Bray, *The History and Antiquities of the County of Surrey* (London, 1814), ii, 445.

PAGE 49
1. Wase MSS., C.C.C. Oxon 391/1, fols. 150, 189.
2. *Considerations concerning Free Schools, as settled in England,* pp. 60–61.

PAGE 50
1. Carlisle, i, 793.
2. *Sussex Archaeological Collections* (Lewes, 1900), xliii, 77, 80.
3. R. Pemberton, *Solihull and its Church* (Exeter, 1905), p. 152.
4. W. Young, *The History of Dulwich College* (London, 1889), i, 151.

PAGE 51
1. Wase MSS., C.C.C. Oxon 390/2, fol. 91.
2. Wase MSS., C.C.C. Oxon 390/2, fol. 120.
3. Bodleian Library, MS. Oxf. Archd. papers Oxon C 160, fols. 265, 268–9.
4. Library Catalogue and Statute Book in the Library of Witney Grammar School, Oxfordshire. See also Guisborough (N. R. W. Stephenson, *A Short History of Guisborough Grammar School,* Guisborough, 1961, p. 8), Abingdon (Wase MSS. C.C.C. Oxon 390/1, fol. 12), Aldenham (*The History and Register of Aldenham School,* seventh edition, compiled by E. Beevor, G. C. F. Mead, R. J. Evans, T. H. Savory, Worcester and London, 1938, p. xxii), St. Albans and St. Bees (Carlisle, i, 156, 157, 516, 517).
5. Carlisle, i, 517, 784.
6. Carlisle, i, 420–1.

PAGE 52
1. Carlisle, i, 602.

2. W. Boys, *Collections for an History of Sandwich in Kent* (Canterbury, 1892), pp. 224, 227.
3. W. B. Wildman, *A Short History of Sherborne* (Sherborne, 1930), pp. 38, 39; Carlisle, i, 380.
4. *V.C.H. Surrey,* ii, 183.
5. G. C. Williamson, *Guildford in the Olden Time* (London, 1904), p. 102.
6. *Sussex Archaeological Collections,* xliii, 77–78.

PAGE 53
1. *The History and Antiquities of Guildford* (Guildford, 1801), pp. 101–2.
2. Library Catalogue and Statute Book in the Library of Witney Grammar School, Oxfordshire.
3. Brasenose College, Oxford, Charlbury, 2, 5.
4. T. Sharp, *Illustrative Papers on the History and Antiquities of the City of Coventry* (Birmingham, 1871), p. 169; Carlisle, ii, 649.
5. W. S. Sampson, *A History of the Bristol Grammar School* (Bristol and London, 1912), pp. 92, 93. See also Sevenoaks in Kent (Carlisle, i, 619, 621), Dorchester in Oxfordshire (MS. Oxf. Archd. papers Oxon C 160, fol. 270).
6. Carlisle, i, 516.
7. *C.C.R.* (1831), xxiv, 96–97.
8. Burn, p. 97.
9. It is, of course, a commonplace that the period of sustained inflation which started in the sixteenth century and continued to the middle of the seventeenth century reduced endowments, which were generous when they were made, to something inadequate at the end of this period. See E. H. Phelps Brown and Sheila V. Hopkins, 'Seven Centuries of the Prices of Consumables, Compared with Builders' Wage-Rates', *Essays in Economic History,* ed. E. M. Carus-Wilson (London, 1962), ii, 179–196.

PAGE 54
1. British Museum, Lansd. MSS. 119, fol. 14.
2. *V.C.H. Suffolk,* ii, 321.
3. J. S. Davies, *A History of Southampton* (Southampton and London, 1883), p. 317; Carlisle, ii, 447–8.

PAGE 55
1. Carlisle, i, 491–2.
2. *V.C.H. Essex,* ii, 540; Carlisle, i, 428.
3. A. F. Leach, *History of Warwick School* (London, 1906), pp. 148–9.
4. S. Rudder, *The History of Cirencester* (Cirencester, 1800), pp. 309–10. An interesting letter written by Dr. Samuel Johnson on 9 January 1770 to Henry Bright, the master of Abingdon School in Berkshire, shows how fees for boarders might be varied in individual cases and might also be used by the schoolmaster as a basis for bargaining. In his letter Dr. Johnson requested Bright to consider admitting another pupil 'in the same manner as Mr. Strahan was taken' and suggested that as he was likely to find this young man more troublesome than the other he should accordingly demand 'a higher price'. (British Museum, Stowe MSS., 755, f. 80.)

PAGE 56
1. *V.C.H. Glos.*, ii, 395.
2. *C.C.R.* (1821), p. 488.
3. *C.C.R.* (8 July 1820), p. 282.

PAGE 57
1. *V.C.H. Suffolk*, ii, 302.
2. *V.C.H. Sussex*, ii, 397.
3. *Schools Inquiry Commission*, ix. 152.

PAGE 58
1. C. Hoole, *A New Discovery of the old Art of Teaching Schoole*, ed. E. T. Campagnac, 'Scholastick Discipline' (Liverpool and London, 1913), p. 238; Sampson, p. 91; Sharp, p. 169; Davies, *Southampton*, p. 317; Bodleian Library, MS. Oxf. Archd. papers Oxon C 160, fol. 267; Brasenose College, Oxford, Charlbury 2, 5, A Copy of the Orders of Charlbury School; Library Catalogue and Statute Book in the Library of Witney Grammar School, Oxfordshire.
2. N. F. Layard, *A Brief Sketch of the History of Ipswich School* (Ipswich, 1901), p. 17; I. E. Gray and W. E. Potter, *Ipswich School 1400–1950* (Ipswich, 1950), p. 40; J. and S. Russell, *The History of Guildford* (Guildford, 1801), p. 97; G. C. Williamson, *The Royal Grammar School of Guildford* (London and Guildford, 1929), pp. 55, 155.
3. New College, Oxford, Statutes of Adderbury School, Oxfordshire; *V.C.H. Northants.*, ii, 212.
4. Sharp, p. 169. See also J. S. Davies, *A History of Southampton*, p. 317, G. C. Williamson, *The Royal Grammar School of Guildford*, pp. 55, 155, Brasenose College, Oxford, Charlbury 2, 5, A Copy of the Orders of Charlbury School.
5. Bodleian Library, MS. Oxf. Archd. papers Oxon C 160, fol. 267; Carlisle, i, 222, 418; *V.C.H. Durham*, i, 394.

PAGE 59
1. Library Catalogue and Statute Book in the Library of Witney Grammar School, Oxfordshire. See also J. Latimer, *The Annals of Bristol in the Seventeenth Century* (Bristol, 1900), p. 284, New College, Oxford, Orders for Adderbury School, Oxfordshire, *V.C.H. Northants.*, ii, 212.
2. Sharp, p. 169; Bodleian Library, MS. Oxf. Archd. papers Oxon C 160, fol. 267; Davies, p. 317; J. and S. Russell, p. 95; *Sussex Archaeological Collections*, xliii, 78; New College, Oxford, The Orders for Adderbury School, Oxfordshire.
3. Latimer, p. 284.
4. Williamson, p. 159; *Sussex Archaeological Collections*, xliii, 78; *The Records of Blackburn Grammar School*, ed. G. A. Stocks (Chetham Society, Manchester, 1909), pp. 72–73; Davies, p. 317; Bodleian Library, MS. Oxf. Archd. papers Oxon C 160, fol. 267; *V.C.H. Lancs.*, ii, 573.
5. A. Macdonald, *A History of the King's School Worcester*, p. 48; A. F. Leach, *Documents Illustrating Early Education in Worcester, 685 to 1700* (Worcestershire Historical Society, 1913), p. 133.
6. *V.C.H. Surrey*, ii, 179.
7. Sharp, p. 169; J. and S. Russell, p. 97; *Sussex Archaeological Collections*, xliii, 79.

8. Davies, *Southampton*, p. 317; *V.C.H. Durham*, i, 395; Carlisle, ii, 718.

PAGE 60

1. Wase MSS., C.C.C. Oxon 390/2, fol. 8; J. Latimer, *The Annals of Bristol in the Seventeenth Century*, p. 284; *V.C.H. Lancs.*, ii, 573.
2. Maxwell Lyte, p. 363.
3. *The Diary of John Evelyn*, ii, 9, 11.

PAGE 61

1. F. J. Baigent and J. E. Millard, *A History of the Ancient Town and Manor of Basingstoke* (Basingstoke and London, 1889), pp. 150, 678–9.
2. See, for example, *Biographical History of Gonville and Caius College, 1349–1897*, compiled by J. Venn (Cambridge, 1896), ii, 7; *V.C.H. Warwicks.*, ii, 346.

PAGE 62

1. *Chigwell Register, Together with a Historical Account of the School by The Rev. Canon Swallow*, ed. O. W. Darch and A. S. Tween (Buckhurst Hill, 1907), pp. 13–14; Carlisle, ii, 737–8.
2. Bodleian Library, MS. Oxf. Archd. papers Oxon, C 160, fol. 267; Carlisle, ii, 9, 560–1, 585–6; *Charter-House, Its Foundation and History* (London, 1849), p. 64.
3. Sharp, p. 170; Carlisle, i, 223, 418, 419.
4. *Orders, Constitutions, and Directions, To Be Observed, For And Concerning The Free-School, in Woodbridge, In the County of Suffolk, And the School-Master, and Scholars thereof. Agreed upon at the Foundation, 1662* (Printed by Robert Loder, 1785), p. 9; Carlisle, ii, 541.
5. G. C. Chambres, *History of Wigan Free Grammar School 1596–1869* (Wigan, 1937), appendix i, pp. 94–95; Row, p. 19; Carlisle, i, 132, 517, 679–80, 729–30, ii, 138, 605, 718, 738.

PAGE 63

1. Maxwell Lyte, pp. 261–2.
2. W. M. Warlow, *A History of the Charities of William Jones* (Bristol, 1899), p. 95.
3. Bodleian Library, MS. Oxf. Archd. papers Oxon C 160, fol. 270; Chambres, appendix i, pp. 94, 95; Wildman, p. 93; W. R. Whatton, The History of Manchester School (1828), *The Foundations of Manchester*, iii, 28–29; Boys, pp. 229–30, 231; Carlisle, i, 133, 161, 223, 420, 492, 604, 606, 660, 680, 729, 730, ii, 218, 358, 561, 586, 717.
4. Sharp, pp. 169–70; Wildman, p. 95; Carlisle, i, 223, 419, 660, ii, 448.

PAGE 64

1. *Milton's Tractate on Education*, ed. O. Browning (Cambridge, 1895), p. 3.
2. D. Defoe, *The Compleat English Gentleman*, ed. K. D. Bulbring (London, 1890), pp. 111, 112.
3. J. Locke, *Some Thoughts Concerning Education*, ed. R. H. Quick (Cambridge, 1880), pp. 2–7, 62–63.
4. J. Boswell, *The Life of Samuel Johnson* (London, 1907), i, 13–14.
5. R. Southey, *The Life of Wesley* (London, 1925), ii, 304, 305.

PAGE 65

1. R. South, *Sermons Preached Upon Several Occasions* (Oxford, 1823), iii, 398.

2. *The Spectator*, No. 157 (August 30, 1711), No. 168 (September 12, 1711), iii, 151, 160, 211, 212.

PAGE 66
1. *The History of Thomas Ellwood Written by Himself* (London, 1885), pp. 12–13; J. H. Brown, *A Short History of Thame School* (London, 1927), p. 135.
2. Mumford, p. 130; J. Aiken, *A Description of the Country from thirty to forty Miles round Manchester* (London, 1795), p. 185.

PAGE 67
1. Carlisle, i, 132–3, ii, 258–9, 631.
2. *Johnson's Lives of the Poets*, ed. Mrs. Alexander Napier (London, 1890), ii, 89, 90.

PAGE 68
1. *Publications of the Dugdale Society*, vii, The Records of King Edward's School Birmingham (London, 1928), ii, 6–7; Carlisle, ii, 632.
2. *Coventry: Its History and Antiquities*, compiled by B. Poole (London, 1870), p. 259.

PAGE 69
1. *V.C.H. Northants.*, ii, 212; *V.C.H. Lincs.*, ii, 445.
2. *Publications of the Dugdale Society*, vii, The Records of King Edward's School Birmingham, ii, 65; A. E. Gibbs, *An Ancient Grammar School, Bygone Hertfordshire*, ed. W. Andrews (London, 1898), p. 132; A. F. Leach, *History of Warwick School*, p. 145; *V.C.H. Glos.*, ii, 419.
3. *Some Thoughts concerning Education*, p. 48.

PAGE 70
1. R. North, *The Lives of the Right Hon. Francis North, Baron Guilford; The Hon. Sir Dudley North; And The Hon. and Rev. Dr. John North*, ed. A. Jessopp (London, 1890), ii, 10, 11, 12, 13.
2. W. O. Lester Smith, *To Whom do Schools Belong?* pp. 62–63.
3. *A New Discovery of the Old Art of Teaching Schoole*, p. ix.

PAGE 71
1. J. Gailhard, *The Compleat Gentleman: or Directions For the Education of Youth As to their Breeding at Home and Travelling Abroad. In Two Treatises* (London, 1678), pp. 14, 15, 18, 19, 21, 22.
2. Carlisle, i, 340, 402, 517, 581, 601, 784, ii, 54, 75, 216, 584.
3. *A New Discovery of the old Art of Teaching Schoole*, 'The Usher's Duty', p. 1.
4. R. North, *The Lives of the Right Hon. Francis North, Baron Guilford; The Hon. Sir Dudley North; And The Hon. and Rev. Dr. John North*, iii, 8.
5. O. Goldsmith, *The Life of Henry St. John, Lord Viscount Bolingbroke* (London, 1770), pp. 5–6.

PAGE 72
1. *A New Discovery of the old Art of Teaching Schoole*, 'The Petty-Schoole', pp. 28–31.
2. H. Woodward, *A Light to Grammar* (London, 1641), p. 47.

3. Carlisle, i, 369, ii, 116, 227, 295, 902.
4. *Chigwell Register, Together with a Historical Account of the School By the Rev. Canon Swallow*, p. 13.
5. Carlisle, i, 282–3, 294, 579, 583.
6. Wase MSS., C.C.C. Oxon 390/2, fol. 231.
7. *Schools Inquiry Commission*, i, Report of the Commissioners, appendix iv, 73; Staunton, p. 421.
8. Carlisle, ii, 235–7, 735.

PAGE 73
1. W. R. Whatton, 'The History of Manchester School', *The Foundations of Manchester*, iii, 28; Stephenson, p. 9; F. Watson, *The English Grammar Schools to 1660*, p. 152.
2. Carlisle, ii, 795, 799.
3. E. H. Pearce, *Annals of Christ's Hospital* (London, 1908), p. 24.
4. Carlisle, i, 402, 517, 581, 601, 784, ii, 54, 75, 216, 584.
5. *A New Discovery of the old Art of Teaching Schoole*, 'Scholastick Discipline', pp. 283–5. See also *Records of Blackburn Grammar School*, p. 73, E. A. Bell, *A History of Giggleswick School* (Leeds, 1912), appendix vii, p. 256.
6. F. Watson, *The English Grammar Schools to 1660*, pp. 189, 191–2.
7. Carlisle, ii, 519.
8. *Schools Inquiry Commission*, i, appendix iv, 71, 74; Staunton, pp. 456, 481.
9. Carlisle, i, 581.
10. Fisher, p. 205.
11. Pearce, pp. 24, 26, 146–7, 154, 304; W. Trollope, *A History of the Royal Foundation of Christ's Hospital* (London, 1834), p. 67.

PAGE 74
1. *Orders, Constitutions, and Directions, To be Observed For and Concerning The Free-School in Woodbridge*, p. 6.
2. Carlisle, ii, 9. See also Brasenose College, Oxford, Charlbury 2, 5, A Copy of the Orders of Charlbury School, E. F. Row, *A History of Midhurst Grammar School*, pp. 10, 19.
3. Carlisle, i, 161; G. C. Williamson, *The Royal Grammar School of Guildford*, p. 57.
4. *V.C.H. Durham*, i, 395.
5. F. Watson, *The Beginnings of the Teaching of Modern Subjects in England* (London, 1909), p. 311; Carlisle, i, 157; Library Catalogue and Statute Book in the Library of Witney Grammar School, Oxfordshire.
6. Row, p. 21.
7. Davies, *Southampton*, p. 317.
8. *Orders, Constitutions, and Directions, To be Observed, For and Concerning the Free-School in Woodbridge*, p. 6.
9. Carlisle, ii, 732.
10. Staunton, pp. 417–552; *Schools Inquiry Commission*, i, appendix iv, 69–79.
11. *Somerset Archaeological and Natural History Society Proceedings During the Years 1865–6* (Taunton, 1867), iii, 40.
12. Carlisle, ii, 624.
13. Ibid., i, 113–4.

PAGE 75

1. E. Cardwell, *Documentary Annals of the Reformed Church of England* (Oxford, 1839), i, 194.
2. C. H. Davis, *The English Church Canons of 1604* (London, 1869), p. 77.
3. F. Watson, *The English Grammar Schools to 1660*, p. 4.
4. *A New Discovery of the old Art of Teaching Schoole*, 'The Ushers Duty', pp. 111–14.
5. See *The History and Register of Aldenham School*, p. xxxv, *V.C.H. Surrey*, ii, 206. An English translation of *Sententiae Pueriles* was prepared by Charles Hoole in 1658 under the title *Sentences for Children, English and Latine. Collected out of Sundry Authors long since by Leonard Culman: And now translated into English by Charles Hoole; For the first enterers into Latin.*

PAGE 76

1. See J. S. Davies, *A History of Southampton*, p. 316; *V.C.H. Surrey*, ii, 206; Carlisle, i, 737.
2. *Visitations and Memorials of Southwell Minster*, ed. A. F. Leach (Camden Society 1891), p. 49; W. A. James, *An Account of the Grammar and Song Schools of The Collegiate Church of Blessed Mary the Virgin of Southwell* (Southwell, 1927), p. 2; J. Brinsley, *Ludus Literarius or The Grammar Schoole*, ed. E. T. Campagnac (Liverpool and London, 1917), p. 219; *A New Discovery of the old Art of Teaching Schoole*, 'Scholastick Discipline', p. 265.
3. *V.C.H. Somerset*, ii, 459; Chambres, p. 95; Davies, *Southampton*, p. 316.

PAGE 77

1. *A New Discovery of the old Art of Teaching Schoole*, 'Scholastick Discipline', p. 265, 'The Masters Method', pp. 137–8, 142–4, 156–7, 161, 173, 177–80, 203.
2. Bodleian Library, MS. Oxf. Archd. papers Oxon C 160, fol. 268; Davies, *Southampton*, p. 316.
3. *V.C.H. Herts.*, ii, 65, *V.C.H. Lincs.*, ii, 458, *V.C.H. Surrey*, ii, 206.
4. Bodleian Library, Rawl. MSS., D. 191, fol. 5.
5. Gloucester Cathedral, Chapter Acts Books, 28 September 1686.
6. Boys, pp. 230–1.
7. *A New Discovery of the old Art of Teaching Schoole*, 'The Masters Method', p. 183.

PAGE 78

1. Bodleian Library, Rawl. MSS., D. 191, fol. 6; *The History and Register of Aldenham School*, p. xxxv.
2. *A New Discovery of the old Art of Teaching Schoole*, 'The Masters Method', pp. 184–5.
3. *The Diary of John Evelyn*, iii, 287–8.
4. *Ludus Literarius*, p. 173.
5. *Milton's Tractate on Education*, p. 6.
6. Wase MSS., C.C.C. Oxon 390/2, fols. 8, 184; Davies, *Southampton*, p. 317; *V.C.H. Lincoln*, ii, 445; A. Macdonald, *A History of the King's School, Worcester*, p. 145; *The Admission Registers of St. Paul's School, from 1748 to 1876*, ed. R. B. Gardiner (London, 1884), p. 13.
7. H. B. Wilson, *The History of Merchant Taylors' School, From its Foundation to the Present Time* (London, 1812), i, 11, 124–5.

PAGE 79

1. Carlisle, i, 131, ii, 50.
2. J. Fischer Williams, *Harrow* (London, 1901), p. 26.
3. *Ludus Literarius*, pp. 226–8; *A New Discovery of the old Art of Teaching Schoole*, 'The Masters Method', pp. 130, 131, 134, 135.

PAGE 80

1. M. H. Peacock, *History of the Free Grammar School of Queen Elizabeth at Wakefield* (Wakefield, 1892), p. 65.
2. Davies, *Southampton*, p. 316.
3. Bodleian Library, Oxf. Archd. papers Oxon C 160, fol. 268.
4. Bodleian Library, Rawl. MSS., D. 191, fol. 5.
5. *Ludus Literarius*, pp. 231–2, 241; *A New Discovery of the old Art of Teaching Schoole*, 'The Masters Method', p. 196.
6. *A New Discovery of the old Art of Teaching Schoole*, 'The Masters Method', pp. 192–4.

PAGE 81

1. Carlisle, ii, 284; J. Sargeaunt, *Annals of Westminster School* (London, 1898), pp. 42, 55; H. B. Wilson, *The History of Merchant Taylors' School*, pp. 11, 39–40; G. H. Box, 'Hebrew Studies in the Reformation Period and After', *The Legacy of Israel*, ed. E. R. Bevan and C. Singer (Oxford, 1927), p. 341. See also C. M. Clode, *Memorials of the Guild of Merchant Taylors of the Fraternity of St. John the Baptist* (London, 1875), p. 408.
2. F. Watson, *The English Grammar Schools to 1660*, p. 529.
3. *The Records of Blackburn Grammar School*, p. 74.
4. T. Cox, *A Popular History of the Grammar School of Queen Elizabeth, At Heath, Near Halifax* (Halifax, 1879), p. 53.
5. Staunton, pp. 470, 498–9, 504; *Schools Inquiry Commission*, i, appendix, 64, 68; Carlisle, ii, 355.
6. *The Works of Thomas Hearne*, vol. iii, Containing the First Volume of Peter Langtoft's Chronicle. The Publisher's Appendix to his Preface, p. cxlvi.
7. McDonnell, pp. 161, 208; *D.N.B.*
8. *The Diary of Samuel Pepys*, ed. H. B. Wheatley (London, 1893), iii, 31.
9. *V.C.H. Herts.*, ii, 65.
10. Sampson, p. 89.

PAGE 82

1. Staunton, pp. 431, 440, 458, 499–500, 529, 546; *Schools Inquiry Commission*, i, appendix iv, 69, 71, 73, 76.
2. Carlisle, i, 244–5.
3. *Considerations concerning Free Schools*, pp. 104, 105.
4. MS. C.C.C. Oxon 390/2, fol. 68.

PAGE 83

1. *A New Discovery of the old Art of Teaching Schoole*, 'Scholastick Discipline', pp. xvii–xxiv, 289–91.
2. MS. C.C.C. Oxon 390/2, fol. 247.

3. MS. C.C.C. Oxon 390/3, fol. 171.
4. MS. C.C.C. Oxon 390/1, fols. 136, 143, 360/2, fol. 10.
5. MS. C.C.C. Oxon 390/2, fol. 26.
6. MS. C.C.C. Oxon 390/2, fols. 79, 91.
7. MS. C.C.C. Oxon 390/2, fol. 137.
8. MS. C.C.C. Oxon 390/1, fol. 201.
9. MS. C.C.C. Oxon 390/2, fols. 36, 72, 243.
10. MS. C.C.C. Oxon 390/1, fol. 94.
11. MS. C.C.C. Oxon 390/1, fol. 21.
12. MS. C.C.C. Oxon 390/2, fol. 29.

PAGE 84
1. MS. C.C.C. Oxon 390/2, fol. 104.
2. MS. C.C.C. Oxon 390/2, fol. 49.
3. MS. C.C.C. Oxon 390/1, fol. 199.
4. MS. C.C.C. Oxon 390/2, fol. 23 v.
5. MS. C.C.C. Oxon 390/1, fol. 114.
6. MS. C.C.C. Oxon 390/1, fol. 157.
7. MS. C.C.C. Oxon 390/2, fol. 155.
8. MS. C.C.C. Oxon 390/3, fol. 26.

PAGE 85
1. MS. C.C.C. Oxon 390/2, fol. 8.
2. See p. 52 above.
3. *A New Discovery of the old Art of Teaching Schoole*, 'Scholastick Discipline', p. 289.

PAGE 86
1. Library Catalogue and Statute Book in the Library of Witney Grammar School, Oxfordshire; Miss M. A. Fleming, *Witney Grammar School 1660–1960* (Oxford, 1960), p. 15.
2. *Considerations concerning Free Schools,* p. 104. See also J. E. Sandys, *A History of Classical Scholarship* (Cambridge, 1908), ii, 175–6.
3. *V.C.H. Notts.,* ii, 233. Alderman John Parker by his will of 26 October 1693 bequeathed rent from lands to enable boys to become apprentices and to set them up in trades, and to begin building up a school library. He directed that the trustees should pay forty pounds in four instalments of ten pounds in alternate years for the purchase of books for the school. Thereafter the rents were to be used to bind apprentices and to set up in trades, and if any apprentice failed in his apprenticeship his annual grant of three pounds was to be paid to the library fund.
4. *Considerations concerning Free Schools*, p. 104.
5. F. Watson, *The English Grammar Schools to 1660*, p. 534.

PAGE 87
1. Bodleian Library, MS. Oxf. Archd. papers Oxon C 160, fol. 266.
2. Carlisle, ii, 717.
3. See J. and S. Russell, *The History of Guildford*, p. 102, G. C. Williamson, *The Royal Grammar School of Guildford*, p. 158, *Sussex Archaeological Collections*, xliii,

R

78, Carlisle, ii, 604, 738, Brasenose College, Oxford, Charlbury 2, 5, A Copy of the Orders of Charlbury School.

4. See Carlisle, i, 223, 419–20, 515, ii, 217, 282, W. Smalley Law, *Oundle's Story* (London, 1922), p. 60, I. E. Gray and W. E. Potter, *Ipswich School 1400–1950*, p. 40, J. S. Davies, *A History of Southampton*, p. 317.

5. Carlisle, ii, 716; *V.C.H. Northants.*, ii, 212.

6. *The Records of Blackburn Grammar School*, p. 72; Carlisle, i, 485.

7. Bodleian Library, MS. Oxf. Archd. papers Oxon C 160, fol. 267; Library Catalogue and Statute Book in the Library of Witney Grammar School, Oxfordshire; Davies, *Southampton*, p. 317; Cox, p. 51; Carlisle, ii, 357.

8. *A New Discovery of the old Art of Teaching Schoole*, 'Scholastick Discipline', p. 267.

9. Mrs. Margaret M. Kay, *The History of Rivington and Blackrod Grammar School*, p. 23. The study of the Bible as an essential part of the school curriculum had been settled by article 79 of the Canons ecclesiastical of 1604 which decreed that it was the duty of schoolmasters on days which were not holy days and festival days to teach the boys 'such sentences of holy Scripture, as shall be most expedient to induce them to all godliness'. (C. H. Davis, *The English Church Canons of 1604*, p. 77.)

PAGE 88

1. Bodleian Library, MS. Oxf. Archd. papers Oxon C 160, fol. 266; Williamson, p. 159; J. and S. Russell, p. 96; *Sussex Archaeological Collections*, xliii, 79; Carlisle, i, 189, ii, 737–8.

2. Bodleian Library, MS. Oxf. Archd. papers Oxon C 160, fol. 266; Davies, *Southampton*, p. 317; Sampson, p. 94.

3. Chambres, p. 92.

4. Carlisle, i, 223, 419, 728, 794, ii, 215.

5. Ibid., i, 157–8, ii, 215; Sampson, p. 94; *The History and Register of Aldenham School*, p. xxxv.

6. *Considerations concerning Free Schools*, p. 92.

7. *A New Discovery of the old Art of Teaching Schoole*, 'The Ushers Duty', pp. 41, 59. See also Carlisle, i, 131.

8. Carlisle, ii, 281, 718.

PAGE 89

1. *Orders, Constitutions, and Directions, To be Observed, For and Concerning the Free-School, in Woodbridge*, p. 9.

2. Boys, p. 229.

3. *V.C.H. Durham*, i, 394.

4. Boys, p. 229; Carlisle, i, 603, ii, 358; S. Rivington, *The History of Tonbridge School*, p. 61; J. P. Hart, *The Parish Council of Bletchingley in the County of Surrey, A Transcription of Parish Documents* (Redhill, Surrey, 1955), p. 10; Williamson, p. 160; *Sussex Archaeological Collections*, xliii, 79.

5. New College, Oxford, The Orders for Adderbury School; Carlisle, i, 224; Peacock, p. 65; Sampson, p. 95; Davies, *Southampton*, p. 317.

6. *D.N.B.*

PAGE 90

1. *'Brief Lives,' chiefly of Contemporaries, set down by John Aubrey, between the Years 1669 and 1696*, ed. A Clark (Oxford, 1898), i, 202–3.

2. Boys, p. 229; Chambres, p. 92; Carlisle, i, 603, 728, ii, 357–8.
3. *V.C.H. Berks.*, ii, 269.
4. Bodleian Library, MS. Oxf. Archd. papers Oxon C 160, fols. 267–8.

PAGE 91
1. *A New Discovery of the old Art of Teaching Schoole,* 'Scholastick Discipline', pp. 224, 250–3.

PAGE 92
1. *A New Discovery of the old Art of Teaching Schoole,* 'Scholastick Discipline', pp. 213–15.

PAGE 93
1. R. H. Quick, *Essays on Educational Reformers* (London, 1910), p. 8.
2. W. O. Lester Smith, *To Whom do Schools Belong?* p. 62.
3. See F. Watson, *The English Grammar Schools to 1660,* p. 261.
4. J. Webster, *Academiarum Examen, Or The Examination of Academies* (London, 1654), pp. 22, 23, 100; S. Hartlib, *The True and Readie Way to Learne the Latine Tongue. Attested by Three Excellently Learned and Approved Authours of Three Nations* (London, 1654), pp. 45–47; G. Miège, *A New French Grammar; Or, A New Method For Learning of the French Tongue* (London, 1678), p. 377; H. Wotton, *An Essay On The Education of Children, In The First Rudiments of Learning. Together With A Narrative of what Knowledge, William Wotton, A child of six Years of Age, had attained unto, upon the Improvement of those Rudiments, in the Latin, Greek, and Hebrew Tongues.* (Published in 1672 and reprinted in London, 1753), pp. 36, 38–39.

PAGE 94
1. *A New Discovery of the old Art of Teaching Schoole,* 'The Ushers Duty', pp. 41, 59.
2. Carlisle, i, 224, 420.
3. *Considerations concerning Free Schools,* p. 91.

PAGE 95
1. British Museum, Sloane MSS., 649, fols. 52–53.

PAGE 96
1. J. Durie, *The Reformed Librarie-Keeper with a Supplement to the Reformed-School, as subordinate to Colleges in Universities,* 1650, p. 5.
2. T. Hobbes, *Behemoth or The Long Parliament,* ed. F. Tonnies (London, 1889), p. 90.
3. *Memoirs, Illustrative of the Life and Writings of John Evelyn, Esq., F.R.S.,* ed. W. Bray (second edition, London, 1819), ii, 217.

PAGE 97
1. *The Grounds and Occasions of the Contempt of the Clergy and Religion Enquired into in a Letter written to R.L.,* London, 1670.
2. Bodleian Library, MS. Aubrey 10, fol. 8.
3. *Some Thoughts concerning Education,* pp. 138–9, 170–1, 174, 175.

PAGE 98
1. *Bishop Burnet's History of His Own Time* (London, 1734), ii, 245–6, 651. As tutor

to the duke of Gloucester Burnet had the opportunity to put his educational theory into practice, going into religious questions very thoroughly and 'thro' Geography so often with him, that he knew all the Maps very particularly,' explaining to him 'the forms of Government in every Country, with the Interests and Trade of that Country, and what was both good and bad in it', acquainting him 'with all the great Revolutions, that had been in the world', giving him 'a copious account of the Greek and Roman Histories, and of Plutarch's Lives', and finally explaining to him 'the Gothick Constitution, and the Beneficiary and Feudal Laws'.

2. *V.C.H. Essex*, ii, 524; *D.N.B.*

PAGE 99
1. *The Records of Blackburn Grammar School*, part i, p. 74.
2. W. Trollope, *A History of the Royal Foundation of Christ's Hospital*, p. 78.
3. Pearce, pp. 99–109.
4. *Schools Inquiry Commission*, i, appendix iv, 73.
5. Charles Hoole gives *Lexicon Geographicum, Poeticum, et Historicum* by Ferrarius, published at London in 1657, as a book 'fitting to be reserved for your Scholars use in the Schoole-librarie'. (*A New Discovery of the old Art of Teaching Schoole*, 'The Masters Method', pp. 162–3.)

PAGE 100
1. *Publications of the Dugdale Society*, vii, The Records of King Edward's School, Birmingham (London, 1928), ii, 92.
2. A. Macdonald, *A History of the King's School, Worcester*, pp. 150–1.
3. Lester Smith, p. 60.
4. J. Webbe, *An Appeale to Truth, In the Controversie between Art, and Use; About the best and most expedient Course in Languages. To be read Fasting; For the greater benefit of the deluded innocencie of our owne, and other Nations* (London, 1622).
5. *The Poetical Works of Robert Lloyd, A.M.* To which is prefixed an Account of the Life and Writings of the Author, by W. Kenrick (London, 1774), i, 5; *D.N.B.*

PAGE 101
1. *C.C.R.* (1830), xxiii, 530–1; *V.C.H. Suffolk*, ii, 322.
2. McDonnell, p. 403.

PAGE 102
1. J. E. G. De Montmorency, *State Intervention in English Education*, p. 182; A. C. Price, *A History of the Leeds Grammar School* (Leeds, 1919), pp. 140–5; S. J. Curtis, *History of Education in Great Britain*, pp. 123–6.
2. Lester Smith, p. 44.
3. Rouse, pp. 120, 133–4, 137–9, 156.
4. *C.C.R.* (1828), xix, 160.

PAGE 103
1. Walker, pp. 263, 264–5.

2. Mumford, pp. 170–1, 192–7, 232.
3. N. Hans, *New Trends in Education in the Eighteenth Century*, pp. 6, 37–41.
4. C. Norwood, *The English Tradition of Education* (London, 1929), p. 13.

PAGE 104
1. T. S. Ashton, *An Economic History of England: The 18th Century* (London, 1955), p. 1.

PAGE 105
1. *V.C.H. Herts.*, ii, 86.
2. *V.C.H. Essex*, ii, 506.
3. Wase MSS., C.C.C. Oxon 390/2, fol. 203.

PAGE 106
1. *C.C.R.* (1819), i, 210.
2. *V.C.H. Essex*, ii, 545.
3. *C.C.R.* (1837–8), xxxii, part i, 569, 570–1, 576.
4. Carlisle, ii, 209, 278.
5. See pp. 53–56 above.
6. W. A. Abram, *A History of Blackburn* (Blackburn, 1877), p. 342.
7. *C.C.R.* (1819), i, 212.

PAGE 107
1. *C.C.R.* (1833), xxv, 570, 573–4.
2. Carlisle, ii, 773.
3. F. Watson, *The Old Grammar Schools* (Cambridge, 1916), p. 129.
4. J. Butler, *A Charge Deliver'd to the Clergy, at the Primary Visitation of the Diocese of Durham, in the year, 1751* (Durham, 1751), p. 5.
5. T. Secker, *Eight Charges Delivered To The Clergy of the Dioceses of Oxford and Canterbury* (London, 1769), pp. 4, 5.
6. G. Berkeley, *A Discourse Addressed To Magistrates and Men in Authority* (Dublin, 1738), p. 41.

PAGE 108
1. Lester Smith, p. 60.
2. S. C. Carpenter, *Eighteenth Century Church and People* (London, 1959), p. 275.

PAGE 109
1. J. Durie, *The Reformed-School: and the Reformed Librarie-Keeper,* London. Printed by William Du-Gard, and are to bee sold by Rob. Littleberrie at the sign of the Unicorn in Little Britain, 1651. The Publisher to the Reader.
2. Fisher, pp. 166–70.
3. *C.S.P.D.* 1655–56, ? January, p. 153. See also p. 125 below.

PAGE 110
1. *Documents relating to the Settlement of the Church of England by the Act of Uniformity of 1662*, ed. G. Gould (London, 1862), pp. 392–3.

2. *The Statutes at Large in Paragraphs and Sections or Numbers, Beginning with the Reign of King James I,* ii, 1320.
3. E. Cardwell, *Documentary Annals of the Reformed Church of England,* ii, 274, 286–7.

PAGE 111
1. *The Reports of Sir Peyton Ventris Kt, The First Part* (London, 1701), p. 41.
2. *Public General Acts,* 19 Geo. III, Cap. xliv (London, 1779), pp. 963–6.
3. A. G. Matthews, *Calamy Revised* (Oxford, 1934), pp. xiv, xxvi, 17–543.
4. E. Calamy, *An Account of the Ministers, Lecturers, Masters and Fellows of Colleges and Schoolmasters, Who were Ejected or Silenced after the Restoration in 1660* (second edition, London, 1713), ii, 841–5.

PAGE 112
1. Bodleian Library, MS. Oxf. Archd. papers Oxon C 160, fol. 266.
2. Wase MSS., C.C.C. Oxon 390/2, fol. 169.

PAGE 113
1. P.R.O., Petty Bag Inquisitions, Bundle 29, No. 15, 19 Charles II. Such was the situation revealed by an inquisition held at Lewes on 24 December 1667 when the Commissioners of Charitable Uses ordered that arrears of rents and also compensation amounting to twenty pounds should be paid to Weston. It appeared that three of the school trustees had objected to the evasion of the founder's intention and had appointed to the mastership Robert Sparke who was a Cambridge undergraduate. Their objection went unheeded since it was shown that they were disloyal to the restored monarchy and the deception was evidently allowed to continue.
2. W. A. Sampson, *A History of the Bristol Grammar School,* pp. 87, 88.
3. *V.C.H. Durham,* i, 394; R. Surtees, *The History and Antiquities of the County Palatine of Durham,* i, 159.
4. Wase MSS., C.C.C. Oxon 390/2, fol. 120. See also Carlisle, i, 130, ii, 805.
5. See, for example, Aylesbury (G. Lipscomb, *The History and Antiquities of the County of Buckingham,* London, 1847, ii, 63, 65), Urswick (*V.C.H. Lancs.,* ii, 608), Fotheringay (H. K. Bonney, *Historic Notices in reference to Fotheringay,* Oundle, London and Edinburgh, 1821, pp. 10, 70), Standen and Stokenchurch (Wase MSS., C.C.C. Oxon 390/2, fol. 123, 390/3, fol. 167).

PAGE 114
1. *Remarks and Collections of Thomas Hearne,* ed. H. E. Salter (Oxford, 1914), ix, 36; C. C. Brookes, *A History of Steeple Aston, and Middle Aston, Oxfordshire* (Long Compton, Shipton-on-Stour, 1929), pp. 329–30; *Brasenose College Monographs* (Oxford, 1909), ii, XII, 33.
2. *Remarks and Collections of Thomas Hearne,* ed. C. E. Dobie (Oxford, 1885), i, 231 (Oxford, 1886), ii, 213; Brookes, pp. 332–3; W. W. Wing, *Annals of Steeple Aston and Middle Aston* (Oxford, 1875), p. 38.
See, for example, Brackley, (*V.C.H. Northants.,* ii, 233, E. G. Forrester, *A History of*

Magdalen College School, Brackley, Northamptonshire 1548–1949, Buckingham, 1950, p. 31), Hertford (*V.C.H. Herts.,* ii, 92, Sir H. Chauncy, *The Historical Antiquities of Hertfordshire,* London, 1700, reprinted 1826, i, 155), Gloucester (S. Rudder, *A New History of Gloucestershire,* Cirencester, 1779, pp. 165, 170, 426), Reading (C. Coates, *The History and Antiquities of Reading,* London, 1802, p. 342, *V.C.H. Berks.,* ii, 257), Chelmsford and Saffron Walden (*V.C.H. Essex,* ii, 512, 524), Colchester (P. Morant, *The History and Antiquities of the County of Essex,* London, 1768, i, 178, *Register of the Scholars Admitted to Colchester School 1637–1740,* ed. J. H. Round, Colchester, 1897, p. 69).

PAGE 115
1. F. Blomefield, *An Essay towards a Topographical History of the County of Norfolk* (London, 1805), ii, 157; *V.C.H. Suffolk,* ii, 305.
2. H. C. Bradby, *Rugby* (London, 1900), p. 27; Rouse, pp. 91–92.

PAGE 116
1. W. Dickinson, *The History and Antiquities of the Town of Southwell* (London, 1819), appendix, pp. 382–3; W. A. James, *An Account of the Grammar and Song Schools of the Collegiate Church of Blessed Mary the Virgin of Southwell,* pp. 18–19; *V.C.H. Notts.,* ii, 193.
2. *V.C.H. Notts.,* ii, 181.
3. P.R.O., Petty Bag Inquisitions, Bundle 43, No. 18, 4 James II.
4. *Schools Inquiry Commission,* vol. i, Report of the Commissioners, appendix iv, p. 74; *V.C.H. Warwicks.,* ii, 368.
5. Wase MSS., C.C.C. Oxon 390/1, fol. 12; *C.C.R.* (4 March 1819), appendix, p. 17; New College, Oxford, Copy of Christopher Rawlins' will, August 7th, 1589; *Hastings, Past and Present* (Hastings and London, 1855), p. 77; *C.C.R.* (1819), pp. 230–1. See also Cuckfield (*V.C.H. Sussex,* ii, 417), Nottingham (*Records of the Borough of Nottingham,* London and Nottingham, 1900, v, 294, 295, 296, 297, 312, 317, *V.C.H. Notts.,* ii, 230–1), Houghton (*V.C.H. Durham,* i, 394. R. Surtees, *The History and Antiquities of the County Palatine of Durham,* i, 159).
6. *C.C.R.* (1834), xxviii, 528–9. See also Wakefield (M. H. Peacock, *History of the Free Grammar School of Queen Elizabeth at Wakefield,* p. 63), Langport Eastover (*V.C.H. Somerset,* ii, 456).

PAGE 117
1. Carlisle, i, 418.
2. H. Fishwick, *The History of the Parish of Preston* (Rochdale and London, 1900), pp. 205, 209; E. Baines, *The History of the County Palatine and Duchy of Lancaster,* ii, 459, 469; *V.C.H. Lancs.,* ii, 572.
3. *V.C.H. Suffolk,* ii, 320–1.
4. Carlisle, ii, 831–2.
5. P. Morant, *The History and Antiquities of the most ancient Town and Borough of Colchester* (London, 1768), pp. 176, 177–8.

PAGE 118
1. P. Thompson, *The History and Antiquities of Boston* (Boston, 1856), p. 285 and footnotes.

2. Mumford, pp. 102, 103, 128, 499.
3. Muniments at Brasenose College, Oxford, Schools, 22, 23.
4. A. T. Lee, *The History of the Town and Parish of Tetbury* (London, 1857), p. 301.
5. Varley, pp. 271–2.
6. Carlisle, i, 418, ii, 8, 585, 605.
7. T. Sandall, *The History of the Stamford Grammar School* (Stamford), pp. 7, 10; *Register of the Scholars Admitted to Colchester School 1637–1740*, p. 80; P. Morant, *The History and Antiquities of the County of Essex*, i, 178.

PAGE 119
1. Wase MSS., C.C.C. Oxon 390/1, fol. 63.
2. *The History and Antiquities of Guildford*, p. 132 footnote.
3. *V.C.H. Lincs.*, ii, 488.

PAGE 123
1. Coates, p. 339; E. J. Climenson, *The History of Shiplake, Oxon* (London, 1894), p. 282.
2. *V.C.H. Berks.*, ii, 256, 269.
3. *V.C.H. Lincs.*, ii, 458; Thompson, p. 285.
4. Coates, p. 341.
5. *V.C.H. Northants.*, ii, 267.
6. *V.C.H. Notts.*, ii, 210–11.
7. *V.C.H. Herts.*, ii, 65.

PAGE 124
1. C. E. Woodruff and H. J. Cape, *Schola Regia Cantuariensis*, pp. 121, 123.
2. A. F. Leach, 'Early Yorkshire Schools', i, 229–30, *The Yorkshire Archaeological Society*, Record Series (London, 1899), xxvii.
3. W. Money, *The History of the Ancient Town and Borough of Newbury* (Oxford and London, 1887), p. 251.
4. Frangopulo, p. 93; *V.C.H. Derby*, ii, 260.
5. Fisher, pp. 138, 153, 160–71, 174–6; J. M. West, *Shrewsbury School* (London, 1937), p. 36.

PAGE 125
1. *C.S.P.D.*, 1654, 30 May, 15 June, 17 August, pp. 190, 212, 308; Firth and Rait, ii, 958–89.
2. J. Sargeaunt, *A History of Bedford School*, edited and completed by E. Hockliffe (Bedford and London, 1925), pp. 32–33; *V.C.H. Beds.*, ii, 164–5.
3. A. Wood, *Fasti Oxonienses* (London, 1721), ii, 100.

PAGE 126
1. W. H. Brown, *Charterhouse Past and Present* (Godalming, 1879), p. 145; Maxwell Lyte, pp. 256, 257, 519.

PAGE 127
1. Coates, pp. 341–2; *V.C.H. Berks.*, ii, 256–7.

2. A. F. Leach, *Educational Charters and Documents 598 to 1909* (Cambridge, 1911), introduction, p. xlvii.

1. D. Masson, *The Life of John Milton* (London, 1877), iv, 148, 152, 225, 250, footnote, 251–2.
2. W. C. Hazlitt, *Schools, School-Books and Schoolmasters* (London, 1888), pp. 145–9.
3. *C.S.P.D. 1649–50*, 1 February, p. 500; *Merchant Taylors' School, Its Origin, History and Present Surroundings* (Oxford, 1929), pp. 46, 47.
4. Stanier, p. 122.
5. A. Wood, *Athenae Oxonienses*, ed. P. Bliss (London, 1817), iii, 942.

1. R. North, *The Lives of the Right Hon. Francis North, Baron Guilford; The Hon. Sir Dudley North; And the Hon. and Rev. Dr. John North*, i, 16, ii, 271–4; *The Gentleman's Magazine* (1850), xxxiii, new series, 40.

1. R. South, *Sermons Preached Upon Several Occasions* (Oxford, 1842), iii, 96.
2. *Admissions to the College of St. John the Evangelist in the University of Cambridge* (Cambridge, 1893), part I, pp. 136, 170; Sandall, p. 7; *V.C.H. Lincs.*, ii, 475; Gray, pp. 40, 48, 50–51, 63; *V.C.H. Northants.*, ii, 238; Cox, p. 26.
3. C. R. L. Fletcher, *Mr. Gladstone at Oxford* (London, 1908), pp. 51–52.
4. *The Palatine Note-Book for 1882* (Manchester, Chester and Liverpool), ii, 58.

1. Mumford, pp. 74–75, 99–102; *The Diary of the Rev. Henry Newcome*, ed. T. Heywood (Printed for the Chetham Society, 1849), 11 and 17 July, 14, 15 and 17 August, 1663, pp. 200, 203, 212, 213.
2. Gray and Potter, pp. 59–60, 161.
3. J. Sargeaunt, *A History of Felsted School* (Chelmsford and London, 1889), pp. 17–18; *Alumni Felstedienses*, ed. G. J. Hornsby Wright (Felsted, 1903), pp. 5–8; Miss C. Fell-Smith, *Mary Rich, Countess of Warwick (1625–1678): Her Family and Friends* (London, 1901), pp. 202–3.

1. Coates, pp. 342–3.
2. H. Fishwick, *The History of the Parish of Preston*, p. 209.
3. Woodruff and Cape, pp. 147–8.
4. *Records of the Borough of Nottingham*, vi, 34.

1. *Rugby, The School and Neighbourhood*, collected and arranged from the writings of the late M. H. Bloxham by W. H. Payne Smith, pp. 26–28, 37.
2. Bradby, pp. 25–27; Rouse, pp. 89–95.
3. Fisher, pp. 191–2, 200–1.
4. *The History and Antiquities of Northamptonshire. Compiled from the Manuscript*

Collections of the late learned antiquary John Bridges, By the Rev. Peter Whalley (Oxford, 1741), ii, 153.

PAGE 134
1. *V.C.H. Northants.*, ii, 268.

PAGE 135
1. A. F. Leach, *History of Warwick School*, pp. 105–6, 133, 136, 140–4.
2. *Publications of the Dugdale Society* (London, 1928), vii, The Records of King Edward's School, Birmingham, ii, 93–94, 95–96, 98, 116, 120, 122.
3. Stanier, pp. 104–5, 124.

PAGE 136
1. *Admissions to the College of St. John the Evangelist in the University of Cambridge,* part II, pp. 95, 99.
2. H. Chauncy, *The Historical Antiquities of Hertfordshire,* ii, 329. Mr. A. F. Leach wrote that 'the only known copy of his immortal poem lies buried in the Hertfordshire Museum. It was printed at London "impensis auctoris, 1683," in a pamphlet of 34 pages, and consists of 835 Latin hexameters, with a dedication to the famous Sir Harbottle Grimston'. (*V.C.H. Herts.,* ii, 66.)
3. P. Morant, *The History and Antiquities of the County of Essex,* i, 177; W. Winstanley, *The Lives of the most famous English Poets* (London, 1687), pp. 204–6.
4. *Poetical Recreations: Consisting of Original Poems, Songs, Odes, &c. With several New Translations. In Two Parts. Part I. Occasionally Written by Mrs. Jane Barker. Part II. By several Gentlemen of the Universities and Others.* London, Printed for Benjamin Crayle, at the Peacock and Bible, at the West-end of St. Pauls. 1688.

PAGE 137
1. D. W. Garrow, *The History and Antiquities of Croydon* (Croydon, 1818), pp. 130–1 and footnotes; E. J. Balley, *Whitgift School and Its Evolution* (Croydon, 1937), pp. 19, 20; A. Wood, *Athenae Oxonienses,* ii, 344, 751–2, *Fasti,* ii, 195. Crowe committed suicide and was succeeded by John Shepherd, B.C.L. of Wadham College, Oxford. Oldham after leaving Croydon acted as a private tutor until his death from smallpox in 1683.
2. A. Wood, *Athenae Oxonienses,* ii, 1011.
3. A. Wood, *Athenae Oxonienses,* ii, 709–10; Burn, p. 97. Provision against the practice of physic by the schoolmasters was included in the new statutes of 1614 for St. Saviour's School, Surrey, and in the orders confirmed by the Commissioners of Charitable Uses on 12 March 1704–5 for Langport Eastover Grammar School in Somerset. (*V.C.H. Surrey,* ii, 179, *V.C.H. Somerset,* ii, 456.)

PAGE 138
1. *A Compleat History of Oxfordshire* (London, 1730), p. 374.
2. Ετυμολογικὸν μικρου sive, *Etymologium Parvum, ex Magno illo Sylburgii Eustathio, Martinio, aliisque magni Nominis Authoribus, Excerptum, digestum, explicatum,* Londini 1654.
3. 'Ονομαστικου βραχύ *Sive Nomenclatura Brevis, Reformata* (London, 1663).
4. A. Wood, *Fasti,* ii, 146–7.

5. *Plutarch's Morals. Translated from the Greek by Several Hands, corrected and revised by W. W. Goodwin* (Boston, 1874), i, 185–250.
6. W. H. Brown, *Charterhouse Past and Present* (Godalming, 1879), pp. 146–7.

PAGE 139
1. 'Felsted School' by an old Felstedian, *The Essex Revue,* ed. E. A. Fitch and Miss C. Fell Smith (Chelmsford and London, 1898), vii, 82–83; J. Sargeaunt, *A History of Felsted School,* pp. 22, 23; *Alumni Felstedienses,* pp. 8, 11; P. Morant, *The History and Antiquities of the County of Essex,* ii, 421.
2. *V.C.H. Essex,* ii, 524; W. Munk, *The Roll of the Royal College of Physicians of London* (London, 1861), i, 433.
3. *Epistolae Medicanales Variis Occasionibus Conscriptae. Authore Ricardo Carr, M.D. Londini 1691.*

PAGE 140
1. F. C. Hipkins, *Repton and its Neighbourhood* (second edition, Repton, 1899), pp. 65–70; G. S. Messiter, *Records and Reminiscences of Repton* (Repton, 1907), pp. 14–19; A Macdonald, *A Short History of Repton,* pp. 100–6.

PAGE 141
1. *Rugby, The School and Neighbourhood,* p. 42; Bradby, pp. 24–25.
2. J. Sargeaunt, *A History of Felsted School,* pp. 22–23; 'Felsted School' by an old Felstedian, *The Essex Revue,* vii, 83; *A Tour Thro' the whole Island of Great Britain, Divided into Circuits or Journeys.* By a Gentleman (London, 1724), i, 135.
3. Fisher, pp. 160–71, 187–8.
4. Hill, p. 38.

PAGE 142
1. British Museum, MSS., 29, 477, James Hume's Commonplace Book; W. Young, *The History of Dulwich College,* i, 215–16, 218.
2. Library Catalogue and Statute Book in the Library of Witney Grammar School, Oxfordshire; *V.C.H. Lincs.,* ii, 445.

PAGE 143
1. *V.C.H. Herts.,* ii, 76.
2. G. Griffith, *The Free Schools of Worcestershire, and their Fulfilment* (London, 1852), p. 230.

PAGE 144
1. *V.C.H. Worcs.,* iv, 517–8. See also *V.C.H. Hants.,* ii, 389, J. S. Davies, *A History of Southampton,* pp. 313, 394.
2. *Records of the Borough of Nottingham* (London and Nottingham, 1900), v, 374, 395, 400, 402 (Nottingham, 1914), vi, 25, 34, 35.

PAGE 145
1. *V.C.H. Northants.,* ii, 213.
2. Fisher, pp. 201–3.

PAGE 146
1. Varley, pp. 88–89.

PAGE 147
1. Young, i, 150, 167, 174–5.
2. Letter from Mayor (John White) announcing death of Mr. Allanson, 5 February 1665, at New College, Oxford.
3. Letter from Corporation (John Parradise, Mayor) recommending Mr. Aspinall to be Master, on retirement of Mr. Willis, 30 July 1683, at New College, Oxford.

PAGE 148
1. Two copies of letter (Henry Beeston, Warden) to Corporation presenting Mr. Aspinall of Emmanuel College, Cambridge, during absence of Mr. Longworth, 8 November 1683, at New College, Oxford; J. Sargeaunt, *A History of Bedford School*, pp. 35–36; *V.C.H. Beds.*, ii, 165–7.
2. *V.C.H. Derbys.*, ii, 260–1; Frangopulo, pp. 93, 95.
3. *V.C.H. Worcs.*, iv, 505.
4. *V.C.H. Oxon.*, i, 471; Burn, p. 97.
5. *V.C.H. Sussex*, ii, 410, *V.C.H. Worcs.*, iv, 517. See also *V.C.H. Hants.*, ii, 381, *V.C.H. Notts.*, ii, 211.

PAGE 149
1. M. Craze, *A History of Felsted School 1564–1947* (Ipswich, 1955), pp. 99–102. See also *V.C.H. Herts.*, ii, 66.
2. See, for example, *C.C.R.* (1826–7), xvii, 229, (1831), xxiv, 503, Carlisle, i, 795, ii, 271.
3. Carlisle, i, 466–7; *Schools Inquiry Commission*, xv, 121; *C.C.R.* (1829), xxi, 164.

PAGE 150
1. Bonney, pp. 10, 70.
2. *C.C.R.* (1819), i, appendix, 8.

PAGE 151
1. *C.C.R.* (1819), i, appendix, 376–7.
2. *V.C.H. Surrey*, ii, 171.

PAGE 152
1. *A New Discovery of the old Art of Teaching Schoole*, pp. x–xi.

PAGE 154
1. Wase MSS., C.C.C. Oxon 390/2, fol. 8
2. Wase MSS., C.C.C. Oxon 390/2, fol. 25.
3. Wase MSS., C.C.C. Oxon 390/1, fol. 199.
4. Walker, pp. 156–7, 160, 164, 171–8, 195–8, 202–4; *V.C.H. Northants.*, ii, 254–6.
5. Vincent, pp. 40–41.
6. C. Wilson, *England's Apprenticeship 1603–1763* (London, 1965), pp. 20, 21.

PAGE 155
1. *V.C.H. Herts.*, ii, 86.
2. *V.C.H. Durham*, i, 391.
3. *V.C.H. Northants.*, ii, 267, *V.C.H. Essex*, ii, 524.

PAGE 156

1. *V.C.H. Lancs,* ii, 598. See also Muniments at Brasenose College, Oxford, Charl-bury 6, Schools 22, 23.
2. J. Sargeaunt, *A History of Felsted School,* pp. 19–20.

PAGE 157

1. R. Pemberton, *Solihull and its Church,* pp. 152–3.
2. New College, Oxford, Copy of letter (Michael Woodward, Warden) to Cor-poration announcing appointment of Mr. John Allanson, Chaplain of New College, 10 December 1663.
3. Letter from Mayor (John White) announcing death of Mr. Allanson, 5 Feb-ruary 1665.
4. Copy of letter announcing appointment of Mr. John Butler of New Inn Hall, on death of Mr. Allanson, 15 February 1665.
5. *V.C.H. Beds.,* ii, 166.

PAGE 158

1. New College, Oxford, Copy of letter (Michael Woodward, Warden) to Cor-poration as to reduction of school fees to townsmen to 2*d.* a quarter, 9 Novem-ber 1668.
2. Letter from Mayor, Thomas Underwood, as to right of reduction of master's salary, 21 February 1668–9.
3. Copy of letter to Corporation as to master's salary, 24 February 1668–9.
4. Copy of letter to Corporation confirming master's choice of John Gascoyne as usher, and expecting continuance of augmentation of master's salary, 8 January 1671–2.
5. Letter from Mr. Butler, resigning, 5 August 1672; Letter from Corporation (Richard Mightnall, Mayor) announcing Mr. Butler's resignation, 6 August 1672.
6. *V.C.H. Beds.,* ii, 167.

PAGE 159

1. New College, Oxford, Agreement between Corporation (R. Walker, Mayor) and Mr. Aspinall as to repairs of school, 30 November 1706.
2. Wase MSS., C.C.C. Oxon 390/1, fols. 93, 124, 390/2, fol. 184.
3. New College Oxford, Letter from Bedford Corporation (Michael Woodward, Warden) announcing the death of Mr. Varney, 16 November 1663.
4. Library Catalogue and Statute Book in the Library of Witney Grammar School, Oxfordshire; J. A. Giles, *History of Witney* (London, 1852), pp. 42–44.
5. British Museum, Lansd. MSS. 119, fol. 14; *V.C.H. Suffolk,* ii, 321.
6. *The Life and Times of Anthony Wood, antiquary, of Oxford, 1632–1695, described by Himself,* ed. A. Clark (Oxford, 1891), i, 108, 124, 223–4 (Oxford, 1892), ii, 116.

PAGE 160

1. Climenson, pp. 282, 285.

2. *Considerations concerning Free Schools*, pp. 67–68.
3. *A New Discovery of the old Art of Teaching Schoole*, 'Scholastick Discipline', p. 227.
4. Miss Anne Whiteman, 'The Re-Establishment of the Church of England', *Transactions of the Royal Historical Society* (London, 1955), v, 128.

PAGE 161
1. Wase MSS., C.C.C. Oxon 390/2, fol. 211.
2. *Publications of the Dugdale Society*, vii, xii, xx, The Records of King Edward's School, Birmingham (London, 1928), 11, 13, 62 (London, 1933), iii, 39, 129, 279 (London, 1948), iv, 3, 5, 13.
3. *V.C.H. Warwicks.*, ii, 346.
4. *V.C.H. Lancs.*, ii, 586.
5. Wase MSS., C.C.C. Oxon 390/2, fol. 211.

PAGE 162
1. Brasenose College, Oxford, A Copy of the Orders of Charlbury School, Charlbury 2, 5.
2. *C.C.R.* (1837–8), xxxii, pt. i, 719–21.
3. *Records of the Borough of Nottingham*, v. 294, 295, 336.
4. G. Chalmers, *An Estimate of the Comparative Strength of Great Britain; and of the Losses of Her Trade, A New Edition, Corrected and Continued to 1803. To which is now annexed Gregory King's Celebrated State of England, with notices of His Life* (London, 1804), pp. 48–49.
5. See P. Laslett, *The World we have lost* (London, 1965), pp. 26–50.
6. Wase MSS., C.C.C. Oxon 390/1, fol. 198, 390/2, fols, 135, 243.
7. Row, p. 10.
8. *V.C.H. Notts.*, ii, 181.

PAGE 163
1. *C.C.R.* (1830), xxii, 140–1.
2. Wase MSS., C.C.C. Oxon 390/1, fol. 268.
3. Wase MSS., C.C.C. Oxon 390/2, fol. 38.
4. Wase MSS., C.C.C. Oxon 390/2, fol. 22.
5. Wase MSS., C.C.C. Oxon 390/2, fol. 153.
6. Wase MSS., C.C.C. Oxon 390/3, fol. 167.

PAGE 164
1. Wase MSS., C.C.C. Oxon 390/2, fol. 115.
2. Wase MSS., C.C.C. Oxon 390/2, fol. 137.
3. *C.C.R.* (1834), xxviii, 505.
4. See p. 161 above.
5. *C.C.R.* (18 September 1820), pp. 403–4.
6. *V.C.H. Durham*, i, 391.
7. See J. M. Gray, *A History of the Perse School, Cambridge*, pp. 15–16, Wase MSS., C.C.C. Oxon 390/1, fols. 46, 256.
8. Wase MSS., C.C.C. Oxon 390/2, fols. 155, 156.
9. Ibid., 390/2, fol. 1.

10. P.R.O., Petty Bag Inquisitions, Bundle 40, No. 11, 35 Charles II.
11. *V.C.H. Herts.*, ii, 86.

PAGE 165
1. *Durham School Register*, second edition, to June 1912, ed. C. S. Earle and L. A. Body (London, 1912), p. 25. See also I. E. Gray and W. E. Potter, *Ipswich School 1400–1950*, pp. 60–63, 161, 163.
2. T. D. Fosbrooke, *An Original History of the City of Gloucester* (London, 1819), p. 116; S. Rudder, *A New History of Gloucestershire*, pp. 166, 171; *V.C.H. Glos.*, ii, 331.
3. See pp. 137–8, 159 above.
4. See pp. 53, 105. See also *C.C.R.* (1830), xxiii, 374–5 (1831), xxiv, 185 (1834), xxviii, 424; A. F. Leach, *English Schools at the Reformation 1546–8* (Westminster, 1896), pp. 147, 149, 151–2, 153.
5. *C.C.R.* (18 September 1820), pp. 403–4.
6. *C.C.R.* (30 June 1821), pp. 618–20.

PAGE 166
1. See P. Morant, *The History and Antiquities of the County of Essex*, ii, 520, P.R.O., Petty Bag Inquisitions, Bundle 26, No. 6, 13 Charles II, *C.C.R.* (1819), p. 162, *C.C.R.* (1835), xxix, pt. i, 113–14, 370, *V.C.H. Northants.*, ii, 278.
2. *Sussex Archaeological Collections*, xliii, 77; J. and S. Russell, *The History of Guildford*, p. 99; G. C. Williamson, *The Royal Grammar School of Guildford*, pp. 56, 156–7; MS. Oxf. Archd. papers Oxon C 160, fol. 70.
3. *V.C.H. Durham*, i, 381.
4. Hill, p. 37; Sampson, p. 97.
5. Hill, pp. 56, 62, 63.

PAGE 167
1. *C.C.R.* (1826–7), xvii, 487; A. F. Leach, *History of Warwick School*, pp. 154, 157, 158, 170.
2. *Considerations concerning Free Schools*, p. 68.
3. M. Nedham, *A Discourse Concerning Schools and School-Masters* (London, 1663), pp. 3, 4.

PAGE 168
1. S. Piggott, *William Stukeley* (Oxford, 1950), p. 84.
2. W. Massey, *The Origin and Progress of Letters*, Part the Second (London, 1763), pp. 115–20.
3. See p. 49 above.
4. J. Lawson, *The Endowed Grammar Schools of East Yorkshire*, p. 19.
5. C. E. Woodruff and H. J. Cape, *Schola Regia Cantuariensis: A History of Canterbury School*, pp. 147–8; *Records of the Borough of Nottingham* (Nottingham, 1914), vi, 34.
6. E. Calamy, *The Nonconformist's Memorial*, ed. S. Palmer (London, 1778), i, 324–7; W. Wilson, *The History and Antiquities of Dissenting Churches and Meeting Houses* (London, 1808), i, 373.

PAGE 169
1. A. Savidge, *The Foundation and Early Years of Queen Anne's Bounty* (London, 1955), p. 9.

2. G. F. A. Best, *Temporal Pillars* (Cambridge, 1964), p. 13.

PAGE 170
1. Other authorities give the date 1647.
2. 1653 (R.); 1648 (V.).
3. 1656 (R); 1657 (C.).

PAGE 171
1. Other authorities say 1466–67.
2. About 1612 (R.); before 1610 (V.).
3. Other authorities say about 1630.
4. Other authorities give the date 1649.
5. About 1552 (R.); 1449 or 1551 (C.); 1448 (V.).

PAGE 173
1. Wase MSS., C.C.C. Oxon 390/2, fols. 184, 186.
2. *Considerations concerning Free Schools*, pp. 82, 83, 84, 85.

PAGE 174
1. *A Discourse Concerning Schools and School-Masters*, p. 4.
2. Wase MSS., C.C.C. Oxon 390/1, fol. 251, 390/2, fols. 169, 171, 390/3, fol. 20.
3. *Schools Inquiry Commission*, i, 245, 274.

PAGE 175
1. P.R.O., Petty Bag Inquisitions, Bundle 43, No. 18, 4 James II.
2. Wase MSS., C.C.C. Oxon 390/1, fol. 91, 390/2, fols. 8, 38.
3. *Schools Inquiry Commission*, i, 245.
4. P.R.O., Petty Bag Inquisitions, Bundle 28, No. 24, 17 Charles II.

PAGE 176
1. *V.C.H. Suffolk*, ii, 342.
2. Wase MSS., C.C.C. Oxon 390/1, fols. 3, 71.
3. Wase MSS., C.C.C. Oxon 390/1, fol. 143.
4. Wase MSS., C.C.C. Oxon 390/2, fol. 155.
5. Wase MSS., C.C.C. Oxon 390/1, fol. 198.

PAGE 177
1. Wase MSS., C.C.C. Oxon 390/1, fol. 146.
2. Wase MSS., C.C.C. Oxon 390/1, fol. 265.
3. Wase MSS., C.C.C. Oxon 390/2, fol. 10.
4. *V.C.H. Glos.*, ii, 406–7.

PAGE 178
1. Carlisle, i, 471–6.

PAGE 179
1. Wase MSS., C.C.C. Oxon 390/1, fol. 239, 391/1, fols. 5, 6.
2. *Schools Inquiry Commission*, i, 254–70.

PAGE 180
1. *C.C.R.* (8 July 1820), pp. 196–7; J. S. Piercy, *The History of Retford* (Retford, 1828), pp. 100, 130–2; Carlisle, ii, 280; *V.C.H. Notts.*, ii, 242–3.

PAGE 181
1. Carlisle, i, 425.

2. *C.C.R.* (8 July 1820), appendix, pp. 516–20.

PAGE 182

1. Wase MSS., C.C.C. Oxon 390/2, fol. 148.
2. Carlisle, ii, 372.
3. *Proceedings of the Somersetshire Archaeological & Natural History Society for the year 1907* (Taunton, 1908), liii, 169; *C.C.R.* (1821), pp. 438–9; *V.C.H. Somerset*, ii, 456.

PAGE 183

1. Varley, pp. 82–88.

PAGE 185

1. Wase MSS., C.C.C. Oxon 390/3, fol. 160.
2. New College, Oxford, Letter from Mr. Rogers, Usher at Bedford to Dr. Cobb, Warden of New College, Oxford, 16 January 1717.

PAGE 186

1. New College, Oxford, Letter from Mr. Priaulx to Henry Levitt, Bursar of New College, 6 April 1718.
2. New College, Oxford, Letter from Mr. Priaulx to Mr. Levitt, Bursar of New College, 10 April 1718.
3. New College, Oxford, Letter of 6 April 1726 to Mr. John Goodhall, Town Clerk of Bedford, from New College.
4. New College, Oxford, Letters from Mr. Priaulx to Dr. Dobson, Warden of New College, 23 November 1723, 7 and 11 January 1723–4, 28 March 1724.
5. New College, Oxford, Letters from William Dixon, 22 and 31 July 1725 to Mr. Bigg, Warden of New College.
6. See pp. 157–9 above.

PAGE 187

1. Fisher, pp. 192–7, 211–13; J. Sargeaunt, *A History of Bedford School*, pp. 37–39.
2. Wase MSS., C.C.C. Oxon 390/2, fol. 1.
3. *Publications of the Dugdale Society*, vii, xii, xx, The Records of King Edward's School, Birmingham (London, 1928), ii, 59, 62, 93, 103, 135, 141, 142 (London, 1933), iii, 38–43, 227 (London, 1948), iv, 9, 10; Carlisle, ii, 622–9, 634, 638–9; *V.C.H. Warwicks.*, ii, 352–4.

PAGE 188

1. Hill, pp. 37–38, 41, 47; J. Latimer, *The Annals of Bristol in the Eighteenth Century* (Bristol, 1893), pp. 96, 119; Sampson, pp. 98–99; *V.C.H. Glos.*, ii, 374.
2. *Considerations concerning Free Schools*, pp. 75–76, 80, 81.

PAGE 189

1. *V.C.H. Suffolk.*, ii, 343.
2. A. Macdonald, *A Short History of Repton*, pp. 129–30.

S

3. *C.C.R.* (1828), xviii, 31–32.
4. B. L. Deed, *A History of Stamford School* (Cambridge, 1954), pp. 33–34.
5. *C.C.R.* (1837–38), xxxii, pt. i, 639.
6. *C.C.R.* (1824), xi, 211–12.
7. Carlisle, i, 446. See also *History of the Cheltenham Grammar School as Collected from the Newspaper Reports*, ed. A. Harper (Cheltenham, 1856), pp. 4–5, 18.

PAGE 190
1. Carlisle, i, xxxv.

PAGE 191
1. Miss Irene Parker, *Dissenting Academies in England* (Cambridge, 1914), pp. 45, 51, 58.
2. Ibid., p. 46.

PAGE 193
1. See pp. 19–20 above.
2. Dr. Hans shows that of the group of 3,000 men, English, Welsh, Scottish and Irish, 2,173 went to universities, 1,324 to Oxford and Cambridge, 542 to Scottish universities, 135 to Trinity College, Dublin and 172 to universities or catholic colleges abroad.

PAGE 194
1. N. Hans, *New Trends in Education in the Eighteenth Century*, pp. 6, 16–17, 24–29, 31 55, 62, 64–66, 69.

PAGE 195
1. T. Birch, *The Life of the Honourable Robert Boyle* (London, 1744), pp. 21, 23.
2. *Historical Manuscripts Commission*, fourteenth report, appendix, part ii, The Manuscripts of His Grace The Duke of Portland (London, 1894), iii, 319.
3. G. F. Russell Barker, *Memoir of Richard Busby*, pp. 121–2.

PAGE 196
1. *Some Thoughts concerning Education*, pp. 45, 46, 48, 67, 68, 69, 71, 75, 77, 78.
2. Miss G. Scott Thomson, *Life in A Noble Household 1641–1700* (London, 1937), pp. 72–73.
3. W. Higford, *The Institution of a Gentleman*, London, printed by A. W. for William Lee at the Turks-head in Fleet street, 1660, The Harleian Miscellany (London, 1812), ix, 591.
4. Scott Thomson, pp. 72–73.

PAGE 197
1. Mrs. Lucy Hutchinson, *Memoirs of the Life of Colonel Hutchinson* (London, 1806), p. 103.
2. J. Gailhard, *The Compleat Gentleman: or Directions For the Education of Youth As to their Breeding at Home and Travelling Abroad. In Two Treatises*, p. 17.
3. T. Morrice, *An Apology for Schoole-Masters* (London, 1619).
4. *The Guardian*, No. 163, 17 September 1713 (London, 1756), ii, 316.

5. *The Guardian*, No. 94, ii, 152. See also *The Tatler*, ed. G. A. Aitken, No, 255, 25 November 1710 (London, 1899), iv, 293–6.
6. *Bishop Burnet's History of His Own Time* (Oxford, 1823), vi, 205.
7. H. Peacham, *The Compleat Gentleman* (third impression, London, 1661), p. 22.

PAGE 198
1. D. Defoe, *The Compleat English Gentleman*, ed. K. D. Bulbring (London, 1890), pp. 71, 87.
2. *The Memoirs of Sir John Reresby 1634–1689 Written by Himself*, ed. J. J. Cartwright (London, 1875), p. 22; *The Memoirs and Travels of Sir John Reresby*, ed. A. Ivatt (London, 1904), p. xv.
3. *Collectanea Curiosa*, ed. J. Gutch (Oxford, 1781), i, 212–13.
4. *Lords' Journals*, ii, 36, 37.

PAGE 199
1. F. Watson, *The Beginnings of the Teaching of Modern Subjects in England*, pp. xxxii–xxxiv, 505; *Collectanea, First Series*, ed. C. R. L. Fletcher, part vi, T. W. Jackson, Dr. Wallis' Letter Against Mr. Maidwell, 1700 (Oxford, 1885), pp. 274–83. For a life of Sir Balthazar Gerbier see H. Walpole, *Anecdotes of Painting in England* (London, 1826), ii, 114–27. See also D. Lysons, *The Environs of London* (London, 1795), ii, 30, 31, and the footnotes in which are printed from newspapers some of the advertisements of Gerbier's lectures.
2. See, pp. 206–7 below.

PAGE 200
1. *Historical Manuscripts Commission*, fourteenth report, appendix, part ii, The Manuscripts of His Grace The Duke of Portland, iii, 366, 371.
2. *The Diary of John Evelyn*, iv, 290.

PAGE 201
1. *A Model for a School for the better Education of Youth*, pp. 7, 8.
2. *Historical Manuscripts Commission*, thirteenth report, appendix, part iii, The Manuscripts of J. B. Fortescue, Esq. (London, 1892), i, 13.
3. *Some Thoughts concerning Education*, p. 139.

PAGE 202
1. *The Lives of the Norths*, ii, 2–4.
2. *A New Discovery of the old Art of Teaching Schoole*, 'Scholastick Discipline', p. 285.
3. *C.S.P.D.*, p. 424.
4. F. Watson, 'The Teaching of Arithmetic and Writing in the Time of the Commonwealth', *The Gentleman's Magazine*, September 1899 (London, 1899), cclxxxvii, 260–1.

PAGE 203
1. M. Misson, *Memoires et Observations Faites par un Voyageur en Angleterre* (A La Haye, 1698), p. 99.
2. Miss Kathleen Lambley, *The Teaching and Cultivation of the French Language in England during Tudor and Stuart Times* (Manchester, 1920), p. 396.
3. K. Charlton, *Education in Renaissance England*, pp. 228–39, 269–71; Mrs. Joan Simon, *Education and Society in Tudor England* (Cambridge, 1966), pp. 316–17, 386.
4. M. M. Verney, *Memoirs of the Verney Family During the Commonwealth 1650 to 1660* (London, 1894), iii, 358.
   S*

PAGE 204

1. E. G. R. Taylor, *The Mathematical Practitioners of Tudor and Stuart England* (Cambridge, 1954), pp. 9–10.

PAGE 205

1. Wase MSS., C.C.C. Oxon 390/2, fol. 41.
2. Ibid., 390/2, fol. 211.

PAGE 206

1. *The Home Counties Magazine*, ed. W. J. Hardy (London, 1904), vi, 32–34.
2. *D.N.B.*, G. V. Bennet, *White Kennet, 1660–1728, Bishop of Peterborough* (London, 1957), pp. 8–9.
3. *Oxford Archaeological Society. Reports for the Year 1907* (Banbury, 1908), pp. 23–33.
4. A. Collins, *Historical Collections of the Noble Families of Cavendishe, Holles, Vere, Harley, and Ogle, with the Lives of the most remarkable Persons* (London, 1752), p. 207.
5. *Historical Manuscripts Commission*, fourteenth report, appendix, part ii, The Manuscripts of His Grace, The Duke of Portland, iii, 324, 364.

PAGE 207

1. A. G. Matthews, *Calamy Revised*, pp. 56–57.
2. J. E. B. Mayor, *Admissions to the College of St. John the Evangelist* (Cambridge, 1893), part ii, pp. 82, 86, 99, 104.
3. *D.N.B.*
4. E. Calamy, *The Nonconformist's Memorial*, ed. S. Palmer (London, 1778), i, 324–7; W. Wilson, *The History and Antiquities of Dissenting Churches and Meeting Houses* (London, 1808), i, 373.
5. See pp. 127–8 above.

PAGE 208

1. E. Cardwell, *Documentary Annals of the Reformed Church of England* (Oxford, 1839), ii, 286–7; F. Watson, 'Unlicensed Nonconformist Schoolmasters: 1662 and Onwards', *The Gentleman's Magazine* (July to December 1902), ccxciii, 295.
2. Wase MSS., C.C.C. Oxon 390/2, fol. 10.
3. W. A. L. Vincent, *The State and School Education 1640–1660 in England and Wales*, p. 9.

PAGE 209

1. *A New Discovery of the old Art of Teaching Schoole*, 'Scholastick Discipline', p. 217.
2. *D.N.B.*
3. A. Wood, *Athenae Oxonienses*, iii, 213–14, 1034–5.

PAGE 210

1. L. Stone, 'The Educational Revolution in England, 1560–1640', *Past and Present*, No. 28 (July 1964), p. 46.
2. *A New Discovery of the old Art of Teaching Schoole*, Introductory Note, p. 10.
3. A. Wood, *Athenae Oxonienses*, iii, 758–9; *D.N.B.*
4. A. Wood, *Athenae Oxonienses*, ii, 472; *D.N.B.*
5. F. Watson, *The English Grammar Schools to 1660*, pp. 183–4.
6. See pp. 109–10, 204–5, 208 above.
7. A. G. Matthews, *Calamy Revised* (Oxford, 1934), pp. lv–lvi.
8. Hans, p. 58; W. H. G. Armytage, *Four Hundred Years of English Education* (Cambridge, 1964), pp. 28–29.

PAGE 211

1. Matthews, p. 95.

2. *V.C.H. Worcs.*, iv, 505.
3. *Past and Present*, No. 28 (July 1964), p. 69.

PAGE 212
1. J. A. Venn, 'Matriculations at Oxford and Cambridge 1544–1906', *The Oxford and Cambridge Review* (1908), iii, 48–66.
2. *Past and Present*, No. 28 (July 1964), pp. 54–56.
3. *The Life and Times of Anthony Wood*, ed. A. Clark, i, 301.
4. See pp. 104–5 above.

PAGE 213
1. J. D. Chambers and G. E. Mingay, *The Agricultural Revolution 1750–1880* (London, 1966), pp. 98–99.
2. Hans, pp. 119, 120, 121, 221–42.
3. *Past and Present*, No. 28, p. 69.

PAGE 214
1. *Past and Present*, No. 28, p. 45.
2. A. Heal, *The English Writing-Masters and their Copy-Books* (Cambridge, 1931). See also W. Massey, *The Origin and Progress of Letters*.
3. *A New Discovery of the old Art of Teaching Schoole*, 'The Petty School', pp. 23–26.
4. See pp. 73 above.
5. Hans, pp. 185–7, 249.

PAGE 215
1. W. Massey, *The Origin and Progress of Letters*, Part the Second, pp. 65, 83, 97, 102, 115–18.
2. E. R. G. Taylor, *The Mathematical Practitioners of Tudor and Stuart England*, p. 278.
3. See p. 99 above.
4. *Collectanea*, First Series, ed. C. R. L. Fletcher, 'A letter from a friend of the universities, in reference to the new project of an academy for riding the great horse &c.' (Oxford, 1885), pp. 313–29.

PAGE 216
1. Taylor, pp. 211, 222, 224, 230, 286, 361, 393, 396, 489, 501, 506, 514, 529, 557, 571.

PAGE 217
1. Hans, pp. 69, 185, 187–9, 210–11, 248–9.
2. See pp. 23–24 above.
3. *Considerations concerning Free Schools*, p. 51.

PAGE 218
1. D. C. Douglas, *English Scholars 1660–1730* (second edition, London, 1951), p. 277.
2. S. Piggott, *William Stukeley*, p. 183.

PAGE 219
1. Hans, p. 212.
2. *Past and Present*, No. 28, p. 73.

PAGE 221
1. *A New Discovery of the old Art of Teaching Schoole*, 'The Petty-School', pp. 23–26.
2. R. F. Young, *Comenius in England*, p. 65; H. R. Trevor-Roper, 'Three Foreigners and the Philosophy of the English Revolution', *Encounter* (February 1960), xiv, No. 2, 13–16.
3. T. Richards, *Religious Developments in Wales (1654–1662)*, p. 61; Vincent, p. 135.

PAGE 222
1. *Considerations concerning Free Schools*, pp. 2, 69.

PAGE 223
1. *Past and Present*, No. 28 (July 1964), p. 73.
2. C. Wilson, *England's Apprenticeship 1603–1763*, p. 347.
3. Miss M. G. Jones, *The Charity School Movement* (Cambridge, 1938), p. 6.
4. Jones, pp. 28–35, 76–84; D. Owen, *English Philanthropy 1660–1960* (Cambridge, Massachusetts, 1964), pp. 27, 28; W. K. Lowther Clarke, *A History of the S.P.C.K.* (London, 1959), pp. 42–43.

PAGE 224
1. Jones, pp. 4, 7–8, 343.
2. Owen, p. 3; Jones, pp. 12–13; Lowther Clarke, pp. 33–35.
3. Lowther Clarke, pp. 20–29; Jones, pp. 36–41.

PAGE 225
1. Jones, pp. 25–26, 57, 65; Lowther Clarke, p. 25.
2. *Schools Inquiry Commission*, i, 120.
3. *Past and Present*, No. 28 (July 1964), p. 45.
4. Jones, p. 18.

PAGE 226
1. Jones, p. 344.
2. A. E. Dobbs, *Education and Social Movements 1700–1850* (London, 1919), p. 91.

PAGE 227
1. J. Fitch, *Educational Aims and Methods* (Cambridge, 1900), p. 194.

BIBLIOGRAPHY

A. Manuscript Sources

BODLEIAN LIBRARY, OXFORD

MS. Ashm. 1820 b (83): 'A Certificat in order to the Collecting and Reporting the State of the present English Free-Schools.'
MS. Aubrey 10: John Aubrey's scheme of educational reform.
MS. C.C.C. Oxon 390/1–3, 391/1: The Manuscripts of Christopher Wase.
MS. Oxf. Archd. papers Oxon C 160: The Statutes of Dorchester Grammar School, Oxfordshire.
MS. Wood D 11: Anthony Wood's notes on Woodstock Free School, Oxfordshire.
Rawl. MSS., D 191: Curriculum at Eton College about 1670.

BRASENOSE COLLEGE, OXFORD

Charlbury 2, 5: A Copy of the Orders of Charlbury School, Oxfordshire.
Charlbury 6: Appointment of Henry Allen, schoolmaster.
Schools 22, 23: Receipt for Henry Allen's pension.

NEW COLLEGE, OXFORD

A copy of Christopher Rawlins's will.
Correspondence between the college authorities and the Bedford Corporation, 1665–1725.
Letter from John Butler resigning schoolmastership of Bedford School, 5 August 1672.
Agreement between corporation and Nicholas Aspinall as to repairs of Bedford School, 30 November 1706.
Letter from Benjamin Rogers, usher at Bedford School, to Dr. Cobb, warden of New College, 16 January 1717.
The Statutes of Adderbury School, Oxfordshire.

BRITISH MUSEUM, LONDON

Lands. MSS., 119: The Statutes of Bury St. Edmunds Grammar School, 1550.
MSS., 29, 477: James Hume's Commonplace Book.
Sloane MSS., 649: John Dury's notes on education.
Stowe MSS., 755: Letter of Dr. Samuel Johnson to Henry Bright, master of Abingdon School, 7 January 1770.

PUBLIC RECORD OFFICE, LONDON

Petty Bag Inquisitions:
  Bundle 26, No. 6, 13 Charles II: Bardfield Grammar School, Essex.

Bundle 28, No. 24, 17 Charles II: Little Thurlow Grammar School, Suffolk.
Bundle 29, No. 15, 19 Charles II: Hartfield Grammar School, Sussex.
Bundle 40, No. 11, 35 Charles II: Ashbourne Grammar School, Derbyshire.
Bundle 43, No. 18, 4 James II: Needham Market Grammar School, Suffolk.

GLOUCESTER CATHEDRAL

Chapter Acts Books: The King's School, Gloucester.

WITNEY GRAMMAR SCHOOL, OXFORDSHIRE

Library Catalogue and Statute Book.

B. Printed Sources

1. SCHOOLS AND SCHOOLMASTERS, 1660–1714

Primary. Educational Records:

Alumni Felstedienses. Edited by G. J. Hornsby Wright. Felsted, 1903.

Deed of Foundation of the Free School of Robert Holgate York. The Holgate Society. Record Series No. 1.

Durham School Register, second edition, to June 1912. Edited by C. S. Earle and L. A. Body. London, 1912.

Gibbs A. E. *The Corporation Records of St. Albans.* St. Albans, 1890.

Goulding R. W. *Louth Old Corporation Records.* Louth, 1891.

Hart, J. P. *The Parish Council of Bletchingley in the County of Surrey. A Transcription of Parish Documents.* Redhill, Surrey, 1955.

Leach, A. F. *Educational Charters and Documents 598 to 1909.* Cambridge, 1911.

Leach, A. F. *Documents illustrating Early Education in Worcester, 685 to 1700.* Worcestershire Historical Society, 1913.

Mayor, J. E. B. *Admissions To the College of St. John the Evangelist, Cambridge.* Parts ii–iii. Cambridge, 1893–1903.

Old Order Book of Hartlebury Grammar School, 1556–1752. Edited by D. Robertson. Oxford, 1904.

Orders, Constitutions, and Directions, To be Observed, For and Concerning the Free-School, in Woodbridge, In the County of Suffolk, and the School-Master, and Scholars thereof. Agreed upon at the Foundation, 1662. Printed by Robert Loder, 1785.

Peile, J. *Biographical Register of Christ's College, 1505–1905.* Two volumes. Cambridge, 1910.

Publications of the Dugdale Society. Volumes vii, xii, xx. The Records of King Edward's School Birmingham. Volumes ii–iv. London, 1928–48.

Records of Blackburn Grammar School. Edited by G. A. Stocks. Chetham Society. Manchester, 1909.

Records of the Borough of Nottingham. Volumes v–vi. London and Nottingham, 1900–1914.

Register of the Scholars Admitted to Colchester School 1637–1740. Edited by J. H. Round. Colchester, 1897.

Repton School Register 1557–1905. Edited by G. S. Messiter. Repton, 1905.

Translation of the Charter of King Edward the Sixth, Whereby a Free Grammar School was Founded for the Benefit of the Town of Louth, In the County of Lincoln. Louth, 1813.

Venn, J. *Biographical History of Gonville and Caius College, 1349–1897.* Volumes i–ii. Cambridge, 1897–98.

Visitations and Memorials of Southwell Minster. Edited by A. F. Leach. Camden Society, 1891.

Walker, T. A. *Admissions to Peterhouse or St. Peter's College, Cambridge*. Cambridge, 1912.
Whitaker, J. *The Statutes and Charter of Rivington School*. London, 1837.

Other Works:
Brief Lives, chiefly of Contemporaries, set down by John Aubrey, between the Years 1669 and 1696. Edited by A. Clark. Volume i. Oxford, 1898.
Diary of Samuel Pepys. Edited by H. B. Wheatley. Volume iii. London, 1893.
History of Thomas Ellwood Written by Himself. London, 1885.
London Gazette. 20 April to 23 April 1674.
North, R. *The Lives of the Right Hon. Francis North, Baron Guilford; The Hon. Sir Dudley North; And the Hon. and Rev. Dr. John North*. Edited by A. Jessopp. Volumes i–ii. London, 1890.
South, R. *Sermons Preached upon Several Occasions*. Volume iii. Oxford, 1842.
Works of Thomas Hearne. Volume iii. Containing the First Volume of Peter Langtoft's Chronicle. Oxford, 1725.

Secondary. School Histories:
Bailey, E. J. *Whitgift School and Its Evolution*. Croydon, 1937.
Banks, M. L. *Blundell's Worthies*. London and Exeter, 1904.
Bell, E. A. *A History of Giggleswick School*. Leeds, 1912.
Brown, J. H. *A Short History of Thame School*. London, 1927.
Brown, W. H. *Charterhouse Past and Present*. Godalming, 1879.
Bradby, H. C. *Rugby*. London, 1900.
Bryant, P. H. M. *Harrow*. London and Glasgow, 1936.
Chambres, G. C. *History of Wigan Free Grammar School 1596–1869*. Wigan, 1937.
Charter-House, Its Foundation and History. London, 1849.
Chigwell Register, Together with a Historical Account of the School by the Rev. Canon Swallow. Edited by O. W. Darch and A. S. Tween. Buckhurst Hill, 1907.
Cox, T. *A Popular History of the Grammar School of Queen Elizabeth, At Heath, Near Halifax*. Halifax, 1879.
Craze, M. *A History of Felsted School 1564–1947*. Ipswich, 1955.
Cust, L. *A History of Eton College*. London, 1899.
Deed, B. L. *A History of Stamford School*. Cambridge, 1954.
Duncan, L. L. *A History of Colfe's School, Lewisham*. Printed for the Governors The Worshipful Company of Leathersellers of the City of London, 1910.
'Felsted School' by an old Felstedian. The Essex Revue. Edited by E. A. Fitch and Miss C. Fell-Smith. Chelmsford and London, 1898.
Fischer Williams, J. *Harrow*. London, 1901.
Fisher, G. W. *Annals of Shrewsbury School*. Revised by J. Spencer Hill. London, 1899.
Fleming, M. A. *Witney Grammar School 1660–1960*. Oxford, 1960.
Forrester, E. G. *A History of Magdalen College School Brackley, Northamptonshire, 1548–1949*. Buckingham, 1950.
Frangopulo, N. J. *The History of Queen Elizabeth's Grammar School Ashburne, Derbyshire 1585–1935*. Ashbourne, 1939.
Gibbs, A. E. *An Ancient Grammar School. Bygone Hertfordshire*. Edited by W. Andrews. London, 1898.
Gray, I. E. and Potter, W. E. *Ipswich School 1400–1950*. Ipswich, 1950.
Gray, J. M. *A History of the Perse School, Cambridge*. Cambridge, 1921.
Griffith, G. *The Free Schools of Worcestershire, and their Fulfilment*. London, 1852.
Hill, C. P. *The History of Bristol Grammar School*. London, 1951.

History and Register of Aldenham School. Seventh Edition. Compiled by E. Beevor, G. C. F. Mead, R. J. Evans, T. H. Savory. Worcester and London, 1938.

History of the Cheltenham Grammar School as Collected from the Newspaper Reports. Edited by A. Harper. Cheltenham, 1856.

Jackson, N. G. *Newark Magnus.* Nottingham, 1904.

James, W. A. *An Account of the Grammar and Song Schools of the Collegiate Church of Blessed Mary the Virgin of Southwell.* Southwell, 1927.

Kay, Margaret. *The History of Rivington and Blackrod Grammar School.* Manchester, 1966.

Lawson, J. *A Town Grammar School through Six Centuries.* London, New York, Toronto, 1963.

Layard, N. F. *A Brief Sketch of the History of Ipswich School.* Ipswich, 1901.

Leach, A. F. *History of Warwick School.* London, 1906.

Macdonald, A. *A History of the King's School Worcester.* London, 1936.

McDonnell, M. F. J. *A History of St. Paul's School.* London, 1909.

Maxwell Lyte, H. C. *A History of Eton College.* London, 1899.

Merchant Taylors' School, Its Origin, History and Present Surroundings. Oxford, 1929.

Messiter, G. S. *Records and Reminiscenses of Repton.* Repton, 1907.

Mumford, A. A. *The Manchester Grammar School 1515–1915.* London, 1919.

Oldham, J. B. *A History of Shrewsbury School 1552–1952.* Oxford, 1952.

Payne Smith, W. H. *Rugby. The School and Neighbourhood. Collected and arranged from the writings of the late M. B. Bloxham.* London and Rugby, 1889.

Peacock, M. H. *History of the Free Grammar School of Queen Elizabeth at Wakefield.* Wakefield, 1892.

Pearce, E. H. *Annals of Christ's Hospital.* London, 1908.

Price, A. C. *A History of the Leeds Grammar School.* Leeds, 1919.

Raine, A. *History of St. Peter's School: York.* London, 1926.

Rivington, S. *The History of Tonbridge School.* London, 1910.

Rouse, W. H. D. *A History of Rugby School.* London, 1898.

Row, E. F. *A History of Midhurst Grammar School.* Brighton, 1913.

Russell, C. F. *A History of King Edward VI School Southampton.* Cambridge, 1940.

Sampson, W. S. *A History of the Bristol Grammar School.* Bristol and London, 1912.

Sandall, T. *The History of the Stamford Grammar School.* Stamford.

Sands, P. C. and Haworth, C. M. *A History of Pocklington School.* London and Hull 1951.

Sargant, W. L. *The Book of Oakham School with Register.* Oakham, 1907.

Sargeaunt, J. *Annals of Westminster School.* London, 1898.

Sargeaunt, J. *A History of Bedford School.* Edited and completed by E. Hockliffe. Bedford and London, 1925.

Sargeaunt, J. *A History of Felsted School.* Chelmsford and London, 1889.

Smalley Law, W. *Oundle's Story.* London, 1922.

Snell, F. J. *Blundell's : A Short History of a Famous West Country School.* London.

Stanier, R. S. *Magdalen School.* Oxford, 1940.

Stephenson, N. R. W. *A Short History of Guisborough Grammar School.* Guisborough, 1961.

Trollope, W. *A History of the Royal Foundation of Christ's Hospital.* London, 1834.

Varley, B. *The History of Stockport Grammar School.* Second Edition. Manchester, 1957.

Walker, W. G. *A History of the Oundle Schools.* London, 1956.

West, J. M. *Shrewsbury School.* London, 1937.

Whatton, W. R. 'The History of Manchester School'. Manchester, 1828. *The Foundations of Manchester.* Volume iii. Manchester, 1848.

Williamson, G. C. *The Royal Grammar School of Guildford*. London and Guildford, 1929.
Wilmot, D. *A Short History of the Grammar School, Macclesfield*. Macclesfield, 1910.
Wilson, H. B. *The History of Merchant-Taylors' School, From its Foundation to the Present Time*. London, 1812.
Woodruff, C. E. and Cape, H. J. *Schola Regia Cantuariensis: A History of Canterbury School*. London, 1908.
Young, W. *The History of Dulwich College*. Volume i. London, 1889.

The Victoria History of the Counties of England:
Leach, A. F. 'Schools'. *Bedfordshire*. Volume ii. Edited by W. Page. London, 1908.
Leach, A. F. 'Schools'. *Berkshire*. Volume ii. Edited by P. H. Ditchfield and W. Page. London, 1907.
Leach, A. F. 'Schools'. *Buckinghamshire*. Volume ii. Edited by W. Page. London, 1908.
Hampson, Ethel M. 'Schools'. *Cambridgeshire*. Volume ii. Edited by L. F. Salzman. London, 1948.
Leach, A. F. 'Schools'. *Derbyshire*. Volume ii. Edited by W. Page. London, 1907.
Leach, A. F. 'Schools'. *Durham*. Volume i. Edited by W. Page. London, 1905.
Fell-Smith, C. 'Schools'. *Essex*. Volume ii. Edited by W. Page and J. H. Round. London, 1907.
Leach, A. F. 'Schools'. *Gloucestershire*. Volume ii. Edited by W. Page. London, 1907.
Leach, A. F. 'Schools'. *Hampshire and the Isle of Wight*. Volume ii. Edited by H. A. Doubleday and W. Page. Westminster, 1903.
Leach A. F. 'Schools'. *Hertfordshire*. Volume ii. Edited by W. Page. London, 1908.
Parsloe, C. G. 'Schools'. *Huntingdonshire*. Volume ii. Edited by W. Page, G. Proby and S. Inskip Ladds. London, 1932.
Leach, A. F. and Chaytor, H. J. 'Schools'. *Lancaster*. Volume ii. Edited by W. Farrer and J. Brownbill. London, 1908.
Leach, A. F. 'Schools'. *Lincolnshire*. Volume ii. Edited by W. Page. London, 1906.
Leach, A. F. 'Schools'. *Northamptonshire*. Volume ii. Edited by R. M. Serjeantson and W. R. D. Adkins. London, 1906.
Leach, A. F. 'Schools'. *Nottinghamshire*. Volume ii. Edited by W. Page. London, 1910.
Lobel, M. D. 'Schools'. *Oxfordshire*. Volume i. Edited by L. F. Salzman. London, 1939.
Fletcher, F. 'Schools'. *Rutland*. Volume i. Edited by W. Page. London, 1908.
Scott Holmes, T. 'Schools'. *Somerset*. Volume ii. Edited by W. Page. London, 1911.
Leach, A. F. and Steele Hutton, E. P. 'Schools'. *Suffolk*. Volume ii. Edited by W. Page. London, 1907.
Leach, A. F. 'Schools'. *Surrey*. Volume ii. Edited by H. E. Malden. London, 1905.
Leach, A. F. 'Schools'. *Sussex*. Volume ii. Edited by W. Page. London, 1907.
Leach, A. F. 'Schools'. *Warwickshire*. Volume ii. Edited by W. Page. London, 1908.
Leach, A. F. 'Schools'. *Worcestershire*. Volume iv. Edited by W. Page and J. W. Willis Bund. London, 1924.
Leach, A. F. 'Schools'. *Yorkshire*. Volume i. Edited by W. Page. London, 1907.

Other Works:
Aiken, J. *A Description of the Country from thirty to forty Miles round Manchester*. London, 1795.

Baigent, F. J. and Millard, J. E. *A History of the Ancient Town and Manor of Basingstoke*. Basingstoke and London, 1889.

Baines, E. *The History of the County Palatine and Duchy of Lancaster*. Volume ii. London, 1870.

Blanch, W. H. *Ye Parish of Camerwell*. London, 1875.

Box, G. H. 'Hebrew Studies in the Reformation Period and After'. *The Legacy of Israel*. Edited by E. R. Bevan and C. Singer. Oxford, 1927.

Boys, W. *Collections for an History of Sandwich in Kent*. Canterbury, 1892.

Burn, J. S. *A History of Henley-on-Thames*. London, 1861.

Carlisle, N. *A Concise Description of the Endowed Grammar Schools in England and Wales*. Two volumes. London, 1818.

Clode, C. M. *Memorials of the Guilds of Merchant Taylors of the Fraternity of St. John the Baptist*. London, 1875.

Coventry: Its History and Antiquities. Compiled by B. Poole. London, 1870.

Curtis, S. J. *History of Education in Great Britain*. Fourth Edition. London, 1957.

Davies, J. S. *A History of Southampton*. Southampton and London, 1883.

Davis, C. H. *The English Church Canons of 1604*. London, 1869.

Dudley, H. *The History and Antiquities of Horsham*. London, 1836.

Goldsmith, O. *The Life of Henry St. John, Lord Viscount Bolingbroke*. London, 1770.

History and Antiquities of Guildford. Guildford, 1801.

Horsfield, T. W. *The History and Antiquities of Lewes and its Vicinity*. Volume i. Lewes, 1824.

Hurst, Dorothea. *Horsham: Its History and Antiquities*. London, 1868.

Johnson's Lives of the Poets. Edited by Mrs. Alexander Napier. Volume ii. London, 1890.

Latimer, J. *The Annals of Bristol in the Seventeenth Century*. Bristol, 1900.

Lawson, J. *The Endowed Grammar Schools of East Yorkshire*. East Yorkshire Local History Society, 1962.

Lester Smith, W. O. *To Whom do Schools Belong?* Oxford, 1943.

Macdonald, A. *A Short History of Repton*. London, 1929.

Manning, O. and Bray, W. *The History and Antiquities of the County of Surrey*. Volume ii. London, 1814.

Morant, P. *The History and Antiquities of the County of Essex*. Volume i. London, 1768.

Notes and Queries for Somerset and Dorset. Edited by F. W. Eaver and C. H. Mayo. Volume iii. Sherborne, 1893.

Pemberton, R. *Solihull and its Church*. Exeter, 1905.

Phelps Brown, E. H. and Hopkins, Sheila V. 'Seven Centuries of the Prices of Consumables, Compared with Builders' Wage-Rates'. *Essays in Economic History*. Edited by E. M. Carus-Wilson. Volume ii. London, 1962.

Piercy, J. S. *The History of Retford*. Retford, 1828.

Proceedings of the Somersetshire Archaeological & Natural History Society for the year 1907. Volume liii. Taunton, 1908.

Quarterly Review. Volume cxlvi. London, 1878.

Quick, R. H. *Essays on Educational Reformers*. London, 1910.

Reports of the Commissioners for Inquiring Concerning Charities. Thirty-two volumes. London, 1819–40.

Rudder, S. *A New History of Gloucestershire*. Cirencester, 1779.

Rudder, S. *The History of Cirencester*. Cirencester, 1800.

Russell, J. and S. *The History of Guildford*. Guildford, 1801.

Russell Barker, G. F. *Memoir of Richard Busby*. London, 1895.

Sandys, J. E. *A History of Classical Scholarship.* Volume ii. Cambridge, 1908.
Schools Inquiry Commission. Volumes i, ix, xv. London, 1868.
Sharp, T. *Illustrative Papers on the History and Antiquities of the City of Coventry.* Birmingham, 1871.
Somersetshire Archaeological and Natural History Society Proceedings During the Years 1865–6. Volume iii. Taunton, 1867.
Staunton, H. *The Great Schools of England.* London, 1877.
Surtees, R. *The History and Antiquities of the County Palatine of Durham.* Volume i. London, 1816.
Sussex Archaeological Collections. Volumes xliii and xlvi. Lewes, 1900–3.
Transactions of the Historic Society of Lancashire and Cheshire, Session 1855–56. Volume viii. London, 1856.
Watson, F. *The Beginnings of the Teaching of Modern Subjects in England.* London, 1909.
Wildman, W. B. *A Short History of Sherborne.* Sherborne, 1930.
Williamson, G. C. *Guildford in the Olden Time.* London, 1904.

(a) The following works contain references to particular schoolmasters.

Primary:

Chauncy, Sir Henry. *The Historical Antiquities of Hertfordshire.* Two volumes. London, 1700, reprinted 1826.
Defoe, D. *A Tour Thro' the whole Island of Great Britain.* Volume i. London, 1724.
Diary of the Rev. Henry Newcome. Edited by T. Heywood. Chetham Society, 1849.
Poetical Recreations: Consisting of Original Poems, Songs, Odes, &c. With several New Translations. In Two Parts. Part I. Occasionally Written by Mrs. Jane Barker. Part II. By several Gentlemen of the Universities and Others. London, 1688.
Remarks and Collections of Thomas Hearne. Edited by H. E. Salter. Volume ix. Oxford, 1914.
Remarks and Collections of Thomas Hearne. Edited by C. E. Dobie. Volumes i–ii. Oxford, 1885–6.
Winstanley, W. *The Lives of the most famous English Poets.* London, 1687.

Secondary:

Blomefield, F. *An Essay towards a Topographical History of the County of Norfolk.* Volume ii. London, 1805.
Bonney, H. K. *Historic Notices in reference to Fotheringay.* Oundle, London and Edinburgh, 1821.
Brasenose College Monographs. Volume ii, No. XII. Oxford, 1909.
Brookes, C. C. *A History of Steeple Aston and Middle Aston, Oxfordshire.* Long Compton, Shipton-on-Stour, 1929.
Climenson, E. J. *The History of Shiplake, Oxon.* London, 1894.
Coates, C. *The History and Antiquities of Reading.* London, 1802.
Compleat History of Oxfordshire. London, 1730.
Dickinson, W. *The History and Antiquities of the Town of Southwell.* London, 1819.
Fell-Smith, C. *Mary Rich, Countess of Warwick (1625–1678): Her Family and Friends.* London, 1901.
Fishwick, H. *The History of the Parish of Preston.* Rochdale and London, 1900.
Fletcher, C. R. L. *Mr. Gladstone at Oxford.* London, 1908.
Garrow, D. W. *The History and Antiquities of Croydon.* Croydon, 1818.
Gentleman's Magazine. Volume xxxiii, new series. London, 1850.

Hastings, Past and Present. Hastings and London, 1855.

Hazlitt, W. C. *Schools, School-Books and Schoolmasters*. London, 1888.

Hipkins, F. C. *Repton and its Neighbourhood*. Second Edition. Repton, 1899.

History and Antiquities of Northamptonshire. Compiled from the Manuscript Collections of the late learned antiquary John Bridges, By the Rev. Peter Whalley. Volume ii. Oxford, 1741.

Leach, A. F. 'Early Yorkshire Schools'. Volume i. *The Yorkshire Archaeological Society, Record Series*. Volume xxvii. London, 1899.

Lee, A. T. *The History of the Town and Parish of Tetbury*. London, 1857.

Lipscomb, G. *The History and Antiquities of the County of Buckingham*. Volume ii. London, 1847.

Masson, D. *The Life of John Milton*. Volume iv. London, 1877.

Money, W. *The History of the Ancient Town and Borough of Newbury*. Oxford and London, 1887.

Morant, P. *The History and Antiquities of the most ancient Town and Borough of Colchester*. London, 1768.

Munk, W. *The Roll of the Royal College of Physicians of London*. Volume i. London, 1861.

Palatine Note-Book for 1882. Volume ii. Manchester, Chester and Liverpool.

Thompson, P. *The History and Antiquities of Boston*. Boston, 1856.

Wing, W. W. *Annals of Steeple Aston and Middle Aston*. Oxford, 1875.

(b) The effects of governmental measures upon schoolmasters have been examined from the following works.

Primary:

Acts and Ordinances of the Interregnum, 1642–1660. Collected and edited by C. H. Firth and R. S. Rait. Volume ii. London, 1911.

Calamy, E. *An Account of the Ministers, Lecturers, Masters and Fellows of Colleges and Schoolmasters, Who were Ejected or Silenced after the Restoration*. Volume ii. Second Edition. London, 1713.

Calendar of State Papers, Domestic Series, 1649–50, 1653, 1654, 1655–56.

Documents relating to the Settlement of the Church of England by the Act of Uniformity of 1662. Edited by G. Gould. London, 1862.

Reports of Sir Peyton Ventris, Kt. The First Part. London, 1701.

Statutes at Large in Paragraphs and Sections or Numbers. Beginning with the Reign of King James I. Volume ii. London, 1695.

Secondary:

Armytage, W. H. G. *Four Hundred Years of English Education*. Cambridge, 1964.

Cardwell, E. *Documentary Annals of the Reformed Church of England*. Volume ii. Oxford, 1839.

Matthews, A. G. *Calamy Revised*. Oxford, 1934.

Richards, T. *Religious Developments in Wales (1654–1662)*. London, 1923.

(c) Reference has been made to the following works to illustrate the financial situation of schoolmasters.

Primary:

Chalmers, G. *An Estimate of the Comparative Strength of Great Britain; and of the Losses of Her Trade, A New Edition, Corrected and Continued to 1803. To which is now annexed Gregory King's Celebrated State of England, with notices of His Life*. London, 1804.

Secondary:
Best, G. F. A. *Temporal Pillars*. Cambridge, 1964.
Fosbrooke, T. D. *An Original History of the City of Gloucester*. London, 1819.
Giles, J. A. *History of Witney*. London, 1852.
Laslett, P. *The World we have lost*. London, 1965.
Leach, A. F. *English Schools at the Reformation 1546-8*. Westminster, 1896.
Savidge, A. *The Foundation and Early Years of Queen Anne's Bounty*. London, 1955.
Whiteman, Anne. 'The Re-Establishment of the Church of England'. *Transactions of the Royal Historical Society*. Volume v. London, 1955.

2. EDUCATIONAL WRITINGS

The following contemporary works express the ideas of reformers and
show the interest in educational problems.

Brinsley, J. *Ludus Literarius or The Grammar Schoole*. Edited by E. T. Campagnac. Liverpool and London, 1917.
Bishop Burnet's History of His Own Time. Volume ii. London, 1734. Volume vi. Oxford, 1823.
Defoe, D. *The Compleat English Gentleman*. Edited by K. D. Bulbring. London, 1890.
Durie, J. *The Reformed-School: and the Reformed Librarie-Keeper*. London, 1651.
Durie, J. *The Reformed Librarie-Keeper with a Supplement to the Reformed-School, as subordinate to Colleges in Universities*. London, 1650.
Gailhard, J. *The Compleat Gentleman: Or Directions for the Educating of Youth As to their Breeding at Home and Travelling Abroad*. In Two Treatises. London, 1678.
Grounds and Occasions of the Contempt of the Clergy and Religion Enquired into in a Letter written to R.L. London, 1670.
Hartlib, S. *The True and Readie Way to Learne the Latine Tongue*. London, 1654.
Hobbes's Leviathan Reprinted from the edition of 1651. With an Essay by the late W. G. Pogson Smith. Oxford, 1909.
Hobbes, T. *Behemoth or The Long Parliament*. Edited by E. Tonnies. London, 1889.
Hoole, C. *A New Discovery of the old Art of Teaching Schoole, In four small Treatises*. Edited by E. T. Campagnac. Liverpool and London, 1913.
Locke, J. *Some Thoughts concerning Education*. Edited by R. H. Quick. Cambridge, 1880.
Memoirs, Illustrative of the Life and Writings of John Evelyn, Esq., F.R.S. Edited by W. Bray. Volume ii. Second Edition. London, 1819.
Miège, G. *A New French Grammar; Or, A New Method for Learning of the French Tongue*. London, 1678.
Milton's Tractate on Education. Edited by O. Browning. Cambridge, 1895.
Moderate Intelligencer: 5 to 12 February 1646.
Nedham, M. *A Discourse Concerning Schools and School-Masters*. London, 1663.
Spectator. No. 157, 30 August 1711, No. 168, 12 September 1711.
Tryon, T. *A New Method of Educating Children*. London, 1695.
Wase, C. *Considerations concerning Free Schools, as settled in England*. Oxford, 1678.
Webbe, J. *An Appeale to Truth, In the Controversie between Art, and Use*. London, 1622.
Webster, J. *Academiarum Examen, Or The Examination of Academies*. London, 1654.
Woodward, H. *A Light to Grammar*. London, 1641.
Wotton, H. *An Essay on the Education of Children, In the First Rudiments of Learning*. Published in 1672 and reprinted in London, 1753.

3. EDUCATIONAL FACILITIES

(a) The following works have been consulted to illustrate the expansion of the grammar schools and educational conditions and facilities before the Restoration.

Primary:

Nelson, R. *The Life of Dr. George Bull.* Second Edition. London, 1714.

Secondary:

Adamson, J. W. '*The Illiterate Anglo-Saxon' and other Essays on Education, Medieval and Modern.* Cambridge, 1946.

Charlton, K. *Education in Renaissance England.* London and Toronto, 1965.

Davies, G. *The Early Stuarts 1603–1660.* Oxford, 1937.

Jordan, W. K. *Philanthropy in England 1480–1660.* London, 1959.

Jordan, W. K. *The Charities of London 1480–1660.* London, 1960.

Richards, T. *A History of the Puritan Movement in Wales.* London, 1920.

Simon, Joan. *Education and Society in Tudor England.* Cambridge, 1966.

Stone, L. 'The Educational Revolution in England, 1560–1640'. *Past and Present.* No. 28. July, 1964.

Trevor-Roper, H. R. 'Three Foreigners and the Philosophy of the English Revolution'. *Encounter.* Edited by S. Spender and M. J. Lasky. Volume xiv, No. 2. February, 1960.

Vincent, W. A. L. *The State and School Education 1640–1660 in England and Wales.* London, 1950.

Wallis, P. J. 'Histories of Old Schools: A Preliminary List for England and Wales'. *British Journal of Educational Studies.* Volume xiv, No. 1. November, 1965.

Watson, F. 'The State and Education during the Commonwealth'. *The English Historical Review.* London, New York and Bombay, 1900.

Watson, F. *The English Grammar Schools to 1660: their Curriculum and Practice.* Cambridge, 1908.

Watson, F. *The Old Grammar Schools.* Cambridge, 1908.

Young, R. F. *Comenius in England.* Oxford, 1932.

(b) For educational conditions in the eighteenth and nineteenth centuries and for the decline of the grammar schools the following sources have been consulted.

Abram, W. A. *A History of Blackburn.* Blackburn, 1877.

Archer, R. L. *Secondary Education in the Nineteenth Century.* Cambridge, 1921.

Ashton, T. S. *An Economic History of England: The 18th Century.* London, 1955.

Berkeley, G. *A Discourse Addressed to Magistrates and Men in Authority.* Dublin, 1738.

Butler, J. *A Charge Deliver'd to the Clergy, at the Primary Visitation of the Diocese of Durham, in the year, 1751.* Durham, 1751.

Carpenter, S. C. *Eighteenth Century Church and People.* London, 1959.

Chambers, J. D. and Mingay, G. E. *The Agricultural Revolution 1750–1880.* London, 1966.

De Montmorency, J. E. G. *State Intervention in English Education.* Cambridge, 1902.

Dobbs, A. E. *Education and Social Movements 1700–1850.* London, 1919.

Douglas, D. C. *English Scholars 1660–1730.* Second Edition. London, 1951.

Fitch, J. *Educational Aims and Methods.* Cambridge, 1900.

Gentleman's Magazine: and Historical Chronicle, For the Year 1804. Part the Second. Volume lxxiv.

Jones, Gwladys. *The Charity School Movement*. Cambridge, 1938.
Livett, G. M. *Southwell Minster*. Southwell, 1883.
Lowther Clarke, W. K. *A History of the S.P.C.K.* London, 1959.
Norwood, C. *The English Tradition of Education*. London, 1929.
Owen, D. *English Philanthropy 1660–1960*. Cambridge, Massachusetts, 1964.
Piggott, S. *William Stukeley*. Oxford, 1950.
Poetical Works of Robert Lloyd, A.M. To which is prefixed an Account of the Life and Writings of the Author, by W. Kenrick. Volume i. London, 1774.
Secker, T. *Eight Charges Delivered to the Clergy of the Dioceses of Oxford and Canterbury*. London, 1769.
Simpson, R. *A Collection of Fragments illustrative of the History and Antiquities of Derby*. Volume i. Derby, 1826.
Venn, J. A. 'Matriculations at Oxford and Cambridge 1544–1906'. *The Oxford and Cambridge Review*. Volume iii. 1908.
Wilson, C. *England's Apprenticeship 1603–1763*. London, 1965.

4. WASE'S INQUIRY

Useful information about Christopher Wase and the Wase School Collection is given in the following modern works.

Curtis, M. H. 'The Alienated Intellectuals of Early Stuart England'. *Past and Present*. No. 23. November, 1962.
Fowler, T. *The History of Corpus Christi College*. Oxford, 1893.
Johnson, J. and Gibson, S. *Print and Privilege at Oxford to the year 1700*. London, 1946.
Madan, F. *Oxford Books*. Volume iii. Oxford, 1931.
Wallis, P. J. 'The Wase School Collection'. *The Bodleian Library Record*. Volume iv, No. 2. August, 1952.

5. PRIVATE ENTERPRISE

For information about private teachers and private schools in the seventeenth and eighteenth centuries the following works have been consulted.

Primary:
Calamy, E. *The Nonconformist's Memorial*. Edited by S. Palmer. Volume i. London, 1778.
Collectanea, First Series. Edited by C. R. L. Fletcher. Part vi. T. W. Jackson, 'Dr. Wallis' Letter Against Mr. Maidwell, 1700'. Oxford, 1885.
Collectanea, First Series. Edited by C. R. L. Fletcher. 'A letter from a friend of the universities, in reference to the new project of an academy for riding the great horse &c.' Oxford, 1885.
Collectanea Curiosa. Edited by J. Gutch. Volume i. Oxford, 1781.
Guardian. No. 94, 29 June 1713, No. 163, 17 September 1713. Volume ii. London, 1756.
Higford, W. The Institution of a Gentleman. London, 1660. *The Harleian Miscellany*. Volume ix. London, 1812.
Historical Manuscripts Commission, Fourteenth Report. The Manuscripts of His Grace The Duke of Portland. Volume iii. London, 1894.
Historical Manuscripts Commission, Thirteenth Report. The Manuscripts of J. B. Fortescue, Esq. Volume i. London, 1892.
Hutchinson, Lucy. *Memoirs of the Life of Colonel Hutchinson*. London, 1806.

Journals of the House of Lords. Volume ii.
Memoirs of Sir John Reresby 1634–1689 Written by Himself. Edited by J. J. Cartwright. London, 1875.
Memoirs and Travels of Sir John Reresby. Edited by A. Ivatt. London, 1904.
Misson, M. *Memoires et Observations Faites par un Voyageur en Angleterre.* La Haye, 1698.
Model for a School for the better Education of Youth.
Morrice, T. *An Apology for Schoole-Masters.* London, 1619.
Peacham, H. *The Compleat Gentleman.* Third Impression. London, 1661.
Tatler. Edited by G. A. Aitken. No. 255, 25 November 1710. Volume iv. London, 1899.
Verney, M. M. *Memoirs of the Verney Family during the Commonwealth 1650 to 1660.* Volume iii. London, 1894.
Wilson, W. *The History and Antiquities of Dissenting Churches and Meeting Houses.* Volume i. London, 1808.

Secondary:
Bennet, G. V. *White Kennet 1660–1728 Bishop of Peterborough.* London, 1957.
Birch, T. *The Life of the Honourable Robert Boyle.* London, 1744.
Collins, A. *Historical Collections of the Noble Families of Cavendishe, Holles, Vere, Harley, and Ogle, with the Lives of the most remarkable Persons.* London, 1752.
Hans, N. *New Trends in Education in the Eighteenth Century.* London, 1951.
Heal, A. *The English Writing Masters and their Copy-Books.* Cambridge, 1931.
Home Counties Magazine. Edited by W. J. Hardy. Volume vi. London, 1904.
Lambley, Kathleen. *The Teaching and Cultivation of the French Language in England during Tudor and Stuart Times.* Manchester, 1920.
Lysons, D. *The Environs of London.* Volume ii. London, 1795.
Massey, W. *The Origin and Progress of Letters.* London, 1763.
Oxford Archaeological Society. Reports for the Year 1907. Banbury, 1908.
Parker, Irene. *Dissenting Academies in England.* Cambridge, 1914.
Scott Thomson, G. *Life in A Noble Household 1641–1700.* London, 1937.
Taylor, E. G. R. *The Mathematical Practitioners of Tudor and Stuart England.* Cambridge, 1954.
Walpole, H. *Anecdotes of Painting in England.* Volume ii. London, 1826.
Watson, F. 'The Teaching of Arithmetic and Writing in the Time of the Commonwealth'. *The Gentleman's Magazine.* Volume cclxxxvii. September 1899.
Watson, F. 'Unlicensed Nonconformist Schoolmasters: 1662 and Onwards'. *The Gentleman's Magazine.* Volume ccxciii. July to December 1902.

6. WORKS OF REFERENCE
Primary:
Diary of John Evelyn. Edited by E. S. De Beer. Volumes ii–iii. London, 1955.
Life and Times of Anthony Wood. Edited by A. Clark. Volumes i–ii. Oxford, 1891–2.
Wood, A. *Athenae Oxonienses.* Edited by P. Bliss. Volumes i–iii. London, 1813–17.
Wood, A. *Fasti Oxonienses.* Volume ii. London, 1721.

Secondary:
Dictionary of National Biography.
Foster, J. *Alumni Oxonienses.* Early Series. Volumes i–iv. Later Series. Volumes i–iv. Oxford, 1891.
Venn, J. and Venn, J. A. *Alumni Cantabrigienses.* Part I. Volumes i–iv. Cambridge, 1922–27.
Venn, J. A. *Alumni Cantabrigienses.* Part II. Volumes i–vi. Cambridge, 1940–54.

INDEX

Endowed Schools Commission, 1868,
47–8; findings, 227
England, changed intellectual climate,
217–18
Erasmus, Thomas, 76, 77
Essex, 11, 31
Estienne, Henri, *Thesaurus Graecae
Linguae*, 86
Etcholls, John, 119
Eton College, 9, 24, 34–5, 65, 80, 125,
126; an exclusive preserve, 19, 20,
193, 194, 214; boarding education, 7;
corporal punishment, 60, 65; dis-
orderly conduct, 62–3; election of
scholars, 13, 81
Evans, John, 182
Evanson, John, 20
Evelyn, John, 25, 60; and modern
language study, 96; education, 60;
on classical accomplishments, 78
Evesham, Prince Henry's G.S., 137, 148
Ewelme G.S., 17
Exeter, Latin and English Schools, 72
Expulsion, for absenteeism, 51, 90; for
indiscipline, 62
Eyans, Richard, 45
Eye G.S., 162–3

Fairfaxes, 9
Farnaby, Thomas, private schools, 209
Fell, Dr. John, and Wase's election, 26
Felsted School, 7, 9, 81; masters, 131,
139, 141, 156; priests-masters, 149;
smallpox outbreak, 141
Ferry Hill, 14
Field, Thomas, 20
Fines, 40, 51–2, 110, 157
Fitch, Sir Joshua, 227
Fock, Sir John, 156
Foots Cray, Kent, 29
Forster (Forrester), Sir William, 8
Fosbrooke, William, curate, 163
Fossan, Thomas, accused of negligence,
143
Foster, Josiah, 156
Foster, William, 153–4
Fotheringay G.S., vicar-master, 149–50
Foubert, Mons. Henry de, Academy,
199–200
Foxcroft, Mr., senior proctor, 31
Franckland, Mrs. Joyce, 178
Frankland, Samuel, 37, 205; and
school salaries, 161, 162; attempted
dismissal, 68
Free grammar schools, 2, 6, 56, 57, 217;
and co-education, 46–8; and the
poor, 225; fee-paying, 40 ff., 225;
founders' intentions, 41–5, 225;

inquiry into, 10, 13; interpretation of,
40–1, 42, 237: 40, 2; open to all
classes, 45–6, 225; payments to
masters, 41–2, 43; resentment at
private schools, 208
Free places, 3, 56, 217
Freeman, Rev. George, dual office,
114
Freind, Nathaniel, congratulates Wase,
32–3

Gailhard, John, on schoolmasters,
70–1
Gainsborough G.S., 163
Garrow, Rev. D. W., 137
Gascoyne, John, usher, 158
Gauden, John, 9
Gell, Sir John, 207
Gerbier, Sir Balthazar, Academy, 199
Gerrard, Thomas, at Reading G.S.,
123, 124, 126–7
Gibbons, William, 35
Gibbs, Rev. Mr., 189
Gifford, Bishop (R.C.), 134
Gilbert, Sir Humphrey, proposed
Academy, 198
Gillett, Thomas, his endowment, 182
Girls, exclusion of, 2, 46, 47; specific
reference to, 47
Gladstone, W. E., 130
Glascock, Christopher, 131
Gloucester Cathedral, 165; sequestra-
tion of estates, 13
Gloucester, King's School, 13, 77,
165
Goad, John, 82
Godmanchester G.S., maintenance, 53
Golding, Thomas, maths master, 215
Goldwin, William, 188
Goodall, John, 189
Goodinge, Thomas, master-usher, 21
Goodread, Thomas, dismissal, 148
Graile, John, 119
Grantham G.S., 30, 36–7, 204
Gratwick, Moses, writing master, 215
Grays Thurrock, Palmer's School, 162
Great Yarmouth G.S., 105
Greenhalgh, Mr., at Chester G.S., 13
Greenwood, Paul, 130
Gregory, Abraham, usher-vicar, 165
Gregory, Dr. Francis, 137–8, 165;
*Instructions concerning the art of Oratory,
The Triall of Religions; Votivum
Carolo,* 138
Gresham's College, 138, 211
Gretton, Mark, usher-vicar, 149
Greys, 8
Griffin, Charles, 33

Leach, A. F., 19, 133–4, 180; and causes of schools' decline, 4, 57, 101, 148–9, 150

Lechmere, Anthony, trustee, 143

Lee, Charles, 166

Leech, Daniel, 183

Leeds, Edward, 136; boarding fees, 159; pupils, 8; *Latinum Compendium*, 136–7, *Methodus Graecam Linguam Docendi*, 137

Leeds G.S., 83; judgement of Lord Eldon, 101–2

Legards, 8

Leigh, Thomas, 26; and Wase's inquiry, 28, 30, 31, 34, 37, 38, 178

Lemprière, Dr. John, 150

Lewes G.S., 42, 60

Lewisham G.S., endowment for writing master, 73–6; founder's intention, 45–6; library, 82–3

Lewisham, English and Latin Schools, 72

Leybourne, William, maths master, 215

Leyden University, 139

Libraries, 27, 82–6 *passim*; bequests to, 84–5, 247: 86, 3; provision of books, 52

Lily's Grammar, authorization of, 75, 79

Lincoln, bishop of, 30, 31, 205; diocesan charity schools, 224–5

Lincoln G.S., 78, 130, 189; book supply, 84

Lincolnshire, 30, 37

Linton, Robert, vicar-master, 149–50

Lips, Joest, professor of history, 84

Little Thurlow, election of schoolmaster, 175

Littlebury, William, 55

Llanbedr, 30

Llanegryn G.S., 174

Lloyd, Edward, writing master, 215

Lloyd, Richard, 133, 145; private school, 210; *Schoole-Masters Auxiliaries*, 210

Lloyd, Robert, usher, 100

Locke, John, advocate of private tuition, 195–6; and grammar schools, 201; and spoken Latin, 76, curriculum, 97; treatment of children, 63–4

London, charity schools, 225; Great Fire, 25, 153; mathematics teachers, 215; merchant wealth, 5–6

Long, George, 50, 156

Long Parliament, and education, 1, 10, 11, 13–14, 16, 221; and election of scholars, 13; inquiry into free schools, 10, 13; interference with teachers,

109; national education in Wales, 14–15

Longworth, John, absenteeism, 147–8

Louth G.S., charter of Edward VI, 42–3

Lubin, Eilhard, professor of literature and theology, 85

Luckin, Sir William, 181

Lydiatt, Simon, 156; *Stachyologia*, 139

Lyon, John, Harrow statutes, 47

Macclesfield, Lord Chancellor, 145, 207

Macclesfield G.S., foundation, 44

Madan, Falconer, 24, 39

Maddy, Meredith, 84

Madeley, co-educational school, 46

Maldon G.S., 106

Manchester Free G.S., 49, 163; 'cock-penny' and 'potation-penny', 42; foundation, 41, 42; high masters, 118, 130–1; salary, 161

Mant, Richard, 18

Market Bosworth G.S., 81

Market Harborough G.S., 132

Martin, John, 28–9

Martindale, Adam, maths teacher, 216

Martock G.S., 76, 209; and holy orders, 116; classical studies, 81; under Darby, 112, 174

Marvell, Andrew, at Eton, 9

Mashbury G.S., ejected master, 111

Massey, William, 'Latin-usher', 168

Masters, Benjamin, 123

Mathematics, 215, 216; teachers of, 193, 203–4, 215–16

Matthews, A. G., 111, 210

Matthews, John, 36

Matthews, Mr., president of Sidney Sussex, 32

Matthews, Robert, 185

Meadows, John, dismissal for negligence, 53, 148

Mercers' School, 125–6

Merchant Taylors' School, 80–1, 82, 154; an exclusive preserve, 19, 193; classical studies, 78; under Dugard, 79, 127–8

Merchants, endowments, 5–6; sons' education, 192, 201, 202–4

Mere, dual foundation schools, 72

Meredith, John, provost of Eton, 62

Meure, Mr., Soho Academy, 201

Middle classes, and grammar schools, 5, 201

Midhurst G.S., 19, 162; free scholars, 45

Steeple Aston G.S., 17; vicar-school-master, 114
Stephens, Henry, 88
Stephens, John, 113
Stevens, Dr. Thomas, 117; and the monarchy, 128–9
Steyning G.S., 21; charges for maintenance, 52–3; holidays, 59; stipulation on numbers, 50
Stickney G.S., 82
Stileman, John, 25
Stockport G.S., 43–4, 118, 146, 183
Stoddart, John, 18
Stokesay G.S., 163
Stone, Lawrence, 209, 213–14, 219
Stoneham, Matthew, private school, 209–10
Stourbridge G.S., 106–7
Stow-on-the-Wold G.S., negligent trustees, 176–7
Stratford on Avon G.S., 33
Strelley, George, 81
Strode, William, endowment of Martock G.S., 112, 116, 174
Stucley, Susannah, and Bedford G.S., 82
Stukeley, William, 218; income as doctor, 167–8
Stump, Thomas, usher, 166
Suffolk, 38; population decline, 57
Sunderland, 14
Surtees, Richard, 18
Sussex, 19; cause of schools' decline, 57
Sutton Coldfield G.S., 161
Syddall's School, Catterick, 165

Tarve, William, 134
Taunton G.S., free places, 56
Taylor, Andrew, 133
Taylor, Professor E.G.R., 204, 215
Taylor, John, maths teacher, 215
Taylor, Joseph, 107
Taylor, Mr., master, 15
Taylor, William, 154
Teachers, and the ministry, 14, 113; disparity in pay, 3; hostility to change, 2, 102; State and Church interference, 109
Tench, Rowland, accusations of neglect, 145
Tenterden G.S., negligent trustees, 176, 177
Tetbury G.S., 118
Thacker, Gilbert, dispute with Repton, 139–40
Thackham, Thomas, 131–2
Thame, Lord Williams' School, 17, 159,

222; and corporal punishment, 66
Theobald, Robert, 175
Thetford G.S., 8, 69–70; pluralist master, 114–15
Thomas, David, at Dorchester G.S., 159, 165
Thomas, Rev. David, at South Stoke, 51
Thompson, Dr. Robert, 31
Thompson, Thomas, 124
Thomson, G. Scott, on tutors, 196
Thomson, Thomas, usher, 164
Thornton, Rev. John, tutor to Russells, 195, 196
Thornton G.S., 168
Thrimby, dual foundation school, 72
Thurlby, Mr., 31
Tipper, John, maths teacher, 216
Tiverton G.S., 44
Tonbridge School, 25
Tooke, Andrew, The Pantheon, 138
Tordiffe, Thomas, usher, 21
Towcester G.S., 33
Tower, Thomas, misuse of school income, 189
Trevor, Thomas Lord, 206
Trustees, 2, 45, 102, 179, 183, 224; and Civil War, 11, 154; payment of salaries, 14, 154, 155, 156, 175, 182; appointment of, 175–6; failure to appoint, 189; for Maintenance for Preaching Ministers, 14, 15; mismanagement by, 177–9, 179–82, 190; rivalry between, 183–7, 188
Tryon, Thomas, New Method of Educating Children, 97
Tucker, Rowland, pension, 166
Tuke, Sir Samuel, 96
Turner, William, 118
Twells, John, 118; Grammatica Reformata, 136
Twelves, Dr. Robert, Registrar of Ely, 27
Twigg, Mr., ejected master, 124

Ullock, William, 7; action for trespass against, 140
Umfreville, Mr., at Lincoln G.S., 130
Unitras Fratrum, 9
Underwood, mayor Thomas, 158
Universities, 17, 74, 96, 112; classes using, 193, 195, 264: 193, 2; decline in entrants, 211, 212, 217; election of scholars, 13; grammar school entrants, 103, 208; private teaching entrants, 208–9, 209 n.; scholarships and exhibitions, 11, 37; trusteeships, 179, 184, 188
Uppingham School, co-education, 47